SITUATIONAL ANXIETY

Also by Dr. Herbert J. Freudenberger
BURN-OUT

SITUATIONAL ANXIETY

Herbert J. Freudenberger, Ph.D.
and Gail North

ANCHOR PRESS

Doubleday & Company, Inc., Garden City, New York

1982

This Anchor Press edition is the first publication of *Situational Anxiety*.
Anchor Press Edition: 1982

Grateful acknowledgment is made to the following for permission
to reprint excerpts from their copyrighted material:

"Marginalia" from *W. H. Auden: Collected Poems,* by W. H. Auden,
edited by Edward Mendelson. Copyright © 1966 by W. H. Auden.
Reprinted by permission of Random House, Inc. and Faber and Faber
Ltd.

"The Love Song of J. Alfred Prufrock" from *Collected Poems 1909–
1962,* by T. S. Eliot. Reprinted by permission of Harcourt Brace
Jovanovich, Inc. and Faber and Faber Ltd.

"At the Ballet," music by Marvin Hamlisch; lyrics by Edward Kleban,
from *A Chorus Line,* copyright © 1975 Marvin Hamlisch and Edward
Kleban. All rights controlled by Wren Music Company and American
Compass Music Corp. International Copyright Secured. All Rights Reserved. Used by Permission.

Library of Congress Cataloging in Publication Data

Freudenberger, Herbert J.
    Situational anxiety.

    Includes index.
    1. Anxiety. 2. Personality and situation. I. North,
Gail. II. Title.
BF575.A6F75 1982   158   AACR2
ISBN: 0-385-17959-6
Library of Congress Catalog Card Number 81–43569

To Arlene, a magnificent, precious woman, and to Lisa, Marc, and Lori, without whom so much would not be possible.

ACKNOWLEDGMENTS

To my many patients, who have helped me to learn and who have promoted mutual laughter and tears.

A special thanks to Rosaire Appel, Kathy Ryan, Jay Siegelaub, and Barbara Zara for their generous and insightful assistance, and to Loretta Barrett, who helped to initiate this project and who has been a much appreciated support.

CONTENTS

SITUATIONAL ANXIETY

ONE

Situational Anxiety

"One cannot remove anxiety by arguing it away."
PAUL TILLICH

EVERYONE HAS IT—NOBODY WANTS IT. IT EMERGES WITHIN THE BEST of us at the worst of times, often unpredictably and sometimes just as expected. The feeling is disconcerting, distracting, and charged with distress. All of us are relieved when it passes away, and, while most of us seek out ingenious methods for avoiding its grasp, no one, including a genuine recluse, can truly manage this feat in every situation.

Anxiety is an ongoing reality of twentieth-century life and an experience that is most common and universal to all people. We all suffer it in varying degrees and are often put at ease by the knowledge that others are prey to the same "bad" feelings. In earlier decades, those feelings were tagged by other names. When baseless fear, helplessness, or self-doubt emerged, "That makes me very nervous!" was a common response. Today, in our culture, whether one has or has not been personally subject to the therapeutic experience, the language of psychoanalytical inner sanctums pervades our day-to-day exchanges. We have become well versed in matters of "neurosis," "regression," "transference," and issues of self-esteem. The popular landscape of apprehension, too, is now easily identified and tagged: we use the code word for the uncertainty in life and speak definitively of being in a state of "anxiety."

There are, however, particular events in our daily lives to

which a high incidence of anxiety is endemic. In a given set of circumstances, a large number of people will experience anxious symptoms—soaring pulse rates, wet palms, a racing heart—yet after disengaging from that event, return again to their "normal" feeling states. Something within that predicament charged them with tension, suspicion, and threat, and although they may later attempt to argue it away or even to plumb the genesis of their feelings and authentically believe they have mastered the dynamics, the next time that identical occasion arises, the same symptoms reappear unbidden. This experience is relived in many different sets of circumstances, yet, to the person who functions smoothly in other areas of his or her life, it can become perplexing. For this reason, anxiety which is suffered on one occasion and not on another is referred to as "situational."

Simply stated, *Situational Anxiety is the condition wherein a specific occasion acts as a catalyst for the emergence of unpleasant, uncomfortable, and unwanted feelings, thoughts, or perceptions from the unresolved past which now intrude upon and threaten one's security base.* These situations are most often time-limited, and the felt anxiety is a conscious or unconscious response to either internal or external stimuli which tend to be repetitive and re-emerge when the individual is confronted with that situation.

Social and private situations abound with anxiety triggers; many of them have become so prevalent as to now be considered universally recognizable. Consider for a moment an activity as benign as taking yourself out to a restaurant for dinner, alone. Few of us can manipulate this event without a twinge of self-consciousness, and those who are hypersensitive to being alone in public will find it difficult, if not impossible, to be comfortable or calm amid the couples and groups, or to refrain from patrolling their self-worth and conduct, and measuring it up against what is perceived as proper, acceptable, and desirable to the other diners in that room. If, however, a friend appeared at the table to your right, the feeling of apprehension, the thought of being devalued, and the perception of yourself as peculiar and out of the mainstream would all vanish. In short, because the situation altered, the security base would be re-established and the anxiety would fade into oblivion.

The situations themselves have many different colorations, are often culturally inseminated, and, depending upon the standards or character of a particular community, occur with greater or lesser frequency. Some situations are based on new sets of circumstances, as on the first morning of a new job. Others are created by an unusual twist in the usual daily story line—waking up late for work, waiting over twenty minutes for a date in a conspicuous public place. Many are fashioned from a unique experience with people that requires a change in behavior or a quick and different adaptation, as at a party, or meeting someone new to whom you are wildly attracted. And, along with the new and unpredictable, some are born from the more conventional activities of daily life—confronting your empty home after a busy workday, or simply facing Sundays. These are all situations which persistently trigger confrontations with apprehension; those merciless little scenarios which, no matter how many times they're encountered, still make the heart beat faster.

Just as no one is immune to the emotional debris of the past, practically no one is exempt from the tyranny of situational anxiety. It perniciously plagues all types of people, from the busy, urban, high achievers to those who lead quieter lives in more pastoral settings. The situations which cue the anxiety are the only variables. We've all developed delicate antennae which signal the emergence of this uninvited interloper, and we all do our best to gracefully control it and keep it under wraps. That signal, however, is one of nature's more profound methods for alerting us to the presence of an inner conflict. When anxiety emerges, there is a private imbroglio taking place between an intellectual notion of who you are and what you are capable of handling, and the substantive emotional reality—how far can you extend yourself into this environment and still remain safe. Caught in the confusion of this distressing double bind, the afflicted person usually feels trapped between the wish to be assertive and seen, and the desire to be passive and hide; between "wanting to stay," and "wanting to run." An inner core is being threatened, and whether it's based on a particular value, an ambition, a control, or a sense of safety, your own very private network of associations is thwarting what you hoped to accomplish in that situation. The result is an implosion of feeling which can range from the mild to the severe.

Quite often, the distinction between anxiety and fear becomes blurred. Because the feelings are so similar, these two different concepts are regularly confused. However, fear is an emotion which is triggered by a reaction to something in the real world—anxiety is the feeling state which is ignited by something out of proportion to the actual danger. To highlight this distinction, consider the following connected situations:

Imagine yourself driving down the highway with a speed demon, someone who is weaving in and out of the three-lane highway, screeching the brakes, hitting ninety miles an hour in a 55-mph zone. It's raining, the lightning seems to graze your arm as you clutch the seat and press the floor-board to activate an imaginary brake. This guy won't slow down! Many cars have pulled off the road to wait out the storm, while others have been subject to violent accidents, and red flares signal their distress.

Believe it—what you're feeling here is real danger—absolute fear!

Now, switch the scene. This time you're driving down that same highway with a cautious, alert, and considerate driver. She uses her signal indicator when changing lanes, drives within the speed limit, and keeps a careful eye on the road from both the rear-view mirror and the front. However, your palms are sweating, and you refuse to speak lest it distract, hope she slept well last night, hope she's had her eyes recently examined, hope she's not stricken with a sudden stroke, hope her hearing's intact, and all the while you're persistently making rapid and noisy intakes of breath, simultaneously pressing your hand against the dashboard—just in case.

This, of course, is a reaction unsupported by a realistic danger, and what you're experiencing is, yes, anxiety!

While these distinctions may seem simple enough, the confusion between anxiety and fear is often compounded by an inability to penetrate the root cause of what is experienced as anxiety.

Parents educate, train, and socialize their children through approval—the showing of love and affection—and disapproval—reprimand, punishment, or rejection. Out of this process the child evolves a sense of his or her inner self. When that sense of self functions well and offers fulfillment, the individual will have developed an ability to tolerate those aspects in situations which arouse anxiety. If the individual's sense of self functions poorly, he or she will feel unprotected, and those same situations will arouse early, unresolved feelings, wishes, needs, and fears. The person may be vaguely aware that something in the situation is wrong or "off," and he or she will feel essentially ineffectual and inadequate to change it. This helplessness will trigger a further perceptual distortion of the situation and its interpersonal relationships which will ultimately culminate in intense anxiety.

Yet, situational anxiety is neither an obsession, a compulsion, nor, *in the main*, neurotic. Neurotic anxiety manifests as an intrusion into every component of the person's life. Situational anxiety is present only if and when the specific set of circumstances arises. However, when anxiety does intrude, judgment and the ability to effectively interact with others becomes impaired, perception and interpretation of the event become distorted, and a preoccupation with the anxious feelings tends to eclipse the reality of the given situation.

While this type of anxiety is "normal" to our culture, the degree and intensity to which impairment and malfunction occurs is the degree to which this behavior is considered neurotic. Anxiety in a specific situation reawakens previously unresolved problems and issues which prevent the individual from seeing the circumstances "whole." As a result, the past is often more "alive" than the present, and neurotic overtones ripple through the consciousness. More often than not, misguided notions of what is being said, thought, or done by others are superimposed on the reality; a simple "Hello, how are you?" can be misconstrued as a direct challenge to one's stature and position. While this occurrence may be disorienting and highly unpleasant, it is not indicative of a severe personality impairment; it is unfinished business from the past that is again asking for sufficient closure. It can become serious, however, when the anxiety is somatized. Some people experience intense bouts of anxiety in too many connected situations with no respite in between. Eventually they find themselves subject to physical symptoms ranging from gastrointestinal, cardiovascular, and dermatological, among others, to starkly felt psychosomatic disturbances based on tension with no physiological basis.

Much of the stress and tension endemic to situational anxiety is born from anticipatory dread concerning the event to come. The situation may cue off anxiety prematurely, and in those weeks, days, or hours preceding the event, anxious symptoms emerge which are often more severe than the situation itself. An approaching birthday may lead the individual to a short-lived depression because he or she is convinced that "no one will remember me." Anticipating a sexual liaison may also cause situational expectancy: when an individual worries excessively about impotency or being "good in bed," he or she begins to behave in an impotent or ineffectual manner prior to the event and, in so doing, prepare themselves for a self-fulfilling prophecy of failure. Anger, short temper, avoidance, irritability, and denial are just a few of the anticipatory responses used to cope with the potential and expected situational anxiety.

Denial is a most significant concept to understanding the dynamics of situational anxiety. A refusal to admit that the particular event does, indeed, arouse apprehension, paradoxically feeds the anxiety and intensifies its effects. There are those who have a substantial investment in denying that certain situations cue discomfort. A shaky self-concept may break down under such scrutiny: if one admits to feeling helpless, doubtful, or threatened, some grandiose but hollow notions concerning self-worth would, by necessity, have to be altered. Therefore, the individual continues to deny the presence of anxiety and, as a consequence, continues to amplify the discomfort. Denial systems tend to increase the measure of unpredictability in a given situation, and they can be likened to the idea of trying to hide a helium balloon by sitting on it. Just as you think you've squashed its visibility, it pops up to the right, to the left, or between the legs, and hits you in the face when least expected. So goes the denial game: you may successfully conceal anxiety from yourself in one situation, but it pops up in the next three with greater force. The longer one persists in upping the denial ante, the more anxiety he or she can expect to feel.

Almost all psychological theories of anxiety are based on one common theme: the relation of anxiety to the unacceptability of one's own conscious or unconscious awareness of danger. Unwanted thoughts, wishes, and feelings may break through and, once again, resurrect early panics and anxieties that were associated with threats from significant people from the past, whether it be the removal of love and approval, or the possibility of being held in disfavor and maybe even punished.

Freud suggested that anxiety is felt by an individual through his or her awareness of formerly repressed unacceptable drives, wishes, or instincts which threaten to float to the surface and incapacitate the person's functioning. His theory of anxiety is closely allied with the loss of love, fear of punishment, and the threat of castration.

Harry Stack Sullivan perceived anxiety as resting within the interpersonal framework of the individual, with its root causes planted in relationships rather than instinctual drives. Anxiety, according to Sullivan, emanates from the fear of anticipated disapproval and loss of love from the original significant people in the individual's life. Later on, this fear of disapproval is transferred from the original people and situations to others with whom the individual is emotionally involved, and feelings of guilt are intimately interwoven with feelings of anxiety. Both Freud and Sullivan believed that disapproval and unacceptability of ourselves experienced early in life through people on whom we were dependent, is sufficient to arouse our anxieties in situations that possess similar qualities in later life.

Otto Rank speaks of the separation anxiety experience at birth as an anxiety which carries itself throughout one's life, and which can be linked to the removal of the mother's breast, weaning, separation from friends, and, ultimately, to the aloneness of death.

Hostility was a prime factor to Karen Horney. She viewed anxiety as closely associated and interwoven with the real, imagined, or anticipated hostility of others toward the individual which would ultimately produce an interruption in the relationship, if not a complete severing.

Psychological isolation and alienation from oneself or the community was suggested by both Eric Fromm and Frank Riesman

as the cause of anxiety in modern society, while Rollo May
defines anxiety as the "apprehension set off by a threat to some
value which the individual holds essential to his existence as a
personality."*

A closer inspection of these theories reveals that all of the psy-
choanalysts and scholars view anxiety as the fear of a loss of a
significant value for the individual, whether that value be a
threatened loss of love, a threat of incipient loneliness, a threat
to one's image, or the threat to needed approval.

No matter what the experts say, each individual handles the
discomfort of anxiety with his or her own particular system and
style. People who are psychologically "healthy" as well as those
who are "disturbed" will do everything possible to avoid, eliminate, or ward off the feelings evoked by a certain situation. Some
people respond by overtalking: they work on the premise that a
moving target can't be hit. Others respond noiselessly, hoping
they will achieve some power in their silence. Nervous gestures
abound—twisting a curl of hair, stroking a beard, cleaning
eyeglasses, smoking, smiling too much, overdrinking, taking
drugs, and the perpetual motion of the wagging crossed leg
speak worlds for the discomfort of the anxiety bully. When
laughter intrudes upon an anxious situation, everyone is relieved
and, often, everyone overreacts to the joke in order to prolong
the feeling of goodwill. However, to openly admit at a business
lunch that you're racked with anxiety is strictly verboten. Ironically, that particular admission of imperfection can be one of the
great social ice-breakers, but few feel easy these days with out-
spoken confessions of implied threats to their value systems. In
the late 1960s and early '70s, during the years that spawned the
"me" generations and mystical gurus, it may have been stylish,
even desirable, to openly parade your situational anxiety quirks,
but the etiquette of the '80s demands a different set of rules.
High achievement has taken the place of execessive self-concern,
and along with dressing for success, there is now a gentleper-
son's agreement to keep a situational silence and noiselessly
master the attendant anxiety.

* *The Meaning of Anxiety*, Pocket Books, copyright 1977 by Rollo May.

Underneath the many complex explanations of how, when, and what anxiety is about lies an engaging though erroneous myth amplifying this popular dilemma. Since anxiety may manifest itself in our thinking processes and cloud our perceptions, it follows that to the very anxious person there seems to be a privileged group of people out there who have been given access to a secret for living to which he or she has not been made privy. Viewed through the eyes of anxiety, this group appears to effortlessly juggle charged situations, events, and new people in their lives, while you remain quietly persecuted by secret threats. What's their secret? How did those people corner the market on confidence, poise, and aplomb, while in the same situation you are a mass of squirming insecurities and pulsating doubts? The underbelly of this disturbing myth (as you will soon discover) is hollow and wanting. The slick and accomplished are also riddled with apprehension, fear of ridicule, and being devalued, and may just secretly be coveting what they perceive as *your* self-assurance and social know-how. It's important to remember that charged situations affect each individual differently: a throat-constricter to you may be a moment of relief to them—a muscle-lock to them may be a refreshing pause to you. Anxiety is simply not socially discriminating.

Yet, the general presumption that those out there are anxiety-free while you are biting your nails to the nub is only one aspect of the perceptual battleground. There are other, more specific camps who view each other through confused and misguided eyes. Women and men are often bewildered by what each perceives as the other's cool front. Many women are convinced that the male ego has been inoculated against the ravages of doubt and therefore often resist the desire to hash out their insecurities with their men. On the other hand, men often view women as unfathomable—people who will secretly ridicule their vulnerabilities, judge them as "unmanly," and take their attentions elsewhere: they too become hard-pressed to reveal or betray any emotional confusions in a given situation. Gay couples, as well, often garnish their relationships with distrust and suspicion. After the initial romance has passed into phase two—regular living—the mutual sharing of situational anxieties becomes measured and guarded. The same threats to self-esteem and loss enter the arena, and thus anxiety's sexual carousel begins its frantic whirl.

The truth here is that we live in an environment which is fraught with gaps in emotional logic. Cultural issues are fast-changing and difficult to follow; meanings that were once publicly shared have undergone extreme metamorphoses. We expect ourselves to keep up with the pace and we pride ourselves on being quick-adapters. When situational anxiety rears, we should not be too surprised. It would be more prudent to simply try to understand that there is an important discrepancy at work within ourselves—a conflict between the present and the past, authentic capabilities and unreal expectations—and that this is the basic flaw in the human equation.

Before going any further, you may want to stop and give a moment's thought to the anxious situations which plague your own life. All of us "make it through" these situations, but are you aware of how the anxiety manifests? Do you know how to cope with the apprehensive feelings? And, how many areas of life do you avoid simply because the experience, well, makes you anxious?

SITUATIONAL ANXIETY INDEX
101 Questions

Take a look at the following questions and give your answers some serious consideration. Score yourself on a scale of 1 to 3: *1=Never. 2=Sometimes. 3=Always.* At the end, when you add up your score, you'll have a better idea of your Situational Anxiety Index, and how much a part of your life it has or has not become.

I. Sexual Anxiety

When you're sexually attracted, does your nervous system feel imperiled? _____

Do you invest the object of your attraction with mythological powers to hurt you or unequivocally change your life? _____

Do you sometimes feel disoriented and out of control? _____

Are you embarrassed at being "caught" attracted? _____

Do you alter your style and content for a mysterious but attractive stranger? _____

Do you go mute, and feel utterly stupid when speaking to a person to whom you are overwhelmingly attracted? _____

Do you exaggerate through innuendo and nuance your sexual expertise? _____

Do you later want to hide under the covers and pretend the attraction never happened? _____

After the initial flirtation, does doubt or apprehension hound your thoughts? _____

Do you worry about sexually measuring up to "them out there"? _____

Do you become confused and anxious over the cultural changes between men and women and feel somewhat inept? _____

Are you worried over whether you'll present yourself to your date as someone who is "as good as you've led him/her to believe you are"? _____

Are you embarrassed to be seen eating food on a first date? _____

Does removing your clothes cue inhibition to come in for a fast ride? _____

Do you leap quickly into the sex act itself to avoid being seen? _____

Are you only comfortable if you conduct an in-depth analysis of your mutual performances in the aftermath of sex? _____

Do you interpret silence as disapproval? _____

Do you double up your efforts to ensure he or she will call you the next day? _____

Do you worry yourself sick that he or she may want a "commitment"? _____

II. Private Aloneness Anxiety

If you work at home alone, do you stay in your robe all day and then feel guilty? _____

Is there an invisible barricade between you and your typewriter, drawing board, telephone, ledger, manuscripts, or dishwasher? _____

Do you put off making "cold calls" when working alone? _____

Do you require a light shining in the other room in order to comfortably fall asleep? _____

Do you fear there may be someone outside your door at night? _____

Do you keep the television or radio going all night? _____

Do you find yourself edgy and restless when you're all alone? _____

Do you feel displaced when the workday ends and blitzkrieg yourself with busy bombs, pieces of inessential activity? _____

Do you often suffer from insomnia, and do you conduct busy dialogues with people from the past in your head? _____

III. Public Aloneness Anxiety

Are you able to take yourself out to a "good restaurant" alone? _____

Can you go to the movies by yourself? _____

When out in a public place all alone, do you believe others are thinking that you couldn't find a friend? _____

Are you hard hit by the reality of Sunday? _____

Do you anticipate Monday morning with suspicion and dread? _____

Do you often believe you've left something incriminating on your desk at the office? _____

IV. Lateness and Waiting Anxiety

When you're late for an appointment, do you rev up and rehearse a thousand false excuses? _____

Do you chronically overbook your schedule and then worry about confronting angry people? _____

When you oversleep and are late for work, do you feel as though you're on the edge of a dangerous precipice? _____

Are you adept at glib excuses? _____

When waiting for someone to show up, do you begin to doubt your memory and judgment? _____

Do you feel disoriented and even suspect you may "never have made this appointment"? _____

Are you humiliated because others may suspect you've been "stood up"? _____

Are you convinced you've been jilted because this person changed his or her mind about you? _____

V. *Dinner Party and Social Anxiety*

As a host or hostess, do you turn your guests into "critics and judges" an hour before they arrive? _____

Do you become suspicious when your guests aren't eating enough? _____

Are you obsessed with making everyone "comfortable"? _____

Do you worry over whether the guests will dislike each other and therefore question your judgment? _____

Do you worry about the guests you did *not* invite? _____

As a guest, do you plan your party personality in advance? _____

Do you often clam up and feel like a nonperson, unseen and disposable? _____

Can you introduce your new lover at a party without flinching? _____

Do you find yourself heading for the bookcase when you enter a crowded room? _____

Do you believe that couples have an easier time at parties? _____

Do you suspect the others are far more informed and intellectually endowed than you? _____

VI. *Birthday Anxiety*

Do you commonly fear you won't be remembered? _____

Do you worry about an empty mailbox? _____

Do you wish someone else would handle the whole miserable day for you? _____

Do you believe, if they cared, even those who are uninformed should divine this is your natal day? _____

Do you become tense when given a gift? _____

Do you suddenly become "by age possessed"? _____

Are you suddenly obsessed by "future fear"? _____
Do you brood over your lost identity as the wunderkind, the
    debutante, the ingenue? _____
Do you fear you're on a treadmill to oblivion? _____

VII. *New Job Anxiety*

The first morning, will you worry over whether you should ar-
    rive two minutes early, two minutes late, or exactly at
    9:00? _____
Will perfection hound your every move? _____
Will you memorize the first memos handed to you to read? _____
Will you act as if you know everything to which everyone is
    referring? (Accounts, clients, organizational structure, ven-
    dors, free-lancers, etc.)? _____
Will you be bent on proving you're a real revenue generator
    between 9:00 and 12:00? _____
Will you be afraid to ask where the bathroom or supply room is
    located? _____
Will you turn down that cup of coffee for fear of appearing like
    a gold-bricker? _____
If you lunch with your boss on the first day, will you suspect the
    food you order will alter your career strategy? _____
Will you suddenly become aware that you may be chewing
    wrong? _____
Will anxiety keep your smile frozen and your lips shaky? _____

VIII. *Body and Beauty Anxiety*

Do you often feel zapped by a "case of bad looks"? _____
If your hair isn't "right," do you lose your power? _____
Has summer become "flesh weather" and a curse on your self-
    image? _____
Do you only buy cover-up clothes and a lot of shoes? _____
Do you avoid exercise classes because you're out of shape? _____
Do you worry about your body-image at the health club? _____
Do you sometimes think of your body as "this thing below my
    neck"? _____
Do you feel ironically more anxious after you've shed a number
    of pounds? _____

Do you usually look at carpets and sidewalks instead of faces and storefronts? _____

Do you overspend at cosmetic counters? _____

Has your poor body-image distorted your spacial perceptions? (Do you often trip over wires, back into walls, or bruise yourself?) _____

Do you often worry about the opinions of those whom you do not like? _____

IX. *Doctors, Dentists, and Shrink Anxiety*

When visiting the doctor, do your symptoms mysteriously vanish? _____

Are you suspicious of the "white coat"? _____

Do you feel like a fool in a paper gown? _____

Does being touched by the doctor force you to pretend you're somebody else? _____

Are you unsure of what to do with the urine specimen? _____

Do you "lose" your mouth and your ears when being examined? _____

Are you afraid of firing your doctor? _____

At the dentist's office, does the sound of the drill calcify all rational thought? _____

Do you delay his procedures by asking the function of instruments and begging off to "rinse"? _____

Are you scared of gagging and having it be known? _____

Do you feel caught in verbal bondage with the hook stuck in your mouth? _____

At a psychoanalytic consultation, do you suspect the analyst has never had a case like you? _____

Do you believe that every nod of the head, blink of the eye, and flex of the ankle is a meaningful portent regarding your case? _____

Do you suspect that you are the only one that has kinky fantasies? _____

Are you convinced the analyst "won't like you"? _____

Are you afraid you'll be "found out" and hauled off in a net? _____

SCORING YOUR SITUATIONAL ANXIETY INDEX

Add up your score and check the results next to the closest category of responses. Next to each score grouping you will see an illustration of how anxiety tends to blot out consciousness. The lower the score, the larger your area of consciousness—the higher the score, the more compressed the ability to consciously judge, perceive, and interpret becomes.

101–181: This means you are well adjusted to our modern world and have learned to cope well with the doubts and uncertainties that plague most of our days. The felt anxiety acts more often than not as a positive awareness factor which may alert you to danger or potential hurt, as well as an aid to creative action and thinking. Consider yourself fortunate, indeed.

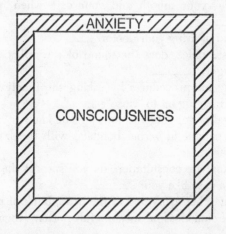

181–202: This indicates that you are often aware of the edges of anxiety's toehold, but are not open-season on red alerts. You may want to explore some of the more potently charged situations in your life and keep the anxiety from closing further in on your consciousness.

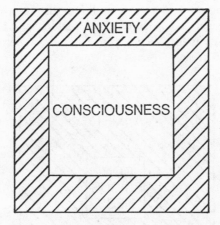

203–258: You're inside the red alert area and very possibly endangering your physical, emotional, and mental well-being. We strongly urge you to take some steps toward slowing down. In many situations, your conscious functioning has been obstructed.

259–303: This is a red alert! You may be in such a high daily stress category that you could very possibly be a candidate for gastrointestinal, cardiovascular, or other serious physical and emotional health hazards. It might be not only wise, but also life-saving to immediately start taking stock of your daily life or else to seek some professional counseling. The incidence of situational anxiety is threatening your conscious functioning in too many areas.

The questions selected for the Situational Anxiety Index Quiz were taken from the nine major categories and thirty situations which seem to perplex many anxious people. These situations were culled from hundreds of variations on a central theme common to the anxiety-prone—the emergence of unpleasant, uncomfortable, and unwanted feelings, thoughts, or perceptions from the unresolved past which now intrude and threaten one's security base. You may not recognize yourself in the first situation you read, or even the first category, but you'll undoubtedly find an accurate reflection in several of the others. Wherever you find yourself, you can now be sure you're not alone!

Additionally, there are some very positive steps, ranging from the analytical to the very practical, which can be taken to defend against the anxiety inherent in these situations. We hope you'll take judicial notice of some new tools to use as emotional aids the next time you enter an anxious situation, and learn how to relax and perhaps laugh as you approach it. Ultimately, you're certain to realize that you're neither crazy nor cowardly—you're simply suffering from situational anxiety.

TWO

Sexual Anxiety

"The basis of optimism is sheer terror."
OSCAR WILDE

ADAM AND EVE MAY HAVE BEEN THE FIRST TO SUFFER SITUA-
tional anxiety. According to legend, after they experienced the
click and understood that they knew what they knew, they
covered their parts with leaves. Through the ages, this foliage
issue has maintained a remarkable durability. Clinicians have
devoted years to dissecting the more profound implications
of the parts motif, and scholars have built towering reputa-
tions researching meanings behind the myth of the quivering leaf. Today, however, the part-covering question is no
longer limited to the naked nether regions alone—it now includes
a wide range of exposed vulnerabilities. The old basic fig protection has metamorphosed into a new emotional shield which is
often summoned up to swiftly hide a situationally anxious heart.

To the sexually anxious, a mere attraction to another can signal the downbeat for internal chaos to begin its dance. Otherwise rational, sane, and centered human beings become convinced that everyone here can see through their coverings and
that their parts will betray them. In these precarious moments,
even the dramatis personae of the emotional life are recast.
Players such as Confidence, Esteem, Assurance, and Poise lower
their eyes and make embarrassed exits, cuing Peril, Doubt, Apprehension, and Inhibition—a few of Anxiety's loyal henchmen
—to enter.

When this scabrous lot takes center stage, all hope of diplomatic relations with cool intelligence is severed. The din of their voices drowns out all sensible inner meanings, and for that moment the sexually anxious are sometimes rendered all but mute. Writer Dan Greenburg gave us a prime example of how Anxiety's good ol' boys manipulate the mind into flight patterns of behavior when physical magnetism strikes the heart. In his book *Scoring,* he tells of a New York party he attended years ago and of an attraction to a young woman he had never met who walked into the festivities around midnight:

"I had never desired anyone so immediately or so powerfully in my life, never before wanted to abandon myself so completely to nakedness and rubbing things . . . I loved her with mind and heart and body and I would cheerfully have written out a proposal of marriage to her on the spot in exchange for even one night in bed with her. So what I did was I went into another room of the apartment and hid."

Other people, both men and women, have been known to gulp magnums of bad chianti, don sunglasses in the dark, feign dying, pop blue valium (or mega-doses of niacinamide), mumble old forgotten mantras, or attack the attractive person with rapier maliciousness simply to avoid displaying their own vulnerable parts. They trust these protections will conceal the voice that has ascended an octave, calm the tremulous smile, or regain the drift of the conversation that's been completely snatched from memory. This is serious stuff.

The whole dimension of sexual attraction seems to dismantle the usual systems for getting through the week. All those tender little nerve centers, so carefully bedded down and peacefully asleep during the average workday, now quite suddenly have the sheets ripped off their backs, are startled into wakefulness, and begin to shriek in utter panic: "Stop! I'm not ready for this yet! I'm still in the raw!" And they leap about, exposed and undefended, blinded by the light, grabbing for the nearest leaf to cover their parts.

The person toward whom the attraction is aimed is immediately charged with the kind of power usually reserved for the Supreme Court. Your sentence, indeed, now pivots on your credibility as a sexually desirable being, and that person over there holds the possibility of your life or your death in his or her erotic hands. The fact that this person could just be an unbalanced crazy who wandered into the party uninvited matters not, for reality here is all but eclipsed.

Further, if your attraction is reciprocated, that is, if you have been able to propel yourself out of the bathroom and over to the bookcase where he or she has beckoned you with a shy but meaningful smile, a new wrinkle emerges which must be cautiously ironed out. At this juncture, every word you utter, every gesture you employ, must be weighed and measured, for the wrong intonation, a poorly timed phrase, an awkward pause, or an untoward lunge could make or break what promises to be a thunderous relationship.

SITUATION #1
Attraction and Peril

Jill Ames went to just such a party and, after sitting on a hard divan for several hours listening to stilted conversations from a handful of strangers, was convinced it was time to leave. But then, somewhere between an appropriate nod at a large man in a velour polo shirt and a sip of lukewarm Chablis, a new crowd arrived and a craggy-eyed man in an open linen vest stepped into the vestibule and pierced her system with what the Italians call the thunderbolt.

Of course she looked the other way—his demeanor was too dazzling—and she landed on the slender woman across the rosewood coffee table who was timidly discussing yogurt cultures. Riveting her eyes to hers, Jill offered a piece of information summoned up from a storehouse of unrelated facts pertaining to proper refrigeration, yet still managed to hear her host cheerfully say, "Good to see you, Paul," and the "Paul" reverberated in her ears. Before she could begin to embarrass herself, she stood and fled to the bedroom, completely missing the introductions.

"Whew!" she murmured to the mirror which reflected the soft slate-gray wraparound dress and the wide gold belt. "Looks good . . ." she said out loud and turned to catch an important rear view, ". . . okay." But as she faced front and began to comb her long ash-blond hair, she caught yet another view—this one of a plump little man in a dark suit perched on her shoulder looking very much like a perfect description of Peril.

"What are you doing here!" Jill screamed, brushing him off as though he was a roach. But Peril was tenacious and clung to her throat.

"Hold it!" he cried out, "and pull yourself together! That guy is a dangerous two-month episode which you can ill afford! You said you'd had it with men, that you'd focus on your life—you promised to re-evaluate your judgment, choose next time and not be chosen, remain 'unfettered by desire,' and here you are hyperventilating over some riverboat gambler in a vest!"

"Get off my back," Jill snapped heatedly, but she remained frozen in front of the mirror. "So what if I contradict myself; I contain multitudes . . . Besides, I'm not attracted that often and it's been a long time . . ." She gave her shoulders a hardy shrug and pursued another line of thought. "What shall I say to him? I need a good opening line. Everything sounds so stupid . . . What do other people say? Maybe I'll have another glass of wine first. Yes . . . I'll just head for the bar and then get my bearings."

Peril wheezed heavily, weakening her knees, and Jill re-entered the room.

The man called Paul was standing in a cluster of people over by the bookcase. She avoided him, got a refill of Chablis, and joined the yogurt lady, who was now seriously discussing sprouts. With her stomach fluttering dangerously, Jill dropped a word or two about protein and tofu, then turned, and, taking baby steps, moved in a zigzag pattern across the room. She adopted the busy-and-popular image, throwing a smooth smile over here, a cocked-head grin over there, and finished her drink in the process. Finding herself in the vestibule corner with nowhere to go but out, she raised her head, saw him looking directly into her face, and instantly pretended a lash had stuck in her eye.

"He's seen you," whispered Peril hoarsely, "it's your move!"

Jill wet her lips, tried to seem as though preoccupied with the parquet floor, but was so stricken that she decided to slip through the door and run. However, it was too late, for the man called Paul walked up to her and said: "Hi . . . I love the way your dress moves."

Peril grabbed her around the larynx. "Thanks," she gulped, then noisily cleared her throat. An awkward pause followed, during which she blinked excessively. My God, she thought, he has a cleft in his chin, and her body registered the miracle of this particular cleft which was like no other cleft in all of the Americas. "What do I say now, what do I do?" she begged of Peril, but he was hanging on to her chin, knocking her teeth against her tongue.

The large man in the velour polo ensemble brushed by, allowing her a moment of grace. "I'm heading for the bar," he said, "can I get either of you something more to drink?" "No," said the man called Paul, whose voice now alerted her loins. "Yes," said Jill, "warm wine, please."

Seemingly absorbed in the folds of her flowy sleeve, the man in the vest reached out and touched the edge of the loose fabric. "It's silk, isn't it?" he said, and his fingers grazed her soft underarm. Peril toppled to the floor and fell on her feet, causing her to pitch backward and land in the center of someone else's conversation. "Sorry . . ." Jill muttered hurriedly to a young woman in a hat. "No, it's a supple synthetic," she ventured, stepping on Peril's face as she re-entered the arena. "I think it would be a good idea for us to sit on the couch," he said, and gently claimed her arm. "Good idea," she answered evenly, and disengaged her foot from the dark shadow on the floor.

Sitting on the hard divan, the man called Paul took her wine from the surrogate host and sipped it. "Party wine," he proclaimed, smiling broadly, and he handed her the glass, simultaneously making serious thigh contact.

"Sooo . . ." she stated, then, totally at a loss for what civilized people say to each other when their muscles have congealed, stopped. Peril rematerialized between them and pointed a stern finger at the spot where the twill slacks pressed against the slate-gray skirt. "Say something! Ask who he is, what he does for a living . . . get going!" he hissed, growing larger and now blurring her vision.

"Are you a vest of the host's . . . *friend!?*" she asked and bit her lip.

"Yes, we're friends, and my name's Paul Wright."

"Oh," she nodded, gaping at his cleft.

"Our host also told me your name and that the two of you work together at Frame Inc. By the way," he went on, now absorbed in her long hair, "he's extremely fond of you . . . you are a very attractive woman."

Peril bucked and swerved against her breast, ricocheting onto her lap.

"Oh . . . are you also in real estate?"

"In a way," he said. "I'm an architect."

"Uh, huh . . ." she murmured with some new anxiety, for now she was convinced he was a serious shaker and mover. "I see." Fondling her glass, she pressed her inquiry further. "Do you design high-rises?"

"Yes . . . I certainly do." The craggy eyes glowed with a sudden intensity. "I'd like to get together with you sometime soon— would you . . . how do you feel about that?"

The small man in the dark suit thrashed around in the remote regions of her lap, then sealed himself in her torso. "Fine," she answered quickly, "that is . . . I think so, I'd have to check my . . . Look, I've got this lash stuck in my thigh, hold my place, this will only take a minute." She unhinged her leg from his, grabbed her bag, and fiercely rubbing her lid, glided into the bathroom where she found Peril sitting on the edge of the tub boning up on Tom Wolfe.

"Listen carefully," she said pacing the tiles, "I think I'm a goner."

"Wise up," said Peril. "The guy's an operator and you're not ready for that! You still have to tackle your intimacy problems."

"I hear you, but we both know I'm going to ultimately do what I want—the attraction is too intense."

"Too risky, you mean," said Peril calmly. "Look how fast he moved in on you. All style, no content. You're repeating an old pattern."

Jill looked into the medicine cabinet mirror and wiped the smudge from beneath her eye. "I know, I know . . . But, look, I won't get serious or fuse up, or ask to meet his kids; I'll just enjoy a simple evening, pleasurable conversation, maybe dinner, oh, sometime next week, and *slowly* see what develops. It's not as if I'm jumping into bed with him tonight," she said, spraying Cerissa on her wrists.

Peril shut his eyes in disbelief. "Tell it to the marines," he said gruffly, and picked up *From Bauhaus to Our House* from where he had dropped it near the drain.

Jill left the bathroom, but had a second thought, and poked her head back in. "Should I agree to see him this week or will that seem as though I'm always free?"

"Get out of here," Peril uttered in a wispy voice, for his power was dwindling, he was almost out of a job, and he could barely summon up the energy to follow her out.

Sauntering confidently through the main room, Jill aimed for the hard divan and, when she arrived, looked the man in the vest squarely in the eye and snapped her bag shut. "I'm ready whenever you are," she finally said, employing her lowest register. She then stepped back, cocked her head and smiled.

The small man in the dark suit did a double take, then leaped up off the floor and planted himself on the center of the architect's back. "She's seen you," he whispered hoarsely, ". . . it's your move!"

THE DYNAMICS OF ATTRACTION

The attraction situation is loaded with energy. The message it throws out is both hopeful and exciting, but to the sexually anxious, its underbelly is fraught with danger and risk. This duality is unsettling, for the attraction/peril pendulum sometimes swings too fast to get an accurate reading on your feelings. Most of us tend to confuse the excitement of attraction with the anxiety of peril and distort the first phase of the mating ritual. Although they may exist simultaneously, they are two separate emotions and each has its own distinct and independent life.

On its own, the voice of attraction can be very compelling, even demanding: "I want you, I must have you . . . if only for this moment," it murmurs heatedly. But when the voice of anxiety intervenes (as it often does), and rudely interrupts this reverie with a different demand, what you hear are the words of impending peril: "Dangerous! Stay away, don't let them catch you without your coverings . . ." This is when you usually get caught in the magnetic double bind. To the timid, the voice of peril is overpowering: a shy person may be prompted to hide in the corner and remain there for the rest of the evening. More often than not, however, attraction's message is the victor, for it speaks in a loud voice and once it usurps peril's bullhorn of threats, it is not easily shut up.

Characteristic of attraction is its domineering power. Once it pierces the system, it's almost futile to protest. It dislikes restraint and is mistress of its own reflexes, and it is stubborn! It refuses to be placated by rational argument and, excepting for its own frame of possessive reference, it has no perspective on the circumstance. In short, attraction knows no immediate reasons for being and has no concern for logic.

So, what's to be done about this tyrant? If you are one of those who secretly admits that you're "always attracted to the wrong people," perhaps you would do well to mull over yet another important distinction, this one focusing on the two aspects of anxiety itself.

In the case of attractions, anxiety is not always a menacing foe bent on destroying your good time. It sometimes acts as a concerned friend forcing you to make contact with your good judgment, which is probably floundering over there by the bookcase. Once your judgment pulls itself together, it can then counsel you against participating in what may or may not be a hazardous frolic. It follows that, in the case of a sudden, hard-core attraction, anxiety can be most useful. It can tap your memory and remind you that this situation looks like another historically painful repetition. Of course, if you're anything like Jill Ames, you may find yourself severely conflicted. On a significant level, she understood that there may have been more than a kernel of truth to what the warning voice of peril was saying to her. When she told him, "I hear you . . . but we both know I'm ultimately going to do what I want—the attraction is too intense," she was making a classic statement, one to which most of us can relate. Even though you may be aware that you could be jeopardizing the next two months of your life in a dead-end affair, nonetheless, you will happily walk into the familiar mouth of the dragon. The attraction is just too tempting.

The negative underpinnings of attraction anxiety and the rather bizarre push-and-pull behavior they provoke are somewhat obvious. However, the reasons behind the negative attraction anxiety are not as clear. Why, for instance, should peril strike out and affect the body with such consuming force? Perception and interpretation are key to this issue.

The eyes are the main conduit for attraction's command. What you *see* over there across the room immediately signals to the brain that something extraordinary, even spellbinding, has been sighted and perceived. A vest, a three-piece suit, a tendril of hair on the nape of the neck, deep-set eyes, a wistful smile, a flowing skirt, a pair of Frye boots—and you become a soft touch for the nostalgic promises this visual summons up from your storehouse of desirable images. You then interrupt the him or the her behind the symbol as crucial to your muted yearnings and unconsciously invest that person with the power to inflate or diminish your entire well-being. When your self-worth is placed on the front lines, your otherwise invincible system for getting through the days goes into threat alert and you proceed to grow doubtful and a bit jumpy. No longer the powerbroker in command here, you find yourself reduced to an unbalanced mass of raw nerves with about as much control as Dr. Strangelove's arm. Your anxiety index now begins to soar, for your social cover is about to be blown and your parts ultimately exposed.

The term "fatally attracted" begins to take on new dimensions when you consider how often people continue to act upon their impulses in these matters simply because they unconsciously recognize a familiar but disturbing attitude from the past and are comfortable negotiating with difficult people. For instance, a challenging smile may trigger an old passion for becoming involved with that person over there whose flickering anger promises to give you "something to push up against." Or, that silent, seductive man who looks as if he has been imbued with the Buddhists' "Aha!" answer to all of life's ironies may actually tap a memory fragment of someone important in your life who was aloof and denied you recognition—a withholding person with whom you learned to feel comfortable. An instantly intimate sensuous woman may give every indication of ending your search for the partner who will fulfill all of your primal and intellectual needs, yet ultimately, like someone else from your past, prove to be frightened of authentic closeness and intimacy. And, of course, there is the ever-magnetic draw of the man or woman who "looked like home to me . . ." Home in this case could mean a withholding parent whom you continue to pursue in your adult life, somehow hoping to make it all come out right the second, third, or eighth time around.

The crux of the attraction anxiety issue revolves around how you handle the situation when it arises. Jill Ames did not handle it well: she landed on a vest and a cleft and interpreted them as an entrée to Nirvana. At that point, she lost her power as well as her control. Therefore, before any of us are stricken by the thunderbolt attraction again, it may be fruitful to decipher a pattern of attractions from the past—which ones were apparently sound, and which were based on old, unresolved situations.

If you are at a party or social gathering and attraction pierces your body, understand that although it's futile to protest, you do have options you can exercise that stand midway between jumping in unprotected or retreating to the vestibule. Turn to the host, hostess, or mutual friends and find out something about this man or woman. Seek out information pertinent to this person's availability, previous history, and even their sanity! This will begin to give you a grounding, an anchor, and help you to lessen anxiety's wild ride. If nothing else, it will give you the desperately needed opening line for your incipient conversation.

Breathe deeply and speak to the person you covet before you allow your "muscles to congeal," your stomach to "flutter dangerously," your vision to begin "blurring." Anxiety has a way of manifesting itself in a variety of clever disguises, which, among others, also include heart palpitations, chest pains, headaches, sweaty palms, and that Machiavellian abomination—dry throat! —which promotes an inability to speak, a growing sense that you have stopped thinking, and the suspicion that you are stupid. Be aware that one of anxiety's bad tricks is to judge your pantry of social statements, questions, and/or chitchat with a ridiculing eye. This can be devastating! Even highly articulate raconteurs have been known to fall victim to the disturbing notion that their usually intelligent, perceptive, and amusing words now sound inane! To circumvent the possibility of being judged a washout, they opt for silence, which places the other person in the unenviable position of supplying all of the words and moves —all in the service of a dry throat.

One way to overcome this jammed feeling is to take the situation and put it into a sane perspective: you *have* most probably overcome it before—you *will* overcome it again! You're stronger than you think. It would be most wise *not* to trust those delaying thought-tactics which suddenly intrude with, "Let me think about it first . . ." or "I swear I'll do it the next time," even, "I'm not dressed right tonight!" But do try to jump in *before* the he or the she who is causing you to panic decides to leave! If you flee in terror now, you're just postponing your life.

You might also try playing the role of attraction sleuth by investigating what could actually happen if you are rejected. Ask yourself why you tend to give so much power over to another individual and, as a consequence, so little to yourself. (After all, there's only so much to divvy up at any given moment!) Make a list of people you know whom you've dubbed as powerful. Next to each name, write out your immediate response to their strong qualities. Then think through the reality of each person and how, if you had the chance, you might change that response and behave differently. Use this list as an anchor for your attraction fears, and when you next meet a desirable person, ask yourself, "What could actually happen to me if I approach, and he or she says, 'No'?" You may find that what you so dreaded is not in reality as frightening as what you imagined.

It will be psychologically advantageous to remember that he or she, like you, is embarrassed by appearing gauche, worries about weight, and probably has the same attacks of morning flatulence. Try to avoid turning him or her into a powerful mythological personality just down from Olympus for the evening whom you must entertain; a sensitive poet-at-the-picnic whom you must protect from your intelligence; or, a bishop here from the Mother cathedral for whom you must lower your voice as well as your thoughts and sensibility. If you alter your style and content for some mysterious stranger at the end of the bar who happens to alarm your system because he or she got stuck

with your symbolic image reference, you'll end up feeling debili-
tated, tense, and probably angry. And further, if that one false
move on your part does send this person fleeing from your life
and out into the night, consider what a full-blown affair would
bring . . .

Finally, attraction is exciting because it is *reciprocated*. Unre-
quited attraction is short-lived at best, and while you may feel
disappointed, even a bit depressed when your attentions are not
returned, very little is lost. It's the reciprocation that counts,
which means that the other person is just as interested in dazzling you and probably just as nervous. If both of you go mute,
there'll be no experience to remember tomorrow and no adven-
ture to explore tonight.

Indigenous to the attraction ritual itself is the transmission of
information about yourself to the other that will ensure he or she
believes you to be a worthy contender for the mating arena.
Leaking data through innuendo and nuance becomes an important part of this exchange: expert seducers have polished the
practice to a fine art—they know well that what they intimate is
as important as what they actually say. However, the novice
seducer, like Jill Ames or Paul Wright, caught in the throes of
attraction anxiety, sometimes ups the attraction ante by trans-
mitting exaggerated, even erroneous, information which later
may prove to be embarrassing. Gripped by the need to appear
fascinating, if not provocative, while guardedly discussing the
who and the what of your life, you simultaneously, but word-
lessly, express your unexpurgated desire to mate. It's not unusual to get lost within the swell of your own momentum and
allude to a readiness and an expertise in these matters that rival
the Kama Sutra and Alex Comfort.

SITUATION #2
Am I as Good as I've Led Her to Believe?

So, you've been to a party and you've met a captivating woman
who, as you now remember, was dressed in wraparound erot-

icism, and in order to impress her with your own male prowess you presented yourself as emotionally footloose, not a bit shy of the road. As you whittled a strategy for looking like a man who truly knows who he is, she, quite spontaneously, led you out of the party and into the night. While sitting in an intimate little bar (talking till 4:00 in the morning), you soundlessly revealed that she could just be the one to end your confused philanderings, and got her telephone number as well.

Now you're dressing to meet her for dinner. As you shave your cheek, you're arrested by an admixture of excitement and fear, for you recall that along with exaggerating your professional accomplishments, you also hinted at an unbridled libido which at the time seemed appropriate, but now, in retrospect, smacks of *macho*, a pose you've been repeatedly warned to avoid with modern women. You wince as you now remember how you voicelessly presented yourself as a sensual libertine whose palms had cupped many a rounded form when the truth is that your fantasies may be full but your reality has been a bit barren. Quite suddenly you begin to measure yourself against the amorphous competition *out there*, and as you stroke the smoothly shaved cheek with the back of your hand, you're visited by one of anxiety's most loyal henchman, the dark elongated one with the perpetually furrowed brow and the loud, stentorian tones— DOUBT, himself.

WELL, PAUL. YOU REALLY *DON'T* KNOW WHAT THEY'RE DOING OUT THERE THESE DAYS, DO YOU?

It's true. Given the past three, five, eight years of being safely tucked in a marriage, you haven't exactly been thrust upon the single scene, and although you've heard a great deal (much more than you'd care to remember!) about the politics of the *new* woman, you're still not sure of how they exactly *manifest* on a simple date. Even though you did orchestrate the evening, selected a small, intimate restaurant where you're known, where the people respond to you, and where you'll look like a confident man-in-the-know, you're just not certain you can sustain that comfortable, uncluttered demeanor for an entire evening alone with her because . . .

YOU DON'T FEEL RELAXED AT ALL, AND YOU'RE

NOT WELL VERSED IN THE IMPORTANT AREAS
THAT REALLY COUNT.

Yes. She might not be at all interested in your topics of discussion, and you suddenly wish you hadn't been so obsessed with work and sports all these years. If you weren't running late, you'd do a quick cram with a few back issues of *Newsweek*, maybe *Time* . . . But you'd better finish shaving—you only have fifteen minutes.

Before leaving the bathroom, you find yourself unwittingly cleaning out the sink, refolding the towels, neatening the array of toilet articles on the shelf—something you rarely think of doing unless . . .

YOU REALLY THINK SHE'S COMING BACK HERE
WITH YOU TONIGHT? DON'T BE SO SURE! SHE MAY
HAVE SECOND THOUGHTS ON THE FIRST COURSE,
JUST ABOUT THE TIME THOSE GREAT GAPS OF SI-
LENCE BEGIN.

You wipe a missed dab of cream off the side of your neck, pat Au Sauvage on your cheeks, and scrutinize your face in the mirror. It's a good face—expressive, craggy-eyed, kind, even rugged. Well, you're not *convinced* all of that will happen . . .

BUT YOU'RE HOPING, WHICH IS WHY YOU BOUGHT
THE BAGELS, EGGS, BACON, AND MILK . . .

No, not really, but you would like to cover yourself just in case . . .

YOU WILL BE HAUNTED BY THOSE ITEMS TOMOR-
ROW MORNING WHEN YOU WAKE UP ALONE.

That's possible, but you do have to eat, too! And, maybe you'll find out that she enjoys quiet people.

THAT'S NOT HOW YOU PRESENTED YOURSELF TO
HER! AND DON'T LAY THAT QUIET BUSINESS ON ME
—YOU MEAN INADEQUATE, MAYBE EVEN DE-
PRESSED . . .

All right. So you are a bit war-torn. After all, you still haven't rid yourself of those stinging honesties your ex flung around at the end—those bitter reproaches for using her badly, accusations for domestic crimes never committed, charges of sexual insensitivity—the kind of acidic confrontations that could only erode your male armor. Well, just because *she* was dissatisfied (she

was still fighting off the ghost of her domineering father—
you explained that to her often enough!) that doesn't mean
that others will find you similarly wanting . . .

THIS NEW ONE HAS A STRONG PRESENCE, PAUL . . .
CAN'T MANIPULATE HER WITH YOUR BATTLE
STORIES—SHE'LL SEE RIGHT THROUGH THEM.
PROBABLY HAS A FEW OF HER OWN.

You know that! Of course, you can always talk about your
work—you did tell her you were an architect, and she did mention she worked in real estate . . . REAL ESTATE! You really
weren't listening, were you? What did you actually say about
your profession? How much embellishing did you do? She may
know much more about your field . . . the whole market! Well,
you can always get around that, just query her on the specifics
of her job. No problem.

In the bedroom, you hesitate for a moment to study your underwear, and after serious consideration pull out the beige and
brown Jockey shorts—new, clean, good fit. If you suck in your
belly, it almost looks as if you've been jogging for more than six
months . . . well, maybe three—you are a little thick on the
sides . . .

THAT'S NOT THE ISSUE! WHAT IS *SHE* GOING TO
THINK OF YOUR BODY? WITHOUT THAT VEST
YOU'RE NOT THE DEFINITIVE PICTURE OF VIRILITY
AND POWER . . .

Yes, but if you wear the three-piece suit . . . No! That's over-
doing it. You do have an Yves St. Laurent sport coat; makes
your shoulders seem a bit sharp, but it cuts in at the waist. And,
with your . . . where's your tie! NO!!! It's at the cleaner's and it's
the only tie that works! It goes with the shirt that goes with the
jacket that goes with the pants—come on!

WITHOUT THAT TIE IT'S ALL OVER, PAUL. YOU'RE
GOING TO NEED ALL THE SECURITY YOU CAN MUS-
TER UP . . . AND, YOU'D BETTER STEP ON IT, YOU'RE
RUNNING LATE.

You know, you know! So, you'll wear this tie, and that shirt,
and . . . God, this is really fatiguing . . . maybe a short nap . . .

ALREADY MAKING EXCUSES? WHAT ARE YOU GOING
TO TELL HER? YOU'VE HAD A BUSY WEEK,

OVERSTRESSED, BURNED-OUT, PREOCCUPIED WITH
WORK? OR, MAYBE YOU'LL HAVE THREE MARTINIS,
THEN YOU CAN SAY YOU HAD A LITTLE TOO MUCH
TO DRINK, IT HAPPENS SOMETIMES.

Well, you aren't so sure you're up to a rousing evening of
steamy sex. But that's not the *only* reason you take a woman out
for dinner. She happens to be bright, good-looking, capable, interesting, and an easy woman with whom to talk, not overly aggressive, soft, yes . . . And you do understand that you've been
lonely for that sexual dimension in your life. You've been filling
it up with quick, empty escapades of late, and, yeah, okay,
certain magazines which you don't acknowledge later. She was
wearing a subtle and stimulating perfume that night which really turned you on. She *is* quite different, and . . . yes, it would
be wonderful if you ended up making hot, steamy love, kissing,
rubbing, biting, claiming each other's turf . . . yeah. Excepting
that . . .

SHE *IS* A CUT ABOVE WHAT YOU'RE USED TO, AND
YOU'RE NOT SO SURE SHE'LL WANT . . .

But the chemistry was so right, you're sure of that . . .

YOU'RE SCARED. YOU COULD MESS IT UP, PAUL.

Nahhhh . . .

MAYBE YOU'D BETTER HAVE A DRINK BEFORE YOU
LEAVE . . .

"Just to take the edge off," you say out loud as you pour yourself a taste of Scotch—you *are* revving up and are ridiculously
nervous.

WHAT IF YOU BOMB OUT?

You decide not to think about that right now, you have to
leave.

WHAT IF YOU . . .

After checking for your Gold Card, you pocket your wallet.

WHAT IF . . .

You stuff your glasses in your jacket, add a comb, loose
change, and stuff the dirty clothes into the corner of the closet.
Checking the living room, you turn on the lamp with the warm,
amber glow, and look to the kitchen . . . wait—two glasses in
the sink. Leave them, it looks as if you have a busy life.

After closing the front door, you smooth your hair down on your neck and just hope you'll be as good as you've led her to believe you are.

SITUATION #3
Am I as Good as I've Led Him to Believe?

On the other side of town, after soaking in a scented milkbath, shaving your legs and other zones where unsightly hair may bloom, you apply Ultima eye shadow in the appropriate shades of brown and rust. After heavily darkening the upper lid, lining the lower, lightening the line near the brow, you blacken all lashes and dramatically step back from the harsh light. Even though you wish there was something you could do about your nose (it could be a trifle smaller, right there!), and your cheek-bones (they should be a bit higher, like that!) as you widen your eyes and blink, you're pleased with the effect.

A thrill attaches itself to your thoughts as you muse over the events of that party—the old despondency that told you not to attend, the sudden, almost crazed decision to go, and then, what a coup! You actually did meet a man whom you would like to pursue, neither married nor gay, of a good age, involved in an interesting profession, and, more important, unafraid to reveal his desire for you. Perhaps it was the new dress, that soft Qiana wraparound that seemed to give you the courage to boldly inti-mate your attraction and move with your body as if you were quite used to its erotic voice. Then again, if you had been wear-ing a sack you would nonetheless have been drawn to this man who silently wooed you through the conversational banalities and into a haven of wishful thinking. He was terribly attractive, attentive (merely kissed your cheek when he said good night at 4:00 A.M.), and now you feel an irresistible pull toward the eve-ning ahead.

But the thrill is soon muted, for as you carefully apply the deep Bordeaux lipstick, it occurs to you that you may have lost all perspective that night and insinuated yourself upon him as a woman whose lusty intentions would ultimately lead him into a musky inner sanctum filled with primitive sexual knowledge.

What you mean is that you led him to believe you're a hot number, Jill.

You grimace as you recognize the slippery voice of *Apprehension,* one of anxiety's more frequent marauders, who seemed to have snaked into the bathroom about the time you were rubbing your lips together and making a sensual O with your mouth.

Cringing, you admit that you certainly did present yourself as flirty and free, matching each of his unspoken challenges with a hint of racy self-knowledge that has nothing to do with your reality! But, after what you've been through, it felt wonderful to be in the running again, exhilarating to be appreciated as a desirable woman . . .

Even if you can't pull it off for an entire evening . . .

Yes, but that idea is a legacy from your ex-husband—he's the one who planted the notion that you're "not good in bed," which, although you now suspect meant he had someone else on the side, was a really cheap shot. But that's old history . . .

Yet it still gnaws at you because you're not convinced it's totally false.

You're also not convinced that you know exactly what that means because you were never desirous, much less *good* when you were angry, while he believed it was the only way to make it all up. At the end he had the nerve to intimate that you had "neutralized" his primal needs, and for some time you felt a bit unnatural, something like an irregular sheet, an ash-blond percale. You haven't been exactly celibate since then, yet the men you've seen—earnest but young, handsome but hostile, terrifically bright but tending toward gay—well, none of them made your skirt seriously flutter in the wind. Then suddenly you were at this party, flouting an alien expertise, blissfully trying out a new personality—exactly as you imagine those in the regular world do out there—and were assailed by a delicious sense of hope.

How do you know what they're doing out there? All you do know is that those people undoubtedly deliver what they promise!

Well, tonight you'll just have to clean up your initial message, because you are a little embarrassed over your somewhat fraudulent portrayal, but then you did have a lot to drink and you're not a *complete* impostor . . .

If you drop the sexual image, you'll lose the relationship before it starts!

That's true, too, which means you'll have to sustain that flirtatious ambience . . .

Which will give him the impression that you're whorey and loose, available to anyone . . .

No, not if you let him know that you simply don't act this way with *every* man you meet . . .

Which he won't believe—he'll continue to view you as a one-night fling . . .

So, you'll have to let him know that you do feel special about him . . .

Which will scare him off . . .

All right. Then you'll *subtly* inform him without seeming to like him too much. You'll even be a bit distant . . .

Then he'll think you don't like him . . .

But, sincere—

And he'll believe you only want a platonic friendship . . .

Not if you sustain a provocative demeanor—

Which could lead him to believe he won't be able to keep up with you.

You're suddenly exhausted. You comb out your hair, even up the side part and let the bulk sweep somewhat seductively over the top of your eye, just enough to enhance the gesture of sweeping it back in place over dinner. If you're going to flop, you'd still like to look good.

You add some blusher to your cheeks, then, wrapping your robe around you, clean up the sink, arrange the folds in the shower curtain, wipe the bath powder off the scale and, while padding into the bedroom, give your freshly cleaned living room a drill sergeant's once over.

Apprehension is sitting in the middle of the bed toying with your new beige lace underwear, and as you clip off the sales tags, slip on the bikini pants, the Barely There bra, and stand before the full-length mirror, it makes a lunge for your eyes.

Not good! Legs should be longer, belly smoother, ass tauter, breasts firmer, hips slimmer, and that cellulite business . . .

You can't lose nine pounds in fourteen minutes, it's impossible. But, if you stand up straight, wear your highest heels, pull everything in, and stay out of fluorescent lights . . .

He looks like a discerning man, even picky, Jill—used to the best . . .

All right. You'll just have to remember to always face front. You smooth on your panty hose, slip into your taupe T-strap heels and new lacy half-slip.

You have eleven minutes!

You know, you know! The cleaner's did a good job on your white silk blouse with the deep-plunge ruffle, and your red-print challis skirt is hanging well, soft and flowy—not bad. But you can't find your thin gold chain and without that chain the effect is all wrong and you remember, yes, your daughter was playing with it yesterday and now she's at her grandmother's for the night . . . dammit to hell! You pick up the tags and plastic bags, stuff them in the wastebasket, straighten the spread, fluff the pillows, close the closet doors, and . . .

Aren't you forgetting something, Jill?

Yes, but, no, okay, you'll bring it with you, although you don't know why right now because it suddenly seems so silly, all this nonsense over a dinner date. You race into the bathroom and stuff your diaphragm into your bag . . .

Because you can't invite him back here, you'll look fast and easy.

So, you won't, but he may suggest having a drink at his place, and you never know . . .

That will be worse—as if you don't care where you go . . .

Then, if it comes down to it, you'll ask him here . . .

But on the first date that will make you seem very knowledgeable.

Then you simply won't do anything!

And he'll experience you as rigid and cold.

All right! Then you *will* ask him back here . . .

And take the chance of seeming slutty.

WHAT THE HELL DO THEY DO "OUT THERE" THESE DAYS? Screw it! It's not worth all this . . . the Women's Move-

ment should have come four years earlier, you're too confused
. . . Right now you neither want to sleep with him nor even
have him in your house!

Excepting that you bought all that food, the bagels *and* rye
bread, Nova Scotia *and* sausages (well, you don't know his tastes
yet), eggs, cream cheese, fresh dill, a special blend of ground
Jamaican coffee beans, orange . . .

Which makes you look as if you expected him to spend the
night all along.

You're not going to think about this anymore.

You spray your hair, wrists, and cleavage with Cerissa, and
have just decided it's imperative to Crazy Curl the bottom of
your hair, when the doorbell rings. After the initial shock to your
heart, you sweep your hair off your eye and walk to the door
only hoping you'll be as good as you've led him to believe you
are.

A serious attraction usually flings its victims into a dervish dance
of excitement and challenge, and at the beginning both parties
put their best feet and faces forward. Later, however, when confronted with those same parts in the mirror, the realities of their
lives—their particular vulnerabilities, weaknesses, experiences—
come back to harass and to haunt. "What possessed me to act as
if I knew so much more than I do?" they ask, cuing Doubt and
Apprehension, who make their dark visitations and respond:
"You were trying to act like *them out there.*"

CONSIDERING "THEM OUT THERE"

This is a phrase usually employed to describe extraterrestrial
objects which dart about in the great unknown expanse of the
skies. Popularly it has come to mean something just as alien and
unreachable—an elitist people who linger at vacation resorts
and smart parties flawlessly exhibiting social dexterity and sexual know-how. Mythology has it that *those out there* do emanate
from a gene pool which has imbued them with the precise
knowledge of what to say, what to do, when, how, and what
color works best with it. It's difficult to compete with this group:

they are distant, amorphous, elusive, and not known for min-
gling where they can actually be seen. In fact, the closest encounters of any kind to be had with them are usually confined to
rich fantasies, fascinating idle gossip, what's been read in magazines, seen in movies, or heard from that one guy you met on
Fire Island whose tales of savoir faire and derring-do mes-
merized you into a willing suspension of disbelief. Nonetheless,
out there endures as a model for upward emotional mobility,
and *those* who inhabit it are strongly rumored to have sexual
clout.

The sexually anxious—straight, gay, old, young—use this spurious order of life as both their externally expected image and
their final criterion for behavior. Once the *out there* concept of
perfection has been incorporated into their thinking, the anxious
then fashion a composite picture of how a person of a certain
age, profession, social class, and education *should* conduct his or
her romantic liaisons and then compound the pressure by trying
to live up to it. This montage includes characteristics of dress,
manners, presence, wit, as well as the business of being well informed and experienced—a surefire checklist for heightened
anxiety.

When you consider, however, that life does include little
human eccentricities like the occasional ragged cuticle, a missed
joke, a book or film not read or seen, or a sudden inability to
speak without interspersing an "er" or an "um" into the sentence,
the composite fails. How could it not? After all, *out there* is only
an acquired notion of what one individual assumes the other
wants, and because it's such hard work presenting yourself as
this idealized person, it's questionable as to whether your front
can be sustained for any length of time.

In this particular situation, both Paul and Jill have passed
through the initial recruiting interview and are now up for the
heavy-duty screening. Identical to the job circuit, each must now
studiously remember what was said on the first meeting in order
to either sustain (or subtly vary) what he or she will say on the
second. Underneath it all, both are simultaneously juggling two
ideas: the authentic reality each knows exists concerning their
individual lives, and the false image each is attempting to project. Along with this precarious split, both are bombarded with

messages concerning relationships and how to get them off the ground without losing face.

Paul is stuck between the old male conditioning which dictates that a real man must be masterful, protective, and seasoned, and the new cultural changes which demand that he be an equal partner—intimate, vulnerable, and sensitive. Yet all of this information is strictly academic, for he has preplanned the entire evening, is preoccupied with his ability to measure up as a sexual sorcerer, and admits he has no idea how the politics of the *new* woman "exactly manifest on a simple date."

Jill is caught between the old female conditioning which dictates that a woman be a passive reactor yet simultaneously exciting and desirable, and the new consciousness which demands that she be independent and assertive, but not in the least frightening. The information is confusing in that she has not yet reconciled the dual qualities and has settled for Chinese menu decisions—a little from Group A, some from Group B, and a few last-minute substitutions.

Both worry over whether they'll be as "good" as they *think* they've led the other to believe, a concern which is misguided and misdirected, for neither makes their decisions based on what they are honestly capable of emotionally handling. Both choose their modes and styles according to the externally expected composite and to that which he or she thinks the other will find most appealing. Ultimately, they've left *themselves* out!

In this situation the false image becomes more important than the actual event. The relationship *per se* is shunted aside for the performance—the content for the style. And, compounding that anxiety, the emphasis on the sexual aspect of the evening has been given top priority! The odds against an enjoyable, comfortable date have now increased, for the harder you try to reflect yourself as a member of the sexual elite *out there*, the faster the potential for real intimacy diminishes. It's here that apprehension and doubt play their finest roles.

The pressure to be all things at once—or even one thing that you're not—encourages and promotes anxiety and panic. For instance, if a man happens to be sexually inexperienced, he may feel compelled to subtly convey that he knows everything. If a woman has "been around," she may find it necessary to dis-

creetly pretend she knows nothing. Of course, as the evening
progresses and new information concerning the other is acquired, the program will have to be adjusted: what if he discovers that she disdains his libidinal mentality? And what if she
finds he is more comfortable with experienced women? As these
variables change, the computations must be altered and some
skillful verbal maneuvers must be rapidly employed. Ultimately,
the entire event will be experienced as more fatiguing than fun,
for unless you are a virtual sleight-of-tongue wizard, the false
image cannot be successfully sustained.

For those who are truly alarmed by first-date pressures, there
are several practical methods you could begin to use to rid yourself of these unfair and unrelenting burdens. Relationships do
take time to build, and only the very naïve expect to be catapulted into a life-long liaison from a one-night success.

In order to diminish the situational anxiety of a first date, it
would be wise to first ask yourself why you tend to overempha-
size the sexual aspect of the evening? Many people use the issue
of sex as their primary proving ground and as a cover for their
intimacy fears. Once the sexual has been disposed of, they are
then ready (maybe) to move on into the relationship itself.
While this sequence may work out for some, for the sexually
anxious it's out of synch—the film is running ahead of the sound
and the experience is disorienting. If you're frightened by the
prospect of being placed in a compromising position, shift the
focus. Instant sex may be an unrealistic demand to place on
yourself. You may need time for sexuality to evolve.

If you do decide to cool out the sexual aspect of the evening,
then don't stock up on breakfast food for the next morning or
lug along birth control accoutrements. These preparations add
even more pressure to an already explosive situation. One sexually anxious woman reports that she relieves herself of this burden by refusing to "clean" her apartment before a first date. In
this way she ensures herself against the possibility of asking him
back later!

To help defuse much of the anxiety inherent in facing an entire evening, instead of jumping into an open-ended Saturday
night date, you could try stepping into the water slowly by
suggesting a time-circumscribed meeting. Limiting a first date to

one or two hours is not suggestive of anything further and will allow you to begin to build a sense of relationship. A lunch date during the week, a drink after work, or a quick bite before an evening class posits a closure and will take the emphasis off the sexual denouement.

If you do make a dinner date and are worried as to how to end it, you might state at the outset that you must be home at a certain time as you have work to complete or an early morning appointment. (If your anxiety miraculously diminishes during dessert, you can, of course, have a sudden change of plan.) This is another way of taking healthy control of a potentially loaded evening.

Along with allowances for time, you might think about place. Once again, for those who are jittery about the expectations of the other, you can lessen those particular fears by neither extending an invitation to your home on the first date, nor accepting one to his or her home. If he makes dinner, you could get caught up in the obligation syndrome and stay longer than is comfortable; if she makes dinner, you could get caught up in the gratitude trap and feel an expectation to perform. These convolutions apply to all frightened first-daters, heterosexual and homosexual—one of the two parties involved feels constrained to jump their own emotional capacity. By choosing a neutral restaurant, coffee shop, bar, or park bench, this lamentable situation can be put to rest.

While you're at it, you might try to leave the negative voices of your ex-husband, ex-wife, ex-lovers, mothers, fathers, or any other significant people who in the past sang destructive tunes, outside with the garbage. These voices are now obsolete and will only attempt to cramp your style and upstage your content. Don't let your anxiety resurrect their words of ill will. Whatever happened between you and them rests in a different time frame, and while the business between you may be unfinished and the impact unresolved, you are not compelled to drag them along on this date—they are just unnecessary baggage.

Anxiety tends to be a great distorter of the senses. Don't be alarmed if your usually sane vision of yourself is suddenly blown all out of proportion and what you see in the mirror tends toward the catastrophic. Try to remember that this is just another one of anxiety's Machiavellian tricks and that the distortion in the mirror is a direct result of having made the him or the her you are about to see too powerful and too important. You haven't changed: you've simply elevated your date to the stature of *them out there* and in so doing have dismissed your own positive qualities.

Finally, pretending to be less frightened than you are promotes yet more anxiety! You might give some thought to the false image you are hoping to convey and what purpose it serves. What qualities in yourself are you hoping to hide? What could happen if they were revealed? A certain degree of anxiety is a normal response to new situations: perhaps you could help yourself to relax by stating at the outset of the evening that you are, indeed, a little anxious. You'll only be exposing a bit of your vulnerable parts and probably hear the other person extend a sigh of relief.

If, however, you've decided to zoom into the evening from the fast track and dazzle your date with a perfectly feigned poise and aplomb, there are several other roadblocks you may incur. Dinner may go well, but what happens later when the two of you, both highly anxious strangers, are left alone sitting on the couch?

SITUATION #4
The Nightcap

"You remind me of a musician I once knew," says Jill, who has now forgotten the notion of appearing chaste and who is intoxicated by the wine, the cleft, and the tendril of dark hair on the base of his neck.

"Who was that?" asks Paul, who no longer fears gaps of silence and who is fixated on her mouth and the plunging ruffle of her blouse.

Propelled by the erotic overtones glutting the table, they have remained locked to each other's words throughout dinner. Although she picked up her fork many times, she could not bring herself to break the intense eye contact and actually allow him to see her eat, but she did discover that she need not shift her eyes to pick up a glass and as a result consumed a great deal of a nice Cabernet. When Paul made a trip to the men's room, she fell upon her food and fiercely scarfed up duck l'orange, wild rice, and a few precious bites of endive. Upon his return, however, she was ready to fuse up once again and regain the image of the perfect non-eating woman.

Since hors d'oeuvre, Paul has been completely smitten by this woman who brushes her hair back from her eyes as though brushing the length of his loins. He is not exactly clear as to how he triumphed here, but suspects it has to do with his relinquishing the traditional male prerogative at the beginning of the meal and letting her taste the wine. They finished a full bottle, another half bottle, and while he ate up everything in sight, including his boeuf bordelaise (it was easy to cut), potato puffs, and creamed broccoli, he was simultaneously transported onto the crest of his randiest anticipation.

Heady with strong wine, Jill is now tingling to the sound of his voice and the richness of his laugh, both of which seem to have blocked out the information he earlier conveyed concerning his ex-wife, a woman he spent some time reminiscing about. And although that incident did cause her to feel as though a third party, an *intruder*, had joined them, she remains seduced by his quiet, occasionally robust boyishness.

Paul did think she spent too much time speaking of her marriage (which made him feel peculiarly *invisible*), and in spite of the fact that she's in a different league and doesn't seem to have enjoyed her food, awed by his success, he has tucked that particular stress aside and now concentrates on how to push his advantage even further and suggest a last drink at home.

"Who was that, the musician you knew?" he now repeats.

"I don't remember his name—just his strong physical presence," she says, and Paul feels her soft bellows waft across his slow burn.

They fondle their espresso cups, lift them in perfect synch, swallow, and smile, acknowledging the significance of this particular juncture.

"Well . . ." Jill sighs, and Paul, who immediately construes this as a mating call, finishes her sentence with "what about a nightcap?"

"I'd love one," she responds, folding her napkin. "Why not come back to my house with me?"

Paul whips out his Gold Card, leans back in his chair, and clasps his hands behind his buzzing head.

But when she opens the door to her home, the air is thick with Scruples who had slipped in ahead of her and are now sprawled on the shag rug making themselves at home. Closing her eyes to will them away, she turns to Paul, and employing a formality that had not been present before, primly utters, "Please come in."

Paul hesitates. The new austerity in her voice weights him with what feels suspiciously like a Qualm, something he hasn't felt since he patted his face with Au Sauvage.

Jill drops her bag on the rolltop desk and turns on three lamps. "Would you like Rémy Martin, Courvoisier, Scotch, or . . ."

"Rémy would be fine," says Paul, loosening his tie, and as she stiffly marches to the kitchen, he senses he has violated a sacred code. Her home reads warmth, intimacy, ease—a complete life. His watch reads 12:20, and his feelings read oddly inessential.

Jill opens the cupboard and is immediately attacked by a group of Scruples viciously nattering near the Wheat Thins: *"You shouldn't have invited him back," "This is your FIRST date," "Your reputation's going straight to hell," "Not nice," "Bad."* She pours the Rémy, Scotch-on-the-rocks for herself, and, with a budding sobriety, carries them into the living room conscious of a lone Scruple rattling the ice in her glass and sounding very much like her mother—*"You weren't brought up this way!"*

As she sits down next to Paul on the rust-colored couch, his Qualm scuttles across the room. *"Something turned her off, she's seen you for what you are, you don't wear well after all . . ."* it cries out, sounding very much like his ex-wife, and lodges itself in the wing chair.

"This is a very comfortable room," Paul observes, affecting a facile ease.

"Thanks . . . I've been here a long time . . ." she responds, feeling tense, and alienated, suddenly aware that his presence is absolutely foreign.

Nervously sipping nightcaps, they launch an awkward conversation discussing topics already covered at dinner, seasoning this "chat" with false starts and forced bursts of enthusiasm. Pressing for that one link which will miraculously make everything right, they switch from I. M. Pei, Van der Rohe, her house and Bauhaus to M.A.S.H., Steve Martin and Mel Brooks, where they pause to stretch their repertoires of comic lines but wear down fast when Paul finds himself recycling a joke concerning garlic and the angel of death. "Well," says Jill, filling in the space, "how about one more drink?" She returns to the kitchen and Paul checks his watch, which now tells him it's 1:45 and that he may have done something horrendously wrong.

"*Send him home!*" demand the Scruples who surprise her in the freezing compartment. "*She thinks she'll feel FREER if she spends four hours talking,*" says a fat sarcastic one; "*she's getting to KNOW him better!*" Jill slams the refrigerator door shut.

In the living room, Paul's Qualm is riding his leg, wresting control of his knee. "*She's changed her mind. She's gearing her conversation to your level. She doesn't think you're as bright as the others . . .*" it pleads and, as Jill returns to her seat, it continues by saying, "*She's about to call it a night!*" Paul angrily wags his leg and, in a privately declared war, inches closer to her on the couch.

Jill hands him his drink, which he sets on the glass coffee table. He reaches out and touches her ash-blond hair, a gesture which startles her. She peers up into his craggy eyes, which now seem a soft, blurred blue, and as he leans in toward her lips, she ducks and grabs for her Scotch, exclaiming with calculated zest, "This has been a wonderful evening!" The lone Qualm slips down Paul's pants to his groin and plays hangman on his member.

"I'd really like to kiss you," Paul says with a knavish edge, feeling much like a sex offender and expecting her to shriek.

"Oh," says a breathy, new Jill, immediately stirred by the personal in his words, and in an unexpected move, tilts her head and murmurs, "then why don't you?"

Her answer flows to his loins, knocking the Qualm silly, and as he covers her mouth with his, the Scruples make a dive for her neckline, freeing her lips to meet his. They fall onto each other's mouths, licking, rubbing, trying out new personalities through their tongues, which are probing ledges and lip lines, for each suspects they'd better make this good, if not memorable, as the sexual future of this relationship now pivots on the impact of this kiss.

But, as they kiss, Jill questions the authenticity of her passion, for she's still not sure she should do *everything* and she's thinking so much she's not certain what she's feeling, except that her veins are filled with a flotilla of The Willies rowing their way to her mind. Diddling with her desire to mate, they remind her of the information Paul passed on at dinner regarding his ex-wife who was, according to him, very special—owned her own boutique, traveled in glamorous circles, and had a biting wit. "What did she look like?" Jill had asked, stroking the stem of her glass. He had paused, then thoughtfully answered, ". . . Marlene Dietrich." Now with his tongue circling her lips and his fingers in her hair, she feels little else but the shiver of her cellulites.

Paul is elated by her spirited response, but hadn't fully reckoned on such *fire,* such *expertise.* Yet, although he is electrified, even elevated, he finds himself wrestling with *Intimidation,* who is commuting up to his mind, threatening to put the kibosh on the rest of the night. Plucking at his nerves, it suggests that her know-how may just be the result of having been with a range of skilled lovers, all like her ex-husband, who she told him earlier was a tad irresponsible, but charming and handsome. He was, she had said, running six miles before marathons were in vogue, conscious of health before whole grains were chic, and prided himself on the European flair of his designer clothes. "And what did he look like," Paul had ventured, meticulously slicing his boeuf bordelaise. "In certain lights," she had said, pondering her empty fork, "he looked exactly like . . . Omar Sharif." Although an almost inaudible moan of pleasure now escapes from her throat, Paul feels little else but the wrongness of his tie and the tightness of his belt.

Jill wants to break this kiss and change her position. Her neck is bent, her leg is nearing charley horse alert, and although her thumb is making circles on his thigh, she is still struggling between the "wants" and the "shoulds" and The Willies are splashing cold against her heated pulse. Paul is haunted by the time, worried about his potency, and wonders how he can be a runaway success if they wait until 4:00 A.M. to enter that promised carnal oblivion, at which time he will need a pulley to hoist him into life.

At 2:15 they break the kiss. Running his finger over her lips Paul murmurs, "It's getting late," which thoroughly alarms her because it means *she* must make the decision, a responsibility she hoped to cleverly circumvent. "Yes, it is," she agrees, shrewdly buying time, which is not what he wanted her to say, and so he kisses her again, this time using his lips in a new imaginative style, and she feels his hand slip down from her neck and onto her breast, which makes her tremble and sends a warm shiver through his hand and down to his thigh which she has resumed stroking.

Quite unexpectedly, his Qualm reappears just then wearing a fright wig, and babbles something urgent in his ear. Paul pulls away from her lips and, looking to his nails, begins the following soliloquy:

"I'd really like to be straight with you. I've only been divorced a short while and I got married when I was quite young, and I don't think I really know what you know because I haven't been out there as long as you have, and, well, you seem to be a woman who knows a lot, you're so attuned to yourself, so natural . . . What I really want is just to *be* with you . . . Why don't we just go into the other room?"

Jill flops back on the couch. Jolted by this confession, which has promoted her from her image as ice maiden to his as hot tomato, she now suspects she must thoroughly convince him that she hasn't had that much experience either. If he continues to think that she knows more than he knows, then he'll be sure to view her as loose and insincere, dooming any emotional connection before it is barely born. The Scruples have returned *en masse* and are making smug, "I-told-you-so" faces, compelling her to defend her spurious know-how.

"Oh, God," she says, ignoring his request, "then I've really given you the wrong impression. I've been thinking all evening of how much I'd like to get to *know* you before . . . I mean, I'm not all *that* experienced! I really don't do this that often and I'm not naturally torrid or tempestuous . . . I'm terribly attracted to you but do think we should wait until we know each other better, don't you?"

Paul is silent. *"You may have blown it,"* whispers his Qualm, who has doffed the wig and is now juggling the rods and cones in his brain. "That's not what I mean," he finally says. "I feel as if I've known you for a long time—I've felt that way all evening, but . . . I may have misread your feelings. I guess I felt comfortable enough with you to be honest . . ."

"Manipulation," whispers a wary Scruple with dangerously narrowed eyes. "Oh, I'm so glad you're being honest . . ." states Jill, wondering whether she should trust his words, for surely he has been with hundreds of wild and exotic lovers. But, fearing she may have overstated her case and lost the sexual edge, her appeal, and him in the bargain, she continues by saying, "You're *very* easy to be with, too."

"She's just turned you into a friend," the timid Qualm mutters. "I'd like very much to be more than friends with you," Paul goes on, reaching out to stroke her cheek, and Jill, not knowing how to reconcile the independent-and-sexual with the respectable-and-good, nervously flashes a cryptic grin, stands, and with both of her hands extended toward his, silently invites him to follow.

They wend their way to the bedroom. She flips on the overhead light which illuminates The Willies now squatting in the middle of the quilted spread holding a sign which blatantly informs: "MARRIAGE BED!" Paul, who is unaware of this particular activity, sits on the edge of that bed and spies a photograph on the nightstand of a well-endowed Jill with a very young girl. "DAUGHTER!" *Intimidation* screams out, momentarily wilting whatever semblance of desire he had on the long voyage from one room to the other.

Jill stands by the armoire wearing a wanton smile; Paul

remains seated on the bed dressed in a seductive grin. Both are fixed in space.

We pause at this precarious juncture to retrace the steps leading up to this moment and to explore a few of the notions endemic to first-date perfection fears, Scruples, Qualms, ghosts of the past and anxieties of the present.

PERFECTION AND EATING

Perfection is the key theme in this situation, and although it became operative way back while both were dressing for the date, it gained its momentum for Jill at the restaurant over duck l'orange. Her perception of *perfect* was embodied right there at the table in her self-created image of a woman so deeply fascinated by the man that mere food could never be rival to the words that fell from his lips. Proving her devotion to the conversation and to his voice, she fused up with his eyes, demonstrating her qualities as an intentive and highly qualified listener. Many sexually anxious people have been known to leave banquets starving in order to perpetuate this image.

However, there are others who have left sumptuously laden tables muffling their hunger pangs in the service of yet another anxiety. These are the people (mainly women) who construe the act of consuming food as intensely intimate and wildly sexual. They believe that using the mouth betrays a range of private impulses and secret flaws which they would rather keep to themselves. Therefore, they choose their social foods wisely, carefully selecting that which can be whittled down to proper bite size, easily measured, portioned, cut, controlled, and appropriately placed into the oral cavity. Foodstuffs which must be licked, sucked, nibbled, chewed extensively, or touched with the hands, edibles that just might dribble, drip, or overflow, are strictly verboten. This eliminates ice cream cones, bottled drinks, fruit, burgers, sandwiches, corn-on-the-cob, chicken, and, of course, duck l'orange. Foolishing forgetting what duck with bones inplies, Jill mistakenly ordered this taboo food. She did redeem herself, however, by refusing to eat while under his visual scrutiny, sustaining her image of "perfect woman."

Logic would dictate that once you have acquired an intellectual understanding of this peculiar eating anxiety, the symptoms would disappear. Unfortunately, there is no such magical prescription for this particular malady. Therefore, if you do suffer its pangs, be sure to order only those foods which you know you are actually capable of ingesting. If you hanker for a chicken dish, first ask if it's deboned; if it's fish you're after, make certain it's filleted; and, if it's pasta you require, stay away from long-noodled linguine. In this way you'll be able to minimize your anxiety and, if your partner selected the restaurant, you'll assuage his or her anxiety as well.

Drinking wine from a controllable glass is allowed here, and in Jill's case it afforded her the courage to invite Paul back to her house for a nightcap, something she struggled against earlier in her argument with Apprehension. Her bravado was short-lived, however, for she was not ready for this abrupt transition.

THE GHOSTS OF THE PAST

The Scruples and Qualm play interesting but not uncommon roles here as voices of anxiety. Anxiety is a function of conflict, and a conflict, of course, is based upon a struggle between the authentic state of your psyche and the externally created composite—that which you are pretending to feel or be. When you invite a new man or woman into your home before you are emotionally ready, you stand the chance of being psychically assaulted by ghost voices from the past—former spouses, lovers, and parents. Your home is a symbol of the authentic you, complete with all of its familiar reminders of what your life has wrought. These ghosts can be dismissed in a neutral restaurant, but they won't be easily shunted aside in your own personal lair. They tend to crowd the room with noisy chatter, showing up in the furnishings, the paintings, books, records, accessories, and especially in the mutually purchased refrigerator, end tables, lamps, and, of course, the bed.

There are numerous people who feel a sense of disloyalty to the past when a new person is brought into their homes. Even though the relationship inspiring this guilt may have ended months ago, the feeling of betrayal persists, for the intimacies shared with the last person are now about to be reopened with a virtual stranger. This circumstance will often provoke memories of your old, broken dreams. This particular anxiety manifests in a number of ways. Women are known to experience an icy chill, to perceive the new person as an intruder, and to begin behaving in a prim, austere, or even formal manner. Men may actively seek out the flaws in the new person's appearance, begin to make sounds of fatigue, talk about the heavy day they must face in the morning, or complain of a sudden physical ailment. All of these manifestations are geared to provide distance from the situation. These people are simply not ready to plunge into an intimate affair—their mourning period has not quite ended.

You can completely avoid this anxiety by carefully assessing your feelings and making peace with the fact that your mourning period may still be in process. Prematurely thrusting yourself into a new affair when your body and your mind are unprepared is tantamount to placing yourself on an emotional rack. By forcing yourself to behave as though you were finished with the past when you're actually still hurting, is overloading yourself with painful demands. The relationship you are contemplating cannot be given the chance it deserves, and when it does go sour and begin to disintegrate, you, of course, will turn the circumstances against yourself and will have provided a new set of abuses with which to be self-critical and self-punishing. Take a rest during this period; this is a time for recuperation. (Do be aware, however, that prolonging a mourning period beyond its natural limits could mean that you are creating a false anxiety in order to avoid facing a new intimacy. This is tricky, for *you* must be the sole judge of the time needed to heal, and you may be postponing your recuperation out of fear.)

The ghost voices of the Scruples and Qualm could also spring from experiences other than a broken love affair. They may be echoing the words of an angry ex-spouse or lover who accused you of being loose, frigid, impotent, passive, aggressive; or, they could be reverberating the judgments of a highly critical parent whose insensitive charges have remained lodged in your head—the possibilities here are infinite. One way to combat these nagging voices is to begin separating them out, one from the other, and learn to distinguish their sources. Once the voices have been identified, you'll be able to sift out that which is valid for your life and begin to dispose of the obsolete trivia. For instance, when one of Jill's Scruples rattled the ice in her glass and said, "You weren't brought up this way!" she was able to identify the voice as that of her mother. Paul, too, was able to distinguish the biting voice of his Qualm as that of his ex-wife. For both, the sting remained intact, but once identified, the impact of the words was negotiable.

CIRCUMVENTING THE SEXUAL

Awkwardness, uneasiness, and tension are natural by-products of the anxiety sexually attracted people experience the first time they're thrown together alone. There's no way it can be completely eliminated and there's no real reason why it should: it's legitimate and it's realistic. The idea of perfection here is gleaned from that same notion that *those out there* do not experience anxiety and its attendant blunders and shakes. Again, this is a false concept! In seeking perfection you're ultimately denying that the human factor exists and are striving for an automaton mentality with no blood, guts, or human frailties.

The desire for perfection is ironically interesting in that it's not a goal unto itself. It's a method for hiding the anxiety from yourself and from others. By allowing yourself to have the anxious feelings, you're on your way to mastering them, for anxiety swells under falseness and diminishes under truth. When you dismiss, deny, or disavow the presence of the anxiety and persist in presenting yourself as solid, together—*perfect*, you've set the stage for a rather severe attack.

In this situation, both Jill and Paul anxiously circumvent any verbal reference to the possibility of becoming affectionate or sexual. By avoiding what they both know they're thinking, the tension increases and the awkwardness grabs out, forcing each into their own isolated little corner. Both are looking for cues as to what the other intends, and, at first, neither is willing to take responsibility for making a first move.

One way to combat this uncomfortable stand-off is to open it

up and address it straight-on. You could be as direct as necessary, perhaps stating that you've been looking forward to this
evening, that you've been hoping to end it by making love, that
now that you're here, you're a little anxious, nervous, maybe unsure. This will relieve you of your tension and open up the conversation. The worst that can happen: the other person will say
that he or she is not ready, doesn't feel close enough, doesn't
know you well enough yet, would like to wait, or—at the very
extreme—that wasn't what he or she had in mind. The facts will
then be disclosed and you'll be able to proceed from there without polluting the rest of the evening with aimless conversations
or slippery manipulations.

However, if you don't want to make love and you do feel
you've overplayed your flirtatiousness, you might say that you do
hope you haven't given out any mixed or double messages by
asking him/her up for a drink, but you really aren't quite ready
to become intimately and/or physically involved. Once again,
the worst that can happen is that your partner could respond
defensively by saying that's not what he or she had in mind at
all, and you could feel foolish for a moment. Nonetheless, the
decks will be cleared of the unnecessary emotional debris.

Of course, in order to come clean about your feelings you
must know what you want and be willing to take responsibility
for your decisions. If you're like Jill and are caught up in the
"wants" and the "shoulds," while you wait for him to make the
first move and the decision you'll end up promoting even more
anxiety for yourself. Try to be clear about your own intentions!
When you wait for the other person to act and to make your decisions for you, you're totally abdicating your power and losing
your sense of self. This is a most confusing issue for women.
Many are caught, like Jill, not having reconciled "the independent-and-sexual with the respectable-and-good" and are stuck
with a disagreeable ambivalence. Yet, it's also bewildering for
men. They fear being branded an exploiter if they make a move,
and a passive bore if they don't. Nonetheless, it's better to risk
making a blunder than not acting at all—there is excitement in
challenge.

Talking and talking till 4:00 A.M. may be the easiest route
around making a final decision, but it will never alleviate the

anxiety. On the contrary, it will promote even more for both parties. Consider this: after working a full week, grappling with
office problems, domestic responsibilities, probably children, a
large dinner, several drinks, and close to eight hours of anxious
tension, is this a good time to engage in the great sexual esca-
pade? If you're hell-bent on making love and this is the first
time, perhaps it would be better to call it a night and resume the
action tomorrow. Many men feel that they must become sexual
because "it's the manly thing to do." If this is your thinking, try
to recognize that you're merely hoping to diminish feelings of insecurity and inadequacy by pushing yourself beyond your physical limits. Nothing kills romance like fatigue.

DISTANCING AND FALSE HONESTIES

One good way to create an overwhelming measure of insecurity
in your prospective lover is to elevate your former lover or ex-
spouse to the stature of a Dietrich or Sharif. There is no possible
way he or she can live up to that image and what it implies;
their feelings will surely begin to careen downhill. This is a
surefire distancing mechanism, one that may temporarily control
your own image anxiety (for it certainly indicates that you have
been desired by the best), but it will work against you in the
long run. If you do find yourself speaking of your last lover (and
you will!), be kind. The new person may become petrified by
the competition and fade away before you've had a chance to
tell the rest of the story.

"I'd really like to be straight with you," is a phrase which has
unfortunately come to mean its complete opposite. Although
there are those who do mean what they say, there are others
who use this opener to announce the arrival of a false honesty.
Paul used this line to introduce a manipulation geared to quell
his anxiety. While his soliloquy sounded "straight" and "honest"
—as if he was genuinely confessing his insecurity—in reality he
was reducing himself to a sexual acorn and enlarging her to a
lustful oak. Of course, his intention was to reduce her expectations, but he only managed to make her defensive. If you'd really like to be "straight," once again, address yourself to your
anxiety. Manipulations tend to backfire, and even when they do

manage to work, by the time you reach the bedroom, the measure of ambivalence and disorientation far exceeds the desire.
Like Paul and Jill, the anxiety will leave you fixed in space, wondering how you can possibly manage the nuts-and-bolts preliminaries to the main event.

SITUATION #5
Sexual Preliminaries and Inhibition

"IF YOU TAKE YOUR CLOTHES OFF ALL AT ONCE
HE'LL THINK YOU LIED ABOUT YOUR EXPERIENCE,"
says INHIBITION, who entered the arena, pointed at Jill, and
seated himself in a director's chair. *Well, I never intended to do
that!* she thinks, wondering just what she's supposed to do since
she's unwilling to be seen walking nude.

"THIS IS THE MOMENT OF TRUTH," the tyrant pro-
claims, now directing himself toward Paul, who is flipping his tie
on his hand and removing his shoes with his toes. *Not if I can
just turn off that light,* he thinks, for he is reluctant to be seen
before he has achieved a dignified proportion.

Jill quickly ascertains the part of her body by which she is
least embarrassed and slowly unbuttons her white ruffled blouse.
Paul apes her movements and, taking great care not to stare at
her breasts, which are now partially revealed in a Barely There
bra, removes his shirt. He pulls down the quilted spread, stacks
the down pillows, and in a burst of appealing boyishness, play-
fully punches them up. "YOU'VE HAD A LOT TO DRINK,"
states INHIBITION clinically, now concerned with his incipient
performance. *I know, I know,* thinks Paul, whisking his T-shirt
up over his head and feeling tense in his calves. Not knowing
what to do with his hands, Paul rests them at his hips and INHI-
BITION asks, "DOES OMAR SHARIF HAVE HANDLES AT
HIS WAIST?" a question steeped in rhetoric, convincing him
once again that Jill has seen and known only the unforgettable
best.

Jill unhooks her skirt, and in spite of the fact that INHIBI-
TION is flashing the famous Eisenstadt photograph of Dietrich-

in-tails before her eyes, she pulls down the red challis and steps out. Catching a glimpse of herself in the mirror, she is stunned by the contrast between the "women-he's-probably-known" and herself, for quite suddenly her curves seem excessive and her hourglass frame old hat. *I am not "what's happening, baby,"* she thinks and, in a perfect imitation of Twyla Tharpe, leaps for the overhead light and shuts it off.

Plunged into darkness, Paul grabs this opportunity to drop his pants and Jockey shorts, which are halfway down when she flicks the bed lamp on. *"COVER YOUR PARTS!"* INHIBITION orders, and Paul hops backward to the bed, jerks them off and, in a fanatical display of neatness, begins to straighten the creases over his lap.

"DON'T LOOK DOWN THERE!" it now directs Jill, who demurely averts her eyes and removes her shoes. She is, however, somewhat dismayed by his adroitness in undressing, a quality which proves to her she cannot trust his words, for he appears to be quite unruffled by this event. And, she's getting nervous because when she does remove her underwear he will discover she is *not* androgynously slim, a body aesthetic she vaguely believes she has gotten away with since they met.

Ensuring he will not be able to examine her flaws, and guaranteeing she will not be able to scrutinize his, they both quickly entwine and fall back onto the bed bent on blinding each other with lust.

Paul works at obscuring her vision by crushing her eyes to his, and calculates how to douse the lamp without appearing to be one of those cloddish men who doesn't know that lights-with-sex is where it's at. Pressing for a rush of erotic momentum, he reaches around her back to unhook her bra, which she knows is futile as it unhooks in front, and as he gropes, she tries to indicate with a negative movement of her head that he's fumbling in the wrong spot, a gesture he construes as a new cry of feminine protest, which only serves to confuse him and mar his credentials as an ace seducer. Alleging a coolness he does not possess, he silkily murmurs, "Why don't you take the rest of this off?" Pretending she's a practiced someone else, Jill tightens her stomach muscles and balletically hoists her hips, tugging down pants, hose, and half-slip. She flings her hair over her face, sits up and pulls them off, unhooks her bra and, making significant cleavage, presses herself to his chest, pleased with her skillful avoidance of his eyes on her less-than-perfect parts.

Paul, who has not yet removed his black socks, and who is now perceiving himself as a porno star, buries his feet in the quilted spread, and as they cling and climb, tumble and twirl, each wondering how to kill that light, it occurs to Jill that her diaphragm is in the other room silently protecting her purse.

"IF YOU GET UP NOW YOU'LL BREAK THE MOOD," says INHIBITION, who is perched on the row of books up on the bedstead. But, thinks Jill stiffening her thighs, I really can't endure two weeks of cold fear with The Willies again! "WELL, YOUR PERIOD ENDED ON THE 17TH WHICH WAS A WEDNESDAY, AND THIS IS THE 29TH. FIGURE THIS IS THE 12TH DAY AND YOU'RE OKAY UNTIL THE 31ST." Not if you count the 17th, which makes this the 13th day, determines Jill who is covering her arithmetic with soft, panty moans, and who believes a perfect woman would never be caught ovulating.

"THEN YOU'LL HAVE TO BACK OUT OF THE ROOM," says INHIBITION, who has now made her acutely aware of the lamp shining on her thighs. Not if I turn it off, thinks Jill, and in a burst of spontaneity whispers to Paul, "Hold it, right there!" disengages from his arms and flips the switch off. Unwilling to trust the moonlight, however, she faces front, sidles her way to the door and disappears.

"YOU CAN RELAX," says INHIBITION now that Paul is alone, "I'M TAKING FIVE." Paul leaps up and whips off his socks. Falling back, he spread-eagles on the bed, stretches and flexes his muscles, then, concerning himself with the quintessential factor, feels his loins—not quite aroused, but definitely in process.

Jill grabs her bag from the rolltop desk, flees to the bathroom and flips the harsh light on. "My God!" she exclaims, widening her blackened eyes in the mirror, "You look decked!" She removes her diaphragm from the blue plastic container, prepares the edges, the pouch, and lifts her foot. But her hands are shaky and the plastic bucks and flips into the air, landing on the soap dish. "Damn!" she says, certain she's lost the knack . . .

Paul flicks the lamp back on and swiftly surveys her bedroom, noting details of her personal life—a mirrored tray of perfumes and colognes, an ebony jewelry box, and on the bedstead behind his head, two long shelves of books. Perusing the titles, his eye is startled by a small grouping nestled between Anaïs Nin and Nabokov: *The Joy of Sex; Older Women, Younger Men; Human Sexual Inadequacy* . . .

On the third attempt, Jill is convinced this night was not meant to be and sits like a stone on the toilet seat staring at a lavender towel . . .

Living Alone and Liking It; No-Fault Marriage; Human Sexual Response; Nice Girls Do; How to Make Love to a Man . . .

On the fourth try it slips in and hooks. She washes her hands, brushes her hair, weighs herself, adds some blusher, and . . .

The Hazards of Being Male . . . Before he can scan the second shelf, he hears the toilet flush and quickly switches off the lamp. As he arranges his elbow on the pillow and his head on his palm, it occurs to him that somewhere around the third book title he lost his edge and now feels alarmingly bland. Nevertheless, he arranges his face into a devilish repose and works up a visual of blackguard ease.

Disturbed by the abrupt jolt of the harsh light and the cold mechanics of this event, Jill's desire is largely flattened. Nonetheless, she puts a sexy lilt into her step, a humid glow on her lips, and sidles seductively back into bed.

It is now 4:00 A.M.

A short digression is in order here to explore some of the pertinent issues surrounding the part-covering theme and the business of preliminaries.

NUDITY AND INHIBITION

Nakedness is a trigger for a wide range of emotional responses to yourself and to the world. Many people find it difficult, if not impossible, to conduct a heated argument while nude and will

run for a robe in midscream. Others cannot hold a serious conversation or even make a grocery list. Still others are able to
function if the top is uncovered, but certainly not the bottom;
and then there are those who can manage if they are partially
clad, although few feel comfortable naked with shoes. Another
subgroup seemingly glows with a sense of pride when completely nude even though they may be quietly entertaining a
high-grade panic!

Quite obviously, garments play a part in our society which far
exceed their original role as protection against the elements. A
very sophisticated language exists in the attire we pick as well as
the styles we choose. Each different ensemble makes its specific
statement containing information pertinent to what we would
like to convey. Much of the bravado anxious people display can
be safely traced back to what they are wearing: one takes courage from appearance and, conversely, may become unhinged if
the outfit *isn't right.*

It follows that when the clothing statement is taken away, the
carefully prepared identity also disappears. Gone are the enhance-
ments, accessories, color, and style—enter vulnerability, exposure, and anxiety.

The following is a list of random comments collected from a
small group of sexually anxious people concerning this issue:

"When I'm naked I'm afraid what I say won't be taken
seriously and that I'll be viewed as foolish."

"I don't really have any personal power when I'm nude."

"I feel that I could get hurt, that I have nothing with which to
defend myself—I'm totally unarmed!"

"I lose my specialness."

"I'm sure she's comparing me to her last lover."

"I know he's comparing me with *Playboy* standards."

"I get embarrassed, taken off guard, self-conscious . . ."

"There was no nudity where I grew up—I can't get used to
it."

"In seventeen years of marriage we always undressed in the
dark."

"She'll see my deficiencies: I *am* a little flabby here, you
know."

"He'll see the discrepancy between the width of my hips and
the size of my breasts."

"I don't like my back!"

"My stomach, my thighs, my cellulites . . ."

"I just don't like to be looked at! It doesn't feel right . . ."

Obviously, the emergence of inhibition while in the nude is
not uncommon: the perfect package—protection and conceal-
ment—disappears and what was hidden is now exposed—
revealed, raw. Because these feelings are so prevalent, the very
complex orchestration of lights, sheets, and blankets, as well as
the sensitive choreography of undressing itself become paramount. In the above situation, visibility and invisibility are priority concerns. Neither Jill nor Paul feels comfortable with their
bodies nor with each other, therefore darkness here is essential.
But the very act of shutting off the light complicates the issue
further, for each considers it something of a disgrace to be
caught feeling inhibited.

For many women, disrobing is fraught with anxiety. Removing your own clothes all at once may imply you are raunchy, experienced, and too assertive, yet it does give you more control
over the sequence of item removal. If, on the other hand, you
disrobe slowly, tentatively, you stand the chance of being
watched, especially if your partner is already undressed and
waiting. Then, again, if you allow him to undress you, you've
placed yourself in the passive, dependent role, a seductive position which also allows you to abdicate responsibility for the entire event. "After all," the thinking goes, "he's doing it, I'm not,
this is happening to me and I have nothing to do with it at all!"
Nonplussed by this dilemma, many women settle for half and
half, thereby assuaging the anxiety of appearing either too passive or too aggressive.

Men are not usually as deeply concerned with the actual removal of their clothes but do become anxious over the degree of
their arousal and, once seen, whether the size will meet with the
approval of their partners. However, if no realistic degree of intimacy has been achieved prior to the undressing, they must
quietly divine through gesture and nuance what the woman
wants of them in terms of helping her. With no sense of the pre-

vailing sensibility regarding this matter of undressing, they often find themselves grappling, like Paul, with garments that prove awkward and confusing in the removal. This can become frustrating and harmful to their image as "ace seducers."

One way to defuse the nudity anxiety is to first understand that your body is indeed private and carries a wisdom your mind sometimes denies. If the spirit of closeness has been shunted aside, the voice of inhibition will undoubtedly take control. In order to unjam yourself, it might be necessary to mention your uneasiness. You don't have to relate your life story of body embarrassment or point out your flaws, but a casual comment could help to lighten up the ambience. Opening this subject up could prove to be a boon for the relationship: it could commence the first *real* conversation of the evening.

BREAKING THE MOOD

The most prevalent stories about unwanted pregnancies come from women who didn't want to stop and "break the mood," were "embarrassed by appearing so absolutely *prepared*," felt "inept over being unprepared," or tricked themselves into "believing it was a safe time to avoid getting up." All of these stories are variations on the same theme: fear that the man will find them disappointing if they interrupt the erotic momentum, an anxiety which takes precedence over the anxiety of suffering the following days or weeks waiting for their periods to arrive. Once again, *perfect* becomes the all-important modus operandi. Leaving the bed in mid-moan destroys the externally created composite picture of how one should conduct a romantic, sexual liaison, something Jill expressed quite succinctly when she thought to herself, "the perfect woman would never be caught ovulating."

One way to quell this anxiety is to dwell for longer than a moment on the larger issue and the *greater* anxiety: becoming pregnant! This topic is far more pressing than the look of love and should act to get you up onto your feet swiftly! If, however, you're paralyzed in his arms, once again, you might verbalize your intention to your partner. Once he's made aware of the fact that you are unprotected, he'll probably take a wide berth around your path off the bed.

However, this is an issue aimed at both women *and* men, and it implies a dual responsibility. It's not "unmanly" to ask about the situation, to voice concern and to share in the problem. As the other half of the act, you may diminish your anxieties greatly in the process and you'll undoubtedly become more real to her.

THE LOOK OF "FREE"

One of the prime anxieties surrounding the preliminaries of sex concerns how "free" you want to appear in this situation. Many people behave as though they've been working the district for years, for they have convinced themselves that in order to be free they've got to act less inhibited than they really feel. This is a method for repressing anxiety under the guise of the motto "Anything goes with me!" In truth, most of these people are scared out of their wits!

This situation can be likened to those who are frightened of the water, yet tell everyone within earshot that they adore water-skiing. They'll even go so far as to travel out to the deepest end of the lake where everyone can witness what a madcap, daredevil he or she can be, all the time hiding an incredible panic! This is called a counterphobic reaction and applies to many who harbor sexual fears. When someone is terrified of sex yet flings off their clothes with wild abandon and begins to attack the parts of the other with much drama and heavy intensity, they are demonstrating this reaction. The whole act becomes false, complete with artificial gestures and superficial lusts, for at this point, the person is quite unrelated to the act and is simply intent on performing.

Of course, this response to anxiety is not without its impact on the other person—homosexual or heterosexual—who may begin to perceive you as the hottest number in gay circles from Muscle Beach to Manhattan, or as the wildest sexual happening from Wilshire Boulevard to Wall Street. However, unless he or she is also acting out of a counterphobic stance, you'll probably scare them to death. If he or she is interested in developing a serious, intimate relationship, they'll most probably be reluctant to call again, unless stricken by a crazed bout of horniness.

The look of "free" can be most deceptive. It not only acts as a way of denying sexual panic and anxiety, it's also a successful method for avoiding intimacy. Feigning "freedom" allows you to race into a fast clinch, thereby circumventing the possibility of being seen with the facial expressions sex, love, affection, and anxiety often promote. Many people are frightened of being caught looking tender, and dive for the nearest part to hide their glow. Others immediately busy themselves as a way of concealing their absence of passion or loss of feeling.

When inhibition has you tied up in knots, it's very difficult to cultivate honest sexual desire. However, pretending to be free of restraint and "ready to try anything" won't transform your feelings: to the contrary, it will only induce more anxiety. If you're scared and feel unsure, try to avoid the counterphobic reaction. Perhaps it would be wiser to slow down, center yourself, and find your own natural rhythm and style. If you ultimately allow your behavior to catch up with your feelings, the voice of inhibition may fade to a hum.

However, as the night moves on, there are other voices with which you may have to contend—voices of authority gleaned from a variety of sources. If you are a sexually anxious person like Jill or Paul, the messages of those other voices, once lodged in your mind, are often confusing, if not frustrating.

SITUATION #6
What the Sex Books Say

Jill has now slipped under the sheets next to Paul. Both offer showy displays of readiness and ease.

JILL: (*Thinking*) I've been fantasizing about this all day, now here he is, here we are, in my bed and . . . I feel so tense!

Something's all wrong, I should be excited, aroused, *ready* . . .

A rustle of pages infiltrates her consciousness. She raises her eyes in an expression of budding recall.

THE SEX BOOKS: WE'RE HERE, LODGED IN YOUR PASSIVE MEMORY!

JILL: Oh, yes . . . now where did I read . . . Never mind. Listen, I'm so afraid I won't be *good,* I can't get into the mood!

HOW-TO SEX BOOK: YOU DIDN'T REALLY CREATE THE PROPER SETTING—WHERE ARE THE FLICKERING CANDLES, THE LUSH GREEN PLANTS . . .

CLINICAL SEX BOOK: GET TO THE POINT! SHE DIDN'T LEARN TO LOVE *HERSELF* FIRST . . .

HOW-TO SEX BOOK: (*Interrupting*) NO, NO, NO. SHE SHOULD HAVE SUGGESTED A WARM STIMULAT-ING BATH, PERHAPS A MASSAGE WITH EXOTIC OILS, APHRODISIACS, RAVEL'S BOLERO . . .

JILL: I can't deal with that! It's not my style—I would have been mortified hauling out a truckload of fancy accoutrements. After all, this is only my first time with him . . .

HOW-TO'S: (*In unison*) YOU'RE NOT SUPPOSED TO FEEL ESTRANGED FROM YOUR BODY. DIDN'T YOU DO YOUR HOMEWORK? DID YOU PRACTICE PLEA-SURING YOURSELF THIS WEEK?

JILL: (*Flinches from guilt*) Ah . . . I didn't have time . . . well, maybe once, but . . .

PERMISSION-GIVING SEX BOOK: (*With motherly concern*) YOU'RE ALLOWED TO LOVE YOUR BODY. JUST ERASE YOUR OLD BAD TAPES, BE GOOD TO YOURSELF, AND . . .

A HOW-TO: *EXCUSE ME!* I WAS SPEAKING. AFTER ALL, I'M *UNDERLINED!* DID YOU SIZE UP HIS LIKES AND DISLIKES?

JILL: Not yet. I was just beginning to do that, but I feel a bit shy. I don't want to upset him in any way . . .

PERMISSION-GIVER: IT'S OKAY TO TREAT HIM AS A SEX OBJECT—YOU HAVE EVERY RIGHT. SOME MEN LIKE . . .

JILL: I can't do *that!* Besides, I read that an aggressive partner can sometimes create secondary impotence . . .

ALL SEX BOOKS: (*Become engaged in a ruckus of infighting*)
WHO WROTE THAT?
IT DOESN'T MATTER—SHE'S GOT IT IN HER HEAD!
WE'RE TALKING ABOUT THE *NEW* ATTITUDE IN MEN, NOT THE *OLD* . . .
YES, BUT SHE MUST BE NONTHREATENING, NONGOAL-ORIENTED . . .
YET, AN ACTIVE PARTICIPANT . . .

JILL: Wait a minute! I can't win for losing . . .

PERMISSION-GIVER: IT'S ALL RIGHT TO BE SELFISH ABOUT YOUR NEEDS, IT'S FINE.

JILL: You mean selfish AND nonthreatening AND nongoal-oriented?

OVERSIZED ILLUSTRATED SEX BOOK: (*With a smug swagger*) NEVER MIND ALL THAT! JUST DWELL ON ME AND BE SEXY. I'M THE ONE WITH THE WELL-WORN PAGES—IN COLOR, I MIGHT ADD.

CLINICAL SEX BOOK: (*Annoyed*) DON'T TELL HER THAT! SHE HAS TO *FEEL* SEXY TO *ACT* SEXY!

PHYSIOLOGICAL CLASSIC: (*With erudition*) SHE'LL NEVER MAKE IT TO EXCITEMENT PHASE I.

JILL: Then, I'll just have to fake it . . . I *do* want to see him again . . .

The Sex Books groan and, flipping their pages in disapproval, focus their attention on Paul. After conferring and turning many dog-earred pages, they proceed to infiltrate his consciousness.

PAUL: (*Thinking*) I knew this would happen! I'm too damned tired. All right . . . I *am* more worried than tired. I don't know if I'm large enough, long enough, thick, strong . . .

THE SEX BOOKS: WE'RE HERE TO INFORM AND REMIND. YOU SIMPLY HAVE THE FIRST-TIME JITTERS.

PAUL: Well, I feel wrecked. Everything hangs on my performance here! I just know it's going to let me down . . .

HOW-TO: YOU'RE TRYING TOO HARD!

PAUL: What the hell else am I supposed to do?

HOW-TO: YOU'RE NOT PRACTICING SENSATE FOCUS!
GET TO IT!

PAUL: I . . . don't remember what that means exactly . . .

ALL SEX BOOKS: YOU DON'T REMEMBER SENSATE? HOW
COME? WE'VE ALL TALKED ABOUT IT . . .

PAUL: Oh, yeah . . . you mean finding her erogenous zones.
Why didn't you just say it? (*He reaches out abruptly.*)
Hey, she's pulling away!

CLINICAL BOOK: STOP GRABBING! SHE NEEDS AFFEC-
TION AND TENDERNESS, JUST LIKE YOU!

PAUL: Oh boy, I've really done it now . . .

PERMISSION-GIVER: IT'S ALL OKAY, YOU'RE ALLOWED TO
MAKE MISTAKES.

PHYSIOLOGICAL CLASSIC: BUT YOU MUST REMEMBER TO
PROLONG THE EXCITEMENT PHASE I. IT MUST
TAKE TIME!

PAUL: I do recall my ex-wife talking about that . . .

THE SEX BOOKS: *SHE* READ US COVER TO COVER.

PAUL: (*Shudders in remembrance*) She said I rushed her . . .
that I behaved as if I'd just come out of a cave . . .

HOW-TO: (*Annoyed*) YOU WANT TO BE A GOOD LOVER?
MEMORABLE? UNFORGETTABLE? THE EARS,
THE NECK, THE UNDERARMS, THE TOES . . .

OVERSIZED ILLUSTRATED SEX BOOK: (*Haughtily butting in*) I
SHOWED YOU THIS *QUITE GRAPHICALLY*—BUT
YOU WERE IN A HURRY TO GET TO THE DIRTY
PARTS. AND THAT WAS WHEN NO ONE WAS
HOME!

HOW-TO: WE KNOW! WE KNOW! . . . BEHIND THE
KNEES, INNER THIGHS . . .

PAUL: Like this, right?

HOW-TO: . . . BUTTOCKS. REMEMBER, THERE'S ROOM
HERE FOR BOLDNESS AND IMAGINATION.

PERMISSION-GIVER: AND YOU HAVE EVERY RIGHT TO USE
YOUR MOUTH *AND* TO WANT HER TO USE HERS.

PAUL: Well, I'd like her to very much, but . . . does that mean
I have to . . . I've never been very good . . .

HOW-TO'S: HOGWASH!

The Sex Books quiet down long enough to observe the arena and, in so doing, notice Jill floundering, and resume command.

JILL: Does this mean I have to do it to him, too? Does this constitute a bargain? I'm terrifically uncomfortable doing that . . . I've never done it well and may get a solid F if I try. If I could just keep him busy up here . . . Well, all right . . .

HOW-TO'S: (*Enthusiastically*) JUST REMEMBER OUR WORDS AND YOU'LL BE FINE.

JILL: What words?

HOW-TO'S: "THE BUTTERFLY FLICK," "THE SILKEN SWIRL" . . .

CLINICAL SEX BOOK: BUT SHE HAS TO WANT TO DO THIS . . .

HOW-TO'S: (*In chorus*) BUTT OUT! KEEP YOUR MOVEMENTS FLUID AND SENSUAL . . . ALL MOTIONS SHOULD BE DONE CONTINUOUSLY . . . CONCENTRATE!

JILL: This feels like work. Have I spent enough time yet? Can I stop now? I mean, it's lonely down here and I don't want him to . . .

CLINICAL BOOK: SHE'S MISSING THE COMMUNICATION, THE INTIMACY! HE SHOULD BE TALKING TO HER, TELLING HER WHAT HE FEELS.

PAUL: She may not like what I say . . . she may be used to something else!

HOW-TO: WELL, SHE SHOULD TALK TO HIM, TOO! IF SHE WANTS TO BE A TRULY EROTIC, SENSUAL WOMAN!

JILL: I may freak him out . . . I may sound foolish, silly . . .

HOW-TO: TELL HIM WHAT YOU FANTASIZED ABOUT TODAY.

JILL: It might make him kinky . . . who knows? I don't know him well enough!

PAUL: (*Mulling over horny thoughts*) If I tell her a fantasy she may want to act it out. And if she tells me one first I'll be forced to pull one—a mild one—out of my bag . . . I can't tell her about the Swedish stewardess and the green olives!

JILL: I can't tell him about the sawhorse and the Cool Whip!

HOW-TO: WHAT DO YOU THINK YOU'RE DOING NOW?

JILL: Keeping my movements fluid and sensual while I fret.

HOW-TO: AND WHAT ARE YOU DOING?

PAUL: Practicing sensate focus while I worry.

CLINICAL BOOK: BUT, SHE DOES SEEM TO BE TURNED ON NOW—EXCITED. LISTEN TO HER . . .

PAUL: I don't trust her sighs.

CLINICAL BOOK: CAN'T YOU PERCEIVE THAT HE'S READY?

JILL: I don't believe he's thinking of me.

PHYSIOLOGICAL CLASSIC: THERE'S NO TIME FOR SUCH SELF-INDULGENCE! YOU'RE BOTH ABOUT TO ENTER PLATEAU PHASE II . . .

PAUL: Leave me alone! I'm losing it . . .

THE SEX BOOKS: (*Heatedly converse, speaking at once*)
HE'S TOO GOAL-ORIENTED, HE HAS TO THINK OF SOMETHING ELSE . . .
ONE CANNOT WILL AN ERECTION . . .
ALL VIRILE MEN EXPERIENCE CRISIS SITUATIONS—IF THEY DON'T, THEY'RE LYING!
GIVE YOURSELF PERMISSION TO FAIL . . .
IT'S A MERE TEMPORARY SEXUAL DYSFUNCTION . . .

PAUL: *WILL ALL OF YOU SHUT UP!*

JILL: I knew it! I did something wrong. What do other women do?

CLINICAL BOOKS: DISTRACT HIM FROM THE CONCERNS OF PERFORMANCE . . . TELL HIM IT DOESN'T MATTER, IT'S OKAY! BE QUICK!

JILL: I can't! I don't want him to know I know it happened! I'll just pretend it never happened, then I won't hurt his feelings . . . Oh, God . . . it really doesn't bother me, but I have to get him off the hook! How I wish this was the third time for us . . .

DIRTY MAGAZINE: (*Enters leering*) PSSST! PAUL!! TAKE A LOOK AT *THIS* AND THIS!!! GOT IT?

THE SEX BOOKS: (*Outraged*) GET HIM OUTTA HERE!

OVERSIZED ILLUSTRATED BOOK: REALLY TACKY!

PAUL: But titillating . . . I think I'm going to be all right . . .

PHYSIOLOGICAL CLASSIC: PLATEAU PHASE II IS ABOUT TO BEGIN!

HOW-TO'S: DID YOU DO YOUR PELVIC EXERCISES, JILL?

JILL: Ah . . . no, should I have? I guess I should have. Does it make a big difference?

HOW-TO'S: TRY IT NOW—EXPERIMENT: IT'S THE SEXY WOMAN'S SECRET.

JILL: Like this?

HOW-TO'S: NO, NO. ISOLATE THE MUSCLE AND TIGHTEN! TILT, ROTATE, CLASP, RELEASE . . .

PAUL: I knew it! She's really been around! Now I've *got to* live up to this, here goes . . .

PHYSIOLOGICAL CLASSIC: REACHING ORGASMIC PHASE III . . .

HOW-TO'S: TOO FAST, PAUL—STOP! GET YOUR MIND ON SOMETHING ELSE.

PAUL: I've got to concentrate, but if I close my eyes she'll think I'm not hip, not into openness . . . (*He shifts his eyes to shelf*) I'll count book spines . . .

JILL: Now I'm really in trouble . . . gassy. What'll I do? (*She coughs excessively*) Whew! And he didn't miss a beat. How am I going to catch up with him?

PERMISSION-GIVER: YOU'RE ALLOWED TO LET YOURSELF MOVE WITH YOUR OWN RHYTHMS, TO FEEL THE HONEST SEXUALITY OF BEING A TOTAL WOMAN . . .

JILL: Okay, fine, but I'm still afraid I won't have an orgasm and end up being an awful disappointment . . .

THE SEX BOOKS: (*Chatter wildly*)

OF COURSE YOU WILL—YOU MAY EVEN HAVE MULTIPLE . . .

A MAXI . . .

SIMULTANEOUS . . .

A CHOICE OF CLITORAL . . .

OR VAGINAL . . .

JILL: (*Embarrassed*) I've never really been able to tell the difference there . . .

THE SEX BOOKS: (*Continuing*)
MANY WOMEN HAVE BEEN KNOWN TO HAVE TWENTY . . .
EVEN THIRTY!
ONE HUNDRED ISN'T UNHEARD OF!

JILL: (*Petrified*) I'm having trouble with one . . . but, something's brewing . . . right now . . .

PAUL: Got to keep going, at least three quarters of an hour . . . thirty-eight, thirty-nine, forty . . .

JILL: I'm getting sore . . .

ALL SEX BOOKS: PAUL! *PAUL!!!* WE MAY HAVE LOST CONTACT WITH HIM!!

JILL: And he didn't even notice! Now I'll be perceived as a woman who can't have orgasms! I'm going to have to make a big one to prove that he's okay to himself so he'll still like me . . .

PAUL: . . . forty-four, forty-five . . . She'd better not forget this night, got to keep this going. It's not totally *in* to give her just one, and I don't trust her shudders . . .

ALL SEX BOOKS: COMMUNICATE! TALK TO HIM! TELL HIM WHAT'S HAPPENING . . . RISK IT!

JILL: I can't! I'll break his mood! No, I'm not going to . . . have to fake it . . . it's the only way . . . here goes . . .

PHYSIOLOGICAL CLASSIC: "RESOLUTION PHASE IV" . . . ACHIEVED, 4:15 A.M.

There are those moments in life when the plethora of wisdom available to us ultimately serves to confuse rather than to clarify. We are a nation of information, with as many opinions as people, and sex is always a hot topic. No matter what sexual area you pursue, you're sure to find out a lot about it from books, lectures, seminars, marathons, and even mail-order cassettes. However, while it's much better to be enlightened than to flounder around in the dark, many people tend to interpret this sexual data as divine revelation, subordinating their own unique sensibilities to what seems to be the Final Word.

What's confusing is that there are so many final words to absorb, and, like having sixteen parents telling you right from wrong, each voice becomes a competing authority. As the pressure to be loyal to all of them mounts, the anxiety spirals and any semblance of natural feeling that happens to be left on the cutting-room floor begins to congeal and erode. At this point, there's only one option: mentally remove yourself from the situation and watch the activity from the critic's corner of the audience.

STAGE FRIGHT, PERFORMANCE, AND THE RATING SYSTEM

When a performer walks on stage, he or she must throw themselves into the part and concentrate on technique, timing, dialogue, movement, blocking, and control, simultaneously hoping to God they can summon up some authentic emotion. If stage fright intervenes and assumes command, the performance is often thrown into critical jeopardy. At that point, an actor may speak of having only "indicated" his role and of having given a superficial performance. This is not unlike the power of sexual anxiety which intervenes when one is under a self-imposed pressure to perform. The players here "indicate" passion, sensuality, and lust, but the feeling rings hollow and false. Backed in a corner, they must now double up on technique, tactics, and skill.

Performance anxiety is directly linked to a rating system which was probably developed years ago when you may have failed (or supposedly failed) to meet someone's lofty expectations. That system has now metamorphosed into a great mythical measuring stick *out there* which poses this question: "How can I be good enough, unforgettable, memorable—the best he or she has ever had?" This would be difficult to answer by even those out there who are supposed to know, because yet another question arises which supersedes the first—"How good is good?" —which is, of course, unanswerable. There are plenty of techniques and nifty little tricks anyone can learn to be "good," but if success is predicated on the desperate and continual need to hear your partners tell you, "Baby, you're the best!" there's the very grim and real possibility that the compulsion to excel will never be sated. There's always someone new you'll have to wow and win over simply because someone back there had expectations you couldn't have met given four full lifetimes. And, if you do manage to live up to them now, you probably won't believe it, because at this point success is not necessarily compatible with your image of yourself—you may be more at home with the striving than the pleasures of the aims.

Therefore, the performance becomes the quintessential issue here, and if your partner does not respond in the manner which will relieve you of your anxiety, you give yourself a low, punishing grade and banish yourself from the human sexual arena. There's nothing left to do but save face, fake it good, and hope to get by with a big, flashy finale.

Lovers Jill and Paul have created the perfect setup for performance anxiety to take command. Since they've given no time to building the relationship or working toward a mutual closeness, they each feel compelled to overwhelm the other and prove themselves worthy through stud-like stamina and eruptions rumored to rival Mount St. Helens. The whole event is ultimately counterproductive to the relationship, for neither actually believes that the other is acting out of genuine desire, and both are right. Paul is obsessed with bringing her to a thousand fruitions, and Jill is determined to show him she's wet and wild, simultaneously not only protecting what she considers her ineptness from his scrutiny, but his from himself. While she's working double time, he's somewhere nearby busily counting time, titles, and strokes.

Not surprisingly, sexual events like this one begin to feel more like labor than love, and the people begin to feel like nonbeings, completely dissociated from eroticism, themselves, and each other, disloyal to their feelings, and disappointed at not being touched on any significant emotional level.

There's no way to change these attitudes overnight or hope to cure them by the weekend. However, if you're stuck with these anxieties, you'll recognize it in the reading and hopefully also begin to perceive the ungratifying nature of these sexual encounters. Try to remember that any kind of faking, lying, or dissembling takes you further away from yourself and, in so doing, greatly increases the anxiety to perform, hide, and conceal, then deny that you're not having a fine, good time. If you can remember, ask yourself if you're attempting to build a reputation or a relationship.

It might also be helpful to remember that you don't have to accomplish everything in one night, especially if it's 4:00 A.M. Being close, sharing good conversations, kissing, hugging, nuzzling, or even falling asleep together in the spirit of intimacy and genuine fatigue may be sufficient for that particular evening, and perhaps more exciting. Everything you know hasn't been pulled out of the bag and abruptly laid on the bed—there's more to look forward to tomorrow.

If, however, you're very much like Jill and Paul, the aftermath anxieties of your estranged sexual encounter may look something like this:

SITUATION #7
Aftermath

"Did you?"

"Yes . . . yes . . . couldn't you tell?"

"Oh, sure . . . but I did sense at one point that you weren't really *there* . . ."

"No, I don't think that's so . . ."

"Well, was it good for you?"

"Oh . . . yes. Did it feel good to you?"

"Yeah . . . But how many times did you?"

"Which kind?"

"Any kind."

"It's hard to say . . . I didn't really count."

"Then you had more than one?"

"Well . . . I *think* so."

"Guess."

"That's not all that important to me. Really. I just like being close."

"Yeah . . . Me too."

In the aftermath of estranged sexuality, anxiety generally manifests itself in one of three ways. In the first, both people aim toward perpetuating the false image and the assumed expectations of the other. One of the parties may become crazed for an okayness fix, however, and force the other into an instant review. Unable to bear the silence which feels more than suspiciously like disapproval, he or she becomes compelled to relieve the pressure by demanding the words which will validate their identity as a perfect lover and, for the moment, allay the anxious fear. But, since neither will want to make a ripple in the supposed ambience of perfection, both pretend incredible satisfaction and hope they've pulled it off.

In the second case, neither says a word. Quite suddenly, one of the parties will begin to wax eloquently on Latin American policy, economic recovery, traffic conditions on Route ⚹1, or something else just as unrelated to the situation, and the other may join in with a swift burst of false enthusiasm, certain that this is what the sophisticated, worldly ones do *out there* in the aftermath of copulation. Both people feel compelled to jump out the window and end this peculiar discourse, but neither does, for to bring the subject back to reality might look as though the event meant more than a casual fling.

The third method is to focus intensely on the sex, take a rapid plunge and begin to discourse at length and in depth on the possible sex problem you may or may not have incurred, but which could surely pose a threat to your future as a couple if it isn't evaluated, assessed, scored, rated, and subtly criticized at this very moment! Minute responses and reactions are microscopically examined, sexual histories exhumed and autopsied, and defenses and fears ostensibly opened up for critical examination. Both people respond to this inquiry as though they've shared a bed for fourteen years and have a corrugated past with which to contend!

All of these eventualities are more anxiety provoking than

relieving. Each works to distance yourself from the possibility of
making a relationship: the basic fear is no longer that of the sexuality, but of being known. The first is a cosmetic cover-up that
will have to be reapplied with each successive meeting; the second is complete avoidance and postponement which will prove
to be defeating; and, the third is a distancing device and a
method for burning out the relationship before it is barely born.

What can you do about this situation? Remember that this is
only the first, second, or even third time you've been together,
and that much of the excitement and joy in these matters comes
from the slow, gradual building of closeness. When you ask for
instant approval, deny that you've just shared your body, or talk
the intricacies of the sex to death, you may ultimately be attempting to control the fear of being known, which will only
serve to maintain the anxiety you initially brought with you into
the bed.

You might try to get a good line on your own real fears of
becoming close or committed and then begin to pinpoint exactly
when and how those fears manifest in distancing techniques.
And while you're at it, during the next few days, while you're
reliving the event in your mind, you could take a look at your
thoughts and feelings to see just what they imply.

SITUATION #8
The Next Few Days

"What did I do wrong?" thinks Jill, poised at the door to her
office, staring at the phone, For four days she has been dodging
the Shadow of Rejection, a tough bruiser, who has been dogging
her steps, gradually gaining ground. Plopping down on her tan
swivel chair, she pushes a stack of mortgage papers aside and
flips through her pink message slips for the third time. "I don't
understand why he hasn't called."

The inescapable sound of footsteps follows her into her room
and Jill recognizes the rhythm of the dragging feet which have
finally caught up with her.

YOU NEVER SHOULD HAVE SLEPT WITH HIM SO

QUICKLY, announces Rejection, sitting on a pile of financial statements.

"I don't think that's it," says Jill, wagging her head in the negative. "He's probably had a very busy week—that *does* happen!"

HE SHOULD HAVE CALLED YOU THE NEXT DAY, MADE CONTACT . . .

"Not really, we were both exhausted. Even *I* didn't feel much like chatting the next night."

HE DIDN'T CALL ON WEDNESDAY EITHER, WHICH MEANS . . .

"Oh, really, it doesn't mean anything! He was probably tied up on the job site working with contractors."

AND THURSDAY? STOP MAKING EXCUSES FOR HIM. PEOPLE ULTIMATELY DO WHAT THEY *WANT* TO DO!

"Haven't *you* ever been unable to get to a phone?"

IF HE'S SO INTERESTED, HOW IS IT THAT HE SLIPPED OUT OF MAKING A DEFINITE DATE WITH YOU WHEN HE LEFT THAT MORNING?

"Well, he did say he'd . . ."

. . . CALL YOU *SOON*. MALE DOUBLE-TALK FOR "SO LONG."

"I simply don't buy that! You're making way too much of this whole thing. I suppose I could call him . . ."

AND HAVE HIM THINK YOU'RE OVERANXIOUS?

"No, I could tell him I have an extra ticket to a concert and see if . . . I mean, I'm fairly liberated, I don't have to wait for him . . ."

HE'LL MAKE SOME WEAK EXCUSE AND YOU'LL BE HUMILIATED.

"Scratch that idea."

YOU LOST YOUR MYSTIQUE, SWEETHEART, the voice of Rejection persists, YOU CAME ON AS TOO READY AND AVAILABLE.

"No, that's not so. He's the one who wanted to go into the bedroom . . . I was trying to get to know him better."

YOU CAME ON TOO STRONG, TOO AGGRESSIVE . . .

"I thought I was restrained . . ."

THEN YOU DIDN'T ACT ASSERTIVE ENOUGH . . .

"But I invited him back for a drink!"

AND, YOU TOLD HIM TOO MUCH ABOUT YOURSELF, TOO FAST . . .

"I perceived myself as a little understated . . ."

YOU WEREN'T PERSONAL ENOUGH . . .

"That's not so! I talked about my marriage, my daughter, friends, my new job . . ."

. . . WHICH WAS A MISTAKE—HE MAY THINK YOU MAKE MORE MONEY THAN HIM.

"That's just foolish, times have changed . . . his wife owned her own boutique!"

AND THEY'RE NOW DIVORCED!

"She's not an issue here."

WELL, YOU'RE NOT EXACTLY IN HER CLASS, says Rejection, who now begins to hum a German lied.

"I don't want to think about that right now." Jill pauses. She watches a knob on her phone light up. With her hand resting on the receiver, she waits for the buzz to her office. Nothing. The light goes off, and Rejection grows larger, blocking out all but the silence from the phone. "I wonder if the receptionist knows I'm still here," she muses, and dials the inner-office code. "Hi, this is Jill. Did I get any calls? No? Yes, I got my messages earlier, I just wanted to make sure you knew I was here. Thanks."

"Maybe I didn't give him my office number," she says, turning to Rejection.

HE KNOWS WHERE YOU WORK! AND, THERE IS A MASTER SWITCHBOARD HERE—THEY'D PUT HIM RIGHT THROUGH. HE ISN'T GOING TO CALL!

"I'm sure there's a good explanation for this . . ."

HOW ABOUT THAT ELABORATE BREAKFAST YOU LAID OUT WHICH HE DIDN'T EVEN TOUCH?

"I think he was pleased . . ."

THINK AGAIN! HE PROBABLY FELT THE DOMESTIC TRAP, FIGURED YOU HAD EVERYTHING PREAR-RANGED . . . NEVER BOUGHT THAT STORY ABOUT KEEPING FOODS IN THE HOUSE THAT YOUR DAUGH-TER LIKES. HE KNOWS EAGER WHEN HE SEES IT.

"But that's not enough to turn someone off, is it? I would have been delighted if I suspected a man had made that much of an effort to please me!"

HE PROBABLY CONSTRUED IT AS DESPERATE AND NEEDY.

"Oh, my God!"

AND, YOU UNDRESSED TOO QUICKLY . . .

"I thought I was too slow, I felt a bit inhibited . . ."

THEN, YOU UNDRESSED TOO SLOWLY.

"No, when I think about it now, it was way too fast . . ."

YOUR BIGGEST BLUNDER WAS BREAKING THE MOOD—THAT WAS STUPID.

"I know."

AND HE KNEW YOU WERE FAKING.

"Only once!"

HE WASN'T VERY AFFECTIONATE AFTER YOU WERE FINISHED . . .

"Well, he did fall asleep with his arm around me!"

BUT TURNED OVER ONTO HIS SIDE VERY QUICKLY.

"Look, it was 4:30 in the morning!"

AND HE KISSED YOU RATHER PERFUNCTORILY WHEN YOU WOKE UP.

"Some men worry about morning breath . . ."

NO . . . HE WAS IN A HURRY TO GET OUT . . .

"He was late!"

HE SAID ALL THE "RIGHT THINGS" AT THE DOOR *WITH NO FEELING!*

"I really messed this up." Jill picks up her briefcase, stuffs a stack of manila folders inside, grabs her bag, and arranges the strap over her shoulder. "I'm getting out of here," she says out loud, and is suddenly furious with herself for refusing a dinner date with her two close women friends. Rejection accompanies her down the corridor, past the reception area, with his arm draped heavily over her shoulders. They pass through the glass doors and wait at the elevator.

"He did say that he had some friends he'd like me to meet . . ."

THAT WAS WHILE YOU BOTH WERE DRINKING AND HE HAD A GLOW ON . . .

The elevator doors open and they both step inside. Jill presses the Down button, rests her head on Rejection's shoulder, and the car makes a swift descent. On the lobby floor, arm in arm, they step out, pass the darkened concession stand and walk out onto the street. "You know," Jill murmurs, looking down at her companion, "I really do wonder what I did wrong."

Over on a construction site, Paul patches up a heated argument between an electrician and a union plumber, checks the time, and in a surprise move trips over DREAD, who is sitting cross-legged on a pile of Sheetrock.

ARE WE READY TO GO? asks DREAD, who refuses to be unacknowledged for any length of time.

"Yeah," says Paul, "but I really should give her a call, just to make contact."

EVEN THOUGH YOU DON'T REALLY WANT TO?

"I do want to call her, but I've got this awful feeling . . ."

SHE LOOKS LIKE A WOMAN WHO WANTS TO GET INTENSELY INVOLVED . . .

"Oh, I'm not so sure that's true," says Paul, rolling up his sheath of drawings.

BUT YOU CAN'T TAKE THAT CHANCE!

"No . . . I'm really not ready for that. She was awfully nice, though, and I haven't been in a relationship for some time now . . ."

YOUR JOB IS TOO DEMANDING, YOU'RE TRYING TO GET A PROMOTION, YOU'RE TOO BUSY, AND IT JUST WOULDN'T WORK OUT.

"I did like that she has her own career and enjoys her work, but . . ."

YOU DON'T WANT A WOMAN WHO IS *THAT* CAREER-ORIENTED—SHE'S PROBABLY A TAD TOO INDEPENDENT.

"She seems to make a lot of money, has nice taste, likes expensive clothes, takes care of herself."

BUT SHE DOESN'T SEEM LIKE A WOMAN WHO WOULD SHARE EXPENSES AND YOU SIMPLY CAN'T AFFORD TO CONTINUE TAKING HER TO EXPENSIVE RESTAURANTS . . .

"Her home is no Quonset hut, either! She obviously is used to the finer things . . . I know I can't show her my apartment, at least not now—she'll see me as beneath her level. And, if I only spend time at her place, she'll begin to get suspicious . . ."

IT JUST WOULDN'T WORK OUT.

"Although she is warm and sexy and attractive . . ."

BUT THERE COULD BE A SEX PROBLEM THERE . . . SHE WAS A LITTLE TOO DEMANDING IN BED, WHICH WORE YOU OUT . . .

". . . and I can't be doing that consistently. I *am* interested in other things. Can't be continually giving in to her extraordinary needs—I'll get burnt out trying to please her nightly!"

YOU'D JUST BETTER NOT GO OUT WITH HER ANY-MORE.

"I did enjoy talking with her, though. She's funny and attentive, smart . . . maybe I should give her a call. I kind of like the way she brushes her hair back from her eyes. Yeah, I think I'll see what she's doing tomorrow night."

Paul attaches red rubber bands to the ends of the roll of drawings, grabs his briefcase, and begins to walk out onto the street. Digging into his pocket for a dime, he is quick to discover that DREAD is holding his wrist in a viselike grip. He stops and leans against a retaining wall for support.

SHE'S JUST WAITING FOR YOU TO CALL TO TRAP YOU INTO A PREMATURE RELATIONSHIP. YOU CAN'T GIVE HER ANY IDEAS!

"That's true. Maybe I'll wait and call her in a week."

AND HAVE TO DEAL WITH HER ANGER? I THOUGHT YOU WERE THROUGH WITH ANGRY WOMEN WHO EX-PECT YOU TO GIVE UP YOUR LIFE FOR THEM!

"Yeah. And she looks like she wants Sundays; that's when I watch football with Jack and Eddie. I mean, we have a standing appointment for the games . . ."

IT JUST WOULDN'T WORK OUT.

"No. And another thing, I asked her how she feels about the cold, and she said she'd like to live in a warm climate, which means we could never go skiing in the winter, and I have a share in a ski lodge."

I'D MAKE TRACKS, FAST!

"And then there's the business with her kid . . . I know she's just looking for someone to step in and be a father and that's not what I have in mind for myself."

IT'S GOOD YOU'RE CATCHING THIS BEFORE IT'S TOO LATE . . .

"It's all coming clear . . . she also had that book on brown rice recipes, and I don't want to be made to feel bad every time I have a steak!"

THAT WOULD CLINCH IT FOR ANYONE!

"I also don't think I'd like her friends; she's into opera and the theater, and even though we both liked *Blazing Saddles*, I don't think she'd fit in with my crowd or appreciate our humor."

NO, IT'S A GOING NOWHERE THING.

Paul walks slowly down the darkened street, submerging himself in the bustling crowds. "You know," he says, pausing at the streetlight and looking beyond his companion, "I'm anxious to meet a nice woman who really wants a relationship."

This two-part finale offers a general overview of the anxious dynamics many women and men—gay and straight—experience in the days or weeks following a date which began with what seemed to have a good possibility for the future. There are a multitude of variations, yet these two particular themes seem to permeate the sexual dating climate.

WHAT DID I DO WRONG?

While this is a lament not exclusively limited to women, it is heard with great frequency as their first line of bewildered complaint. It would be impossible to tally the possibilities of "what I did wrong"; the painful musings over this issue range anywhere from "my voice may have been a little too grating" to "he didn't like my coffee." The list is endless. There is an answer here, however, and it might prove indispensable to those who repeatedly bemoan their ostensible failings: *You're asking the wrong question!*

There is literally no way you can win, place, or show when

this dynamic takes control. If you happen to be strong, self-sufficient, and competent, you'll turn those qualities into self-crit-cal failings and label them harsh, aggressive, or domineering. If you're predisposed to timidity, reticence, and quiet talks, you'll change these characteristics into inept gaucheries. This is the re-sult of years of conditioned thinking, most likely carried over from childhood when the notions of women as care-givers, nur-turers, and earth mothers—people who made everything *nice*—prevailed. (In their adult years, some women even go so far as to consciously make themselves mediocre to avoid losing an anx-ious man!) You may still be negotiating with old, passive, self-effacing roles which consistently plague you with demeaning questions of self-worth, such as, "How could I have been more pleasing to him?"

Ironically, by taking this position, women not only keep them-selves in check, they perpetuate a false climate and keep men in childlike positions of false expectations. Anyone who is con-tinually excused, exonerated, or protected from their part of the responsibility in any situation acquires a distorted sense of truth. That person is completely taken off the hook, given nothing to push up against, fight for, or, ultimately, to learn. This position becomes quickly and firmly established: one of the parties is wrong and finds fault with her- or himself—the other is right and directs all blame elsewhere.

One way to beat this rap is to understand at the outset that he or she may have fused up too quickly, burned out the excite-ment before it had a chance to begin, be terrified of commitment and unable to make a significant connection with another human being at this time in his or her life.

You may be thoroughly accustomed to giving him or her the full treatment and routine—listening well, giving much, making it right, dancing around his or her personality quirks, eccen-tricities, likes or dislikes. If this is the case, it would be wise to begin conveying a sense of your own life, your own plans, aspirations, needs, wants, and, yes, realistic expectations, to the other person. What he or she does with this information, how they may act upon it, is out of your control. If you continue to convey a false image, later, if and when the relationship does get off the ground, resentment and anger will emerge on both sides, and it will boomerang. When he or she discovers you aren't a super service and when you begin to feel unseen, the feelings will begin to disintegrate.

You might begin to look at the swiftness with which the electric sexuality takes off and be a little suspicious if he or she moves in too fast, offering up what seems to be highly intimate information which immediately pierces your vulnerable core. Almost everyone craves the feeling of being desired, recognized, liked or loved, but enchanted moments can be deceptive: you cannot fly to anyone's side and make them your own in just one evening! Like Jill Ames, you could find yourself courting anxious rejection and a completely missing man.

WHY HE DOESN'T CALL

Once again, this issue is not strictly limited to the male domain; however, the dynamic occurs so frequently in our society, it has almost become a cliché. While she worries over why he isn't calling, he's working hard somewhere else to create a roster of crimes and problems she may or may not ultimately commit or pose.

If a man comes from a home where his father was depressed, passive, or ineffectual, and his mother complained, provoked, and perhaps yelled out her frustration or went into silent suffering, he may now perceive all relationships as similar traps. If he does involve himself with a new woman, he could just lose himself, be taken over by her demands, and be cast in the subordinate position of devoting his life to pleasing her. In the days subsequent to an interesting evening, this frightening specter may follow him around. He may fear he's taken on the mantle of his father's life and does not want to live out the same experience.

Circumventing these disastrous consequences, he puts himself into an unattainable position, and will subtly begin a fault-finding expedition which ends up in blatantly blaming her for a trillion wrongdoings.

If you find yourself in and out of one-night, two-week, or three-month relationships; in the position of continually berating the women you meet; or complaining to friends about being alone and never meeting women who are seriously considering a future, perhaps it would be wise to take a long look at the pattern behind you. You might even list the women you've recently dated and fill in a column with their faults and their flaws. Next, try to ascertain how many of these characteristics are truthful, and how many function as a method for avoiding anxiety and closeness. You may discover you simply don't want to be involved, that you're too frightened of commitment, and that you'd be much happier in casual but friendly sexual encounters free of the demands and future fears.

On the other hand, if you find that you ultimately do wish to find a mate, you may be consistently pursuing the wrong people. Although you may be attracted to the confident, self-assured, independent woman, she may be the precise type with whom you find most fault: you may be using those qualities to reject her and quell your own anxiety. That could speak of a strong fear which may not be disposed of easily. You may want to shift your focus to a different type of woman, someone who isn't immediately dazzling, but with whom you feel comfortable and whom you may gradually come to know without the anxious fear of losing your identity.

A LAST WORD FOR THE TELEPHONE

If you find that you've overextended yourself and want to back off, the phone is a good place to begin: it's distant, disembodied, and can't go for your throat! You might telephone the person with whom you've just shared the bed and communicate that you did enjoy the evening, simultaneously conveying that you are seeing a number of people and it may be a few weeks before you'll be in touch again.

Women, too, can pick up the receiver and either pass along the same information or get a better grasp on a situation that is confusing and possibly hurtful. The telephone is a nonsexist instrument of communication.

Ultimately, sexual anxiety affects each person differently, and each must be prepared to bring his or her own background and particular set of circumstances into that arena. Romantic fantasies are filled with notions of instant openness, honesty, and the intimate sharing of secret thoughts. Yet, romantic realities rarely measure up—it's too difficult to jump your own network of doubt and immediately clear the abyss of situationally intrusive anxieties. However, while you're covering up your vulnerable parts, it might be wise to remember that a certain amount of anxiety is normal, if not essential. Without it, that sense of sexual challenge, risk, and excitement would quickly fade into a dull oblivion.

THREE

Private Aloneness Anxiety

"When it comes to the important things one is always alone."
MAY SARTON

ALONENESS IS A HUMAN CONDITION AND ALTHOUGH YOU MAY FEEL
very much alone in believing *only you* suffer the palpitations
and shakes from its attendant situational anxieties—you are
wrong. This paradoxical message, of course, in no way diminishes the miseries of private aloneness anxiety, it merely positions it properly: it places the condition in the realm of what is
a real, palpable, and often unpleasant experience for most of the
human race.

Consider for a moment your own particular day-to-day situations, those boxes of time spent hugging your own vulnerable
and naked needs. If you work alone at home, or even in a one-
person office, how much time is spent battling the void before
forging a path to the typewriter or files? How do you confront
the emptiness of the night with its dark and silent spaces? How
do you fill up the hours at the end of a busy day when there's no
one at home to greet you? What can you "do" with yourself in
the insomniac hours? And, how do you survive the solitude of
Sunday? These situations are all charged with private anxieties,
and often, to contain those amorphous feelings, we tend to write
them off to "restlessness," "boredom," or "loneliness."

The Aloneness/Loneliness Controversy

Not surprisingly, these two distinctly different concepts are often confused. At times they seem to overlap, mesh, and even harmonize; at other times they seem to be mutually exclusive, singing their separate arias on different stages.

Quite simply, *aloneness* is the condition wherein you find yourself *without other people in your presence, and aloneness anxiety signals a lack of intimacy with yourself*. The issue of aloneness grows murky when it's mistaken for yet another unsavory acquaintance—isolation. On the surface, both aloneness and isolation appear as twin propositions. However, unlike aloneness, isolation can be likened to a quarantine on the self and experienced as though disconnected from the world and set adrift in a tank of deprivation. Mistaking one for the other tends to perpetuate the negative notions already surrounding aloneness and eclipse both its positive and its powerful values. To be alone implies more than idle, morose moping or jumping when your shadow appears; it's a time to treat the body with rest, to reflect on what your behavior has wrought, to renovate ambitions gone astray, renew old resolutions, revamp expectations, and, ultimately, to let yourself have the pleasure of quietly growing—creatively and intellectually.

Loneliness is the condition wherein you find yourself *wanting and/or missing other people in your presence,* and *loneliness anxiety signals an absence of intimacy with others*. Loneliness is experienced as a yearning for someone familiar, and perhaps predictable, to fill up the lost, empty space inside and out. There is a longing for the comfort of another, the desire to touch or to talk, the need to be validated by the company of a firm friend. Admitting to loneliness, however, is a little like contacting skin rash: it must be covered up, as many fear they may "catch" it. Interestingly, we all have the capability for loneliness and, though fearful of appearing to others as dependent, desperate, or needy, simultaneously harbor the wish to be needed by someone else, to be important to them, and to be wanted.

The confusion between the two concepts is highlighted when,

for instance, you find you are alone and intensely seek out others
to escape your own self; or, conversely, find you are lonely in the
midst of a crowd and long to go off alone. Compounding that
potpourri of emotional possibility is the perception that the feelings both provoke are often quite similar, and because the nature of anxiety is so diffuse, it takes some concentrated self-
exploration to distinguish between the two. However, it is
aloneness we are addressing in these upcoming situations—
private aloneness and the many protean guises of its attendant
anxiety.

Anxiety stalks the shadow of aloneness in many diffuse costumes: often it emerges as an internal terrorist, a spooky figure
who seems to keep a constant vigil on our lives canceling out all
immediate plans; sometimes it appears as an annoying intruder
who interrupts with nagging chatter; and, at other times, it
manifests as a mugger who makes a sudden raid and just as
quickly leaves. Consider, for instance, the plight of the lone laborers.

The Lone Home Worker

Experts tell us that in the near future we may all be working
alone, set up in private spaces where information on every level
will filter in via home computers hooked up to central terminals
located all over the world. Naturally, for those who find refuge
from aloneness smack in the bosom of the work family which a
busy office provides, this prophecy is a little unnerving! However, as it stands now, there are already millions of sturdy people who, by choice or necessity, spend their creative, productive
hours absolutely alone in the starkness of their own homes,
fighting the good fight against the scourges of the anxiety
mugger.

Writers, artists, housewives and husbands, small business en-
trepreneurs, accountants, travel and celebrity agents, consultants
of all persuasions, and free-lancers of all professional shapes already know about the hidden stress of the self-starting home
worker. With no coffee-wagon bell to signal a midmorning
break, no lunch hour to formally justify a simple walk in the sun

or even a frivolous purchase to perk up the spirit, no interoffice memos flying from out-box to in-box to keep them informed and anchored in space, no impromptu meetings to test their verbal mettle, and no good gossip to warm the cockles of their humanity, the lone laborers must constantly rally against the isolation and anxiety endemic to the alone at home.

Working out of one's home is filled with special problems that the office-bound rarely consider. Those who must drag themselves out of bed and dress smartly each day sometimes harbor mini-resentments against the homebound whom they consider to be free agents, unfettered by the voice of authority or time. The home worker must set up firm ground rules for their nine-to-five friends, those people who fail to comprehend that this "free agent" makes himself or herself available to either chat on the phone or join in an unexpected shopping expedition on the day that the office worker has picked as a "mental health day," at the expense of their own special professional or domestic obligations. The office worker unwittingly preys on the weakest part of the home worker's will when he or she poignantly suggests, "You certainly have to take *some* time off, don't you?" or, "Why don't you work later tonight to make up for it?" To the alone at home, these words ring out as an alluring escape-hatch to Nirvana, meaning, of course, that they must instantly double up their efforts to remain loyal to an already sagging discipline.

Working at home alone is indeed fraught with struggle, and resisting the temptation to avoid the day's tasks is akin to swimming upsteam in chilled molasses. Just getting oneself outside of the bed area is a noteworthy accomplishment for some, and for others, relieving the bladder is the only motivation real enough to move them through space. Getting dressed (as if you were a *normal* person) poses another special problem which is then compounded by the worry that someone will "catch" you in your sleeping ensemble during the daylight, which could be as early as ten or as late as five. Morning television—*The Today Show, Good Morning America*, and especially *Donahue*—are very tricky propositions for lone laborers: they sound as tempting sirens across the room luring you into the arena of real people with real anecdotes and problems, making you soft on the seductions of real life when you are inescapably unvalidated and alone. And even though you may have just sent the kids off to school, your spouse off to the office, your lover off to the unemployment office or a precarious breakfast meeting, and, even though you may live alone but are not wanting for a snappy evening which is lined up for later with a multitude of friends, the invisible barricade between you and your typewriter, you and your dishwasher, you and your account books, telephones, or briefs sets the stomach to churning and the dread fluttering dangerously.

In truth, you are never really alone: the meddling anxiety mugger, that troublesome acquaintance of long standing, is always present in your rooms posing a substantial threat to your identity as a certifiable human being.

How do most lone laborers send this intruder packing? The known methods are inexhaustible, but only offer temporary relief, are usually most habit-forming, and must be changed and revised from minute to minute. When anxiety begins to flow through the calves, hits the belly, crashes through to the chest, and harnesses the head, there's little chance of doing any of the work demanded of you. The only alternatives seem to be repelling the attack by stuffing, stifling, or anesthetizing the anxiety mugger who is obstinately increasing your dose of adrenaline.

Fourteen Ways to Elude Your Labor

Sleep	Dial-a-Friend
Smoke	Swallow-a-Pill
Eat	Putter
Clean	Pose
Fix	Watch-the-Soaps
Fantasize	Make-a-List
Drink	Masturbate

At the outset, it must be stated that these activities are all performed in secret. Although you promise to do your work later and do it even harder, no one must "catch" you doing these things, for if you are found out, you must then attempt to lie, deny, or alibi. The anxiety will then accelerate and you may forget what you were avoiding in the first place. And even if you do remember, the selected excuse for your behavior loses its potency in the telling and you're left feeling like a complete jerk, for in your mind the rest of the world functions smoothly and efficiently, while you are at best inept, at worst a candidate for Creedmore.

So, before you can settle down and tackle the job at hand, you must find an immediate way to circumvent the "awful feeling" which is steadily rendering you incompetent, and you must do it without letting even yourself know the full import of what you are avoiding. These fourteen choices are immediately accessible and the variations are infinite. Exactly how they are put into practice does depend upon the individual temperament, but the sex of the sufferer matters not. Men and women alike utilize these methods with the same frequency, secrecy, and expertise.

Here's how two different anxiety sufferers do it:

SITUATION #1
The Free-Lancer at Home Alone

That man walking down the street with the brown envelope tucked under his arm, the one with the fast, intrepid gait, has just triumphed over two solid weeks of combat with the anxiety mugger. A fairly successful free-lance magazine writer, he's about to deliver his finished article and is so thoroughly relieved he'd like to sing.

Two weeks ago he clinched an assignment to write a piece entitled "The New Man for the New Woman," the feature article in a major magazine. Happy as a clam, he zipped back to his apartment and began organizing his stash of research materials. He alerted his friends that he "wouldn't be answering the phone except for an emergency," changed the cartridge in his electric typewriter, neatened up his work space, used Fantastick to clean the desk top, sharpened pencils, lined up pens, adjusted the Venetian blinds, surrounded himself with the appropriate books and files, sat down, and in a flurry of determination fiercely inspected his nails.

It was then that he became agitated over the barely discernible street noises and leaped out of his chair to silently admonish the offenders eight floors below, but that distraction was short-lived. Assuming the posture of a serious biblical scholar, he then thoughtfully stroked his chin while perusing the bookcases. After giving an authoritative nudge to the bridge of his glasses, he hooked his thumbs through his belt loops, caught his reflection in a wall mirror, which propelled him over for a closer look at his moustache, which was definitely due for a trim. Clipping the single but visibly offensive hair, he gave himself the okay nod and sat down in his work chair.

"THE NEW MAN FOR THE NEW WOMAN," he wrote, after which seemed the appropriate time to light up a cigarette. Gazing out of the window, he dragged deeply and smoked in the silence that was only broken by the steady hum of the machine. Turning back to the blank paper, he was charged with a pure bolt of "nothingness" which set his heart to palpitating.

"Are you ready for the feminist fatale?" he tapped out, then looked at his watch and discovered it was 2:00 on the nose. Since no one was around, he thought he might just as well see what was stirring on the soaps, turned directly to *One Life to Live*, a show he believed to have "plot merit," and waited for the appearance of arch-villain Asa Buchanan, whose son, Clint, was just opening up his mother's crypt as the show commenced. Suspending logical disbelief, the writer settled in for the duration of the drama. At 3:00, annoyed by his procrastinations, he slapped off the set, but then decided he was just too keyed up to concentrate effectively. Pouring himself a vodka-on-the-rocks, he returned to the typewriter.

"Have you met the new feminist fatale?" he cleverly revised, and then proceeded to go blank.

The apartment suddenly seemed extraordinarily empty and the writer was just lighting up another cigarette when the anxiety mugger, looking remarkably like himself, made a glaring appearance. The following dialogue ensued:

MUGGER: Thought you were a big-deal writer, huh?
WRITER: (*Slinking into profound passivity*) Maybe I was wrong . . .
MUGGER: You can't live up to your last piece!

WRITER: Maybe that's true, maybe I've shot my bolt . . .

MUGGER: (*With a withering glance at the blank sheet in the typewriter*) Fraud, pure fraud! You've never had the intellectual capacity of *them out there*—go get a regular job. You need a timeclock and an authority to tell you what to think.

WRITER: Yes . . . I need people around me—I need to exchange ideas . . . how the hell do I get out of this? (*He rests his forehead in his palms*)

MUGGER: There's no way out, you're stuck with me until you come to your senses and give up this creative stuff!

WRITER: (*Slumping insensibly into his chair*) If I could just come up with a good face-saving excuse, I'd return the assignment. (*He begins to yawn*) If I could just slink out of town and find a job as a caretaker in the backwoods of a lonely estate where no one would know me . . .

MUGGER: (*Simultaneously growing weary*) No matter what you tell them, they'll all know—they'll all laugh and agree that you couldn't cut it, that you were a momentary lapse in their otherwise fine judgment. (*The Mugger suddenly comes to life again and begins to dance a wild gavotte as he throws a rough-hewn lariat around the Writer's chest, and yanks! He sings out with great cheer*) Failure!

WRITER: Yes . . . and I feel so sleepy . . . maybe a short nap will refresh my mind. (*He rubs his brow and prepares to exit*)

MUGGER: (*Once again growing smaller. His voice recedes into the background as he whispers*) I'll be . . . back . . . (*And disappears*)

The writer barely made it into the bedroom, where he blocked out the sun with a down pillow and slipped off into a deep coma of sleep.

However, upon awakening, he heard the anxiety mugger rattling the typewriter in the living room and the writer's muscles began to calcify right on the chenille bedspread. Trying to muffle the voice he would all too soon confront again, the writer's mind took a leap to more erotic levels, and before he could even begin to consider the social ramifications of "The New Man for the New Woman," the image of a lusty stranger wafted through his mind and his hand became a blur of self-love.

At the close of his impassioned interlude, he sat up with a jolt, and with renewed determination stomped into the living room where he found his visitor had temporarily disappeared. Writing with the speed of the damned, he rough-drafted his article and at 6:oo, when his wife returned home from her regular-person's job that takes her to a warm, busy office, he smugly reported that "the writing went fine today."

SITUATION #2
The Small Business Entrepreneur at Home Alone

The woman sitting up on the edge of the double bed with traces of black beneath her eyes, books and papers scattered around the scrambled sheets, and the telephone propped on top of the pillow, is now on her third cup of coffee. Although she frequently reaches out toward the receiver, as yet she has been unable to make the business call she has been revising in her head for over an hour: "*Hi, this is Janice Jones. I'm calling to make an appointment with . . .*" "*Hello! This is Janice Jones. We spoke two days ago about the possibility of my coming in to show you some of my samples . . . ?*" "*Yes, this is Janice Jones . . . Oh, you do remember? Good. Well, how about lunch?*"

Unable to come up with the masterpiece opening which will bedazzle her potential client with sincerity and wit, plus convince him long before seeing her work that she is indispensable to his greeting card company, Janice takes another nervous sip of her cold coffee. Suspecting she should wait until tomorrow when she will be "up to it," or later in the afternoon when she will be "more into the day," she forsakes the call and, with nightgown trailing behind her, eases into the tiny studio she has set up in the back of the house for her work.

She is disliking this summer intensely. An art teacher at a junior high school nine months out of the year, on her three-month summer furlough she devotes herself to her small greeting card business. She is currently finishing up the last three Christmas card cartoons from a package of ten and must hustle more work in order to obtain the tuition money she needs for her son's schooling.

Ordinarily she would not feel so anxious, but with her young daughter off at camp and her son vacationing with a friend at the beach, the sounds from her usually raucous home are missing, and the silence is deafening. "Where's the action?!!" the voice in her head bellows out and, after inspecting her drawing board as if she's never seen it before, she shuffles into the kitchen, where she makes herself a toasted bagel with butter and cream cheese.

"Hello, this is Janice Jones. I'll be in town today and wonder if . . ." Drawn to the small sketch pad lying on the butcher-block table, she decides that a grocery list reflecting her resolve to lose fifteen pounds is an absolute priority today. "Cottage cheese, carrots, green peppers, cantaloupe, fish, chicken, skim milk." Short and unsatisfying. She drops the pad, picks up a bread stick, eats it up with the speed of a gopher, and returns to the studio where she sits, gets up, and returns to the kitchen. She reaches for a can of Chinese fried noodles and crunches a handful while constructing an important new budget which denotes her assets—checkbook balance, savings account, and cash-on-hand—as well as her projected expenses, including all capricious purchases for herself and the kids for the next seventeen years.

Since the can is now empty, she walks into the bathroom, where she discovers that the grouting between the tiles has grayed, and it becomes imperative that she scrub down the wall with detergent, which, of course, is unsuccessful. It's here she realizes that somewhere between the bed and the kitchen the anxiety mugger slipped in, that she has unconsciously been rubbing her thigh with her fingers and digging her index nail into her thumb in an effort to ward off the "awful feeling" that has slowly been gaining ground.

"Enough!" she says out loud, shaking her hands in space, and returns to the studio, where she flounces herself down in the swivel-tilter chair and quickly doodles a fat Santa jogging through Tahoe followed closely by eight lean reindeer all wearing green Adidas shoes. Delighted with this accomplishment, she returns to the bathroom, where she seemingly has earned the right to wash her face. Now she's ready for the heavy artillery.

"Janice Jones here! I'm free tomororrow at 11:00 and would like to set up an . . ." But wait! Maybe before actually calling she'll clean up the kitchen, which is creating a terrible eyesore. She washes the dishes, scours the sink, and, enjoying this surge of creative momentum, defrosts the refrigerator, too, and, while she's at it, she could just as well toss the Swanson's Frozen Fried Take-Out-Variety Chicken into the oven, which will give her forty-five minutes of something pleasant to anticipate. Good.

At 1:00, after finishing the entire box of crisp, assorted pieces, she picks up the receiver, puts it down, and turns on *All My Children,* "just to keep up with the story line," but basically to find out if Nina Courtland will accept her husband's out-of-wedlock baby. At 2:00 she watches Clint Buchanan open his mother's crypt, and at 3:00 she finds she has eaten a small bag of Hershey's Kisses which she was saving for her daughter's return from camp. Thoroughly disgusted with her pig-out avoidance and completely irritated at finding herself still in her nightgown, now glittering with silver foil, she picks up her sketch pad and knocks off a drawing of a dancing Christmas wreath, smiling up at a Santa hung from a nail on a wooden door.

Time is running out, and Janice, crazed by the frantic grip of the anxiety mugger, finally succumbs to swallowing just a half of a half of a yellow Valium. While she waits for the attack to subside, she changes her nightgown for a comfortable Indian print dress, combs her hair, puts on some makeup, makes the bed, then reaches for a pad and pencil and carefully writes: "Hi, this is Janice Jones. We recently met at a luncheon and you suggested I call for an appointment to show my samples . . ."

Holding the note in her lap, she picks up the telephone receiver and dials. Her approach is direct and firm. Without faltering, she delivers her prescribed script, after which a decidedly male voice on the other end of the wire replies: "I'm sorry, he's out of the office today. May I take . . ."

"No," says Janice staring blankly at a lamp, "no message . . . I'll try again on Monday."

Painted against a landscape of clammy fear and quivering doubt, these two portraits spotlight the scourges of apprehension and avoidance common to the alone-at-home worker. While the writer and Ms. Jones focus their anxious emphasis on two distinctly different targets, they are both wizards at warding off confrontations with their labors.

The writer, cursed with the masterpiece theory of perfection, is driven by the dire notion that his every concept, idea, phrase, and word must be definitive, riveting, incisive, and pure—nothing less than worthy of the honor bestowed upon him by the POWER who gave him the job over on Second Avenue. However, with his expectations towering above his human function and his aspirations crowding the room, there's little space for the writer who has now catapulted himself into the creative freeze.

Lurking beneath his scholarly posturing is the terrible suspicion that he may know absolutely nothing about men and women, and less about the New Man (whoever he is!) or the New Woman (whom he vaguely suspects he resents, even though his wife carries a lizard briefcase to work). Further, who the hell is he to inform the world of what's in store for the future of the sexes? He's just a little guy from a small town who still thrills to the scent of sachet.

He *could* use his past successes to shore up his confidence in this project—all those compliments and kudos he's received for his essays and articles. But . . . the editors he worked with were too new to the game to catch his flaws; his readers were not very sophisticated; the magazines, well, they were kind of second-rate; and, given those other contributors, the competition wasn't exactly stiff. No, those pieces don't really count, not in the light of *this* assignment, which could prove to be truly *pivotal* in his career.

He *could* give himself the appropriate time to think the project through, to allow himself permission to putter and pose without the ravages of guilt. For the lone laborer with no one there to bounce back ideas but the anxiety mugger (who is cer-

tainly not trustworthy), this is essential and constitutes an important part of the creative process. But, there are too many old
voices in his head telling him that his work is not "legitimate,"
that he should be sitting behind a curved desk in an established
office, collecting a weekly paycheck, using up "sick" days, planning his paid vacation and working toward the retirement that
comes from a "respectable job," instead of indulging this
"hobby" which his father unrelentingly calls his work.

As for his overwhelming need to sleep, it might be fruitful for
the writer to learn that, before commencing his work, Thomas
Alva Edison is rumored to have taken to his bed. Lying on his
back, the scientist is said to have placed one arm out over the
edge of the bed with two ball bearings placed in the center of
his outstretched palm. As he fell into a twilight slumber, his
hand would drop, releasing the ball bearings, which would crack
onto the floor, instantly awakening him. In this quasi-conscious
state, Edison would fly back to his work area where, as the story
goes, he proceeded to develop most of his most brilliant theories.
Who can say for certain that this genius was not also threatened
by that same anxiety mugger?

It's difficult to determine which particular method will ultimately propel the alone-at-home into the thick of their work.
The writer gained mobility via rest and erotic release—but what
of Ms. Jones?

Janice has little difficulty executing the creative end of her
small business. Her aloneness anxiety manifests in a totally
different area—the horror of making a "cold call." However, the
tenor of her inner dialogue is much the same. Working on the
masterpiece theory of presentation, she is driven by the panicky
notion that the rhythms, accent, tone, and timbre of her telephone voice, plus the words she selects, could all, individually or
collectively, irrevocably make or break this potential account.
After all, she reasons, she's only been in this business for five
years, is still a bit unseasoned, and just needs to learn a few
more tricks of the trade before ultimately perfecting her sales
pitch.

Although Janice, too, could use her past successes in calling clients to shore up her confidence, those contacts were mostly
penny-ante stuff—schlock little outfits filled with ordinary peo-

ple like herself who were just trying to make a buck. This new contact, however, is no mom-and-pop outfit: this is national corporate stuff, big enough to advertise on television, to have become a household word.

If that's the case, then where does she get off knocking on their door? Are her samples slick, clever, and professional enough to compete with all those other illustrators who work at their business all year round?

Furthermore, this man is undoubtedly very busy juggling a full schedule of high-powered appointments and will be hard pressed to find an hour to see her for at least twelve weeks. And then, of course, he'll somehow divine over the telephone that she's neither in demand nor dressed, which will assure him he's dealing with an odd duck. What was his name? Lord. Miles Lord, which must mean he comes from old wealth, while hers is Jones, as in "keeping up with the . . ." which is rather bourgeois and a perfect reason to postpone the call until tomorrow, for she'll be damned if she'll end up pressing her nose against the palace glass visibly panting for a handout. She's been through too much in her life to play that number and deserves a bit more respect, which she may get later in the afternoon when she has leveled out and realizes that Miles Lord is a perfect stranger who routinely speaks with new illustrators as part of his job.

"Cold calls" are but one of the more difficult hurdles the at-home small business entrepreneur must conquer. In the emptiness of the work space, the mysterious client at the end of the phone can become a giant of ridicule and rejection. For this reason, many lone laborers insist on treating their homes in the same manner as they would a storefront business. Employing a strict but necessary discipline, they shave, shower, dress, and groom themselves to meet the day in spite of the fact that they may not be seen at all. They have found that by looking the part they ultimately become the person they wish to project and therefore present themselves as confident professionals.

Another method for vanquishing the anxiety mugger is to warm up to the cold call by speaking with a friend before calling the client or contact. This exchange acts as a dress rehearsal for the business call and accustoms you to the sound of your own voice. Or, if the anxiety mugger is stifling your breath and you fear stuttering or even forgetting what you wanted to convey, like Janice, you might write out the opening message, as on a cue card. Hopefully, this will all begin at the start of the day and without the aid of a tranquilizer.

Whatever type of occupation in which you may be engaged at home alone, that initial barrier or anxiety between you and the work itself is difficult to penetrate: before you can actually sit down and write, calculate, paint, draw, or make calls, you may have to ease yourself into it, slowly. If you are approaching a particularly confusing task, you might talk it over with someone in a related field before you commence, then take a short walk and think it through, or write a brief letter to a good friend to warm up your mental mechanisms. At that point, your ideas should begin to take over for themselves and you will have broken the barrier.

However, it's imperative for lone home workers to set up a pattern for work. Choose the part of the day or night in which you are most energetic and creative and use the remainder of your time for other domestic or personal tasks. Many people are night workers—between 10:00 P.M. and 2:00 A.M. they are the most productive. Others thrive from dawn till noon and are finished for the day. It might also be sensible to work in spurts, two- or three-hour slots as opposed to an eight-hour day. You might also approach the work in small pieces, not in big chunks, which can be overwhelming and promote more anxiety.

When your work is of an intensely cerebral nature, it would be helpful to have a change-of-pace activity at hand with which to alter your schedule, perhaps cooking, cleaning the stove or refrigerator, making a piece of jewelry or refinishing furniture. It's also important to take breaks and get yourself out of your home. If you remain in the same environment for both work and living, day after day, you could eventually build up a dislike, sometimes even an outright loathing, for your profession. Isolation feeds on itself and perpetuates the feeling of imprisonment.

Many self-employed home workers initially feel guilty about their ability to set a work-style for themselves which clashes with the "regular" world, out there, and find it difficult to explain their patterns to others. Try to recognize that having chosen to work alone you have already made a statement for yourself and that you may be different from the general work force. Consider yourself a trend-setter.

In the future, many more alone-at-home workers may find themselves confronted by the unannounced raids of the anxiety mugger who comes and goes chattering gleefully and dispensing portents of doom. English historian Edward Gibbon was once quoted as declaring, "I was never less alone than while by myself," a piece of wisdom you as an independent laborer will have confronted and thoroughly understand. Perhaps eventually you may come to view yourself as just a little ahead of your time.

There are many other situations which also inspire private aloneness anxieties, yet have less to do with interrupted tasks or goals than with the issue of being abandoned to the starkness of yourself.

THAT "AWFUL FEELING" OF ALONENESS

The existentialists, whose main philosophical thrust is to accept their lone individuality in this world, are fond of saying that "the moment is the sole reality." Their relentless grappling with this issue makes sense when you consider that a piece of every waking day is spent stripped of the routine devices we all use to avoid that eerie quality of aloneness. Those moments when we are absolutely alone with ourselves are the prelude to the emergence of what has popularly been dubbed that "awful feeling." Absented from other people, domestic tasks, professions, and business or entertaining diversions that regularly bolster the experience of human frailty, we're left with only our private vulnerabilities and what is experienced as delicate links to the center of self-worth. Sadness, uncertainty, helplessness, and doubt—a few of the elements in that great primordial soup of your emotional life—are all serious candidates for recall when private aloneness anxiety springs its ancient attack.

Much vital energy is habitually used up circumventing that "awful feeling." You might be surprised to discover just how much of your life may be spent protecting against this anxiety, especially when alone in the night. There are two main issues at work within the nighttime situations: darkness anxiety generated by external danger—the real or imagined threat of someone or something breaking into your space—and darkness anxiety perpetuated by the internal touch-and-go terrors of what your own conscious or unconscious thoughts may summon up. In the dark and empty silence, there are no outside voices of friends either to muffle the sounds from within your mind, or to reflect back any skewed perceptions of the situation. Alone at night, the mind sometimes acts as its own internal terrorist.

SITUATION #3
Dark Places—Silent Spaces

Like a barely discernible sound, the moment of anxiety begins with the subtle consciousness that "something is off." This unsettling notion is quickly followed by the uncomfortable awareness that you are, for certain, alone now, with yourself, unsupported by external banisters.

You may have just shut off the television, given a yawn, and are about to turn off the lamp in the living room when a rattle at your mind's door alerts you to the presence of the internal anxiety terrorist who has just gained a foothold. It's clear at this point: your emotional security system has been jimmied and the sound you shrink from is the silence.

"I hope that's what it is," you may think as you finally flip the switch off, "I feel so edgy." In the bedroom, you begin to undress, are suddenly aware of a *real sound*, and freeze on the spot. "What's that!" You listen, stretching your ears throughout the house . . . "There's something wrong. Stop . . . relax. It's just your nerves . . ." Nonetheless, you hoist your pants back up, edge your way out to the hall, into the living room, where you switch the lights back on, and then move into the kitchen. Holding yourself quite still, you listen again. "That's it!" you think, identifying the sound of a single drop of water that drips from the tap and, tightening the spigot, breathe deeply in profound relief. Concentrating on how to jump past this awful time-frame of aloneness, you resolve to stifle your fluttering heart by losing yourself in a deep sleep.

"I don't like this feeling . . . makes me too tense," you think, heading back toward the hall. Passing the bathroom, you suddenly stop, check behind the door, in the shower, then head toward the bedroom, where you continue undressing. However, you find you're talking out loud, uttering calculatedly neutral phrases to trick yourself into thinking you're on top of this situation. "Whew, it's been some day . . ." "Hmmm, think I'll just get in bed and read my book." "Better do a load of laundry tomorrow . . ." Now, having convinced the emptiness that you are without a psyche, you get into bed and douse the light. But, although your body is tired, your mind is a seething mass of scuttling sounds, and there's nothing to do but turn the lamp back on. While moving your eyes around the room, you realize that you did not check the closet and immediately begin to hum.

Easing out of bed, you sidle against the wall and one-step over to the closet, where you yank open the door and quickly jump back. Nothing. "Well, I thought there was nothing there, but you just never know . . . think I'll leave this light on though . . ." and you begin to wonder if any of your friends would mind if you called this late because, really, "it would be nice to hear someone else's voice." But it is a little too late, and perhaps if you could just concentrate on something substantial in your life, something tangible, then you wouldn't feel so hollow and alone. "Think about money . . . if I pay off the department stores, plus Visa and American Express, then I'll be able to save enough for a new car, get this place fixed up . . ." you mentally plan as you amble back to the bed. Once under the covers, the silence drowns out your rational thoughts and you realize you didn't check *under* the bed. "Why should I check under the bed?" you think, questioning your own impulse. "Because that's what you must do," you think, answering your previous thought. Up again, you kneel down, raise the fabric near the floor, and cautiously peruse that bad dark place, simultaneously perceiving that you could bring the television in from the living room. Straightening up, you begin to walk out the door, but something taps your peripheral vision and you make a sharp intake of

breath! Turning, you stare directly into the full-length mirror
and are confronted by, yes, the internal terrorist itself.

"My God," you say out loud, holding your heart. Ultimately,
what can you do when you look it squarely in the eye and find
that you're looking at you?

THE DARKLY ANXIOUS

"Turn up the lights; I don't want to go home in the dark," are
the last words master writer O. Henry is rumored to have uttered. This sentiment could easily be usurped by any of us who
experience aloneness anxiety when confronted with the night.
Think of how many nightlights are sold and attached to bedroom baseboards, how many flashlights grace the surfaces of
crowded nightstands, how many lamps stay lit all through the
night. Granted, there are many practical reasons for keeping a
bright home-fire burning, but a close questioning of the afflicted
reveals that these people do feel safer with themselves when a
light penetrates the dark.

Here are some common remarks from a handful of the darkly
anxious on this sensitive issue:

• "Walking into an unlit apartment makes me very wary. I don't
know what's waiting for me—my heart pounds, my breath
comes short. I make a lot of superfluous noises outside the door
hoping that the person inside will hide and I won't have to see."
• "I can't sleep unless there's a light on in the next room."
• "Before I go to sleep, I check under the bed, then behind the
shower curtain, and then I get into bed and turn off the light.
I'm immediately convinced I didn't make a *thorough* check, and
am up again. I look under the bed, in the shower, and this time
add the closets. Down again, off with the light . . . still uncon-
vinced. Up again. Exhausted and angry, I switch on the living
room light and leave it on. With my house now in order, I instantly fall asleep . . . maybe."
• "I think I still believe in the boogeyman myth. You know, he
waits until the apartment is dark to materialize and scare me."
• "I sleep with the covers over my head and pretend it's the
middle of the day."

• "I'm sure to have my old whopper nightmare if I don't sleep with a light blazing in the room. It's a recurring dream: I've left the front door open or the windows ajar—something like that. In any event, there's an opening to my rooms and something ominous is about to enter."

• "When it's dark, I lose my boundaries . . . I can't control what I can't see with my eyes."

• "Me? I try to never sleep alone."

As in the above situation, many people with dark places anxiety also fear silent spaces. It's the noiselessness that ignites their "awful feeling," and their hearing becomes acutely sensitive. A creak in the roof, a footstep in the hall below, the rattle of a shutter, the single "ping" of a radiator, or a lone drip from a leaky faucet charges them with a startle response so electric, it could easily make their hair stand on end. "Who's there?" "What's that?" the inner dialogue begins, and as adrenaline floods their systems, and their eyes dilate in the dark, their ears become fiercely alert to the follow-up noise which will surely validate cause for the severest of alarm.

James Thurber once wryly observed that "most men lead lives of noisy desperation." But, how are these people, men and women, supposed to deal with the desperate terms of the anxiety terrorist when the quiet drives them to proverbial distraction?

Most of them have become completely enamoured by the electronic revolution. An innovation which absolutely captivated the public and was guaranteed to hold the terrorist at bay was the Sony Walkman. This piece of delicate equipment, complete with mini-headphones, was cleverly fashioned not only to act as armor for the street-anxious among us, but also to provide a sleeping companion for aloneness sufferers. The major Walkman benefit is ingenious: it allows its wearer to prevent aloneness anxiety and to completely control his or her aural environment by blocking out that which is alarming or distasteful with a blend of musical anesthesia. Those not given to attaching machines to their bodies may choose a radio instead which provides both music and the silky tones of a late-night D.J. to bust up the terrible silence. An air-conditioner at full blast offers the "white noise" necessary to muffle the sporadic floorboard creak, and a television, of course, will fill the quiet with the familiar voices of movie stars past while simultaneously helping the sufferer to deny that the darkness ever existed.

Without the aid of these electronic protections, what do you really think is lurking in the silence, in the dark? What unnameable person or thing has the power to so threaten the night? Even after a prudent check of the potential hiding spots, why does your internal anxiety terrorist persist?

"I have a better idea since that hair-raising night I spent camping," says Sam, a soft, sensitive man who, since returning from a trip to the Canadian woods, is trying to explore this issue. Sam did not go alone, yet he experienced the same terrors out in the woods that he does at home in the city protected by four bedroom walls. "Every form of wild beast was seemingly growling outside in the night. I affixed my flashlight to the opening of the tent, lay with my Swiss Army knife clutched in my hand, then finally got up, ducked outside, and built a fire beside which I sat, staring at the flames until they had died. There was literally nothing out there," he says with a touch of ironic disappointment. When he crawled back inside the tent, however, the growling resumed. His woman-friend then opened an eye and demanded he eat something. ". . . at least a piece of bread. Your stomach sounds like St. Helens," she mumbled and slid back into her enviable slumber.

Relieved, albeit somewhat embarrassed, Sam, too, succumbed to sleep, but the incident has provided him with a clue to his bouts with aloneness anxiety. Feeling helpless in the hostile, unknown world of the woods, he did a bit of fancy juggling and rearranged his psychic focus. Unknown to his conscious mind, he turned his helplessness into anger (unacceptable to Sam), his anger into aggression (unconscionable to this gentle being), and then projected the whole mess out onto the night, where it metamorphosed into fierce beasts menacing his life.

Back home in the city where the soft-spoken Sam works as a computer programmer for a large banking corporation, he also feels helpless in a seemingly hostile world. But, since his dark-woods journey, he has a better grasp on the identity of the terrorist in his living room. He's beginning to understand that the anxiety he experiences is a creation of his own psychic inventiveness and that he has a few "forbidden wishes" and "taboo impulses" that refuse to behave in a fit manner. In the still of the night, when he feels most vulnerable, his hidden urges, so carefully harnessed during the day, commence a castle revolt and storm the barricades of his conscious mind by confronting him with the internal anxiety terrorist who reveals himself to be none other than the underbelly of Sam's own outlaw desires.

Though many of the darkly anxious attempt to deny that these fears exist, ironically, they know much about assuaging the nighttime terrors. Until actually humbled by it, most of us, however, tend to play down the anxiety: not everyone is as blatant about the condition as Woody Allen, who baldly asserts, "I'm afraid of the dark and suspicious of the future." Most of us try holding our heads up high and whistling a happy tune so no one will know we're afraid, which, of course, only works in the bright daylight when you're trying to protect your image.

Those who secretly suffer dark places or silent spaces know that watching or reading a spine-tingling thriller alone at night is a direct challenge to hidden fear terminals and that they are particularly sensitive to Hitchcockian scenes from films and books. As Stephen King, master of the macabre, points out, the work of horror "is looking for what I would call phobic pressure points. The good horror tale will dance its way to the center of your life and find the secret door to the room you believed no one but you knew of . . ." For this reason alone, novels by King, Peter Straub, and a host of others steeped in the literary or cinematic terror trade should only be read or viewed while the sun still shines.

Unless you're willing to drink until you slump insensibly into bed, the brandy bottle is no panacea for dealing with the dark. Alcohol distorts the world view and tends to enlarge old pent-up passions. If you're trying to ward off seething angers from the near or distant past, stiff drinks will only augment and inflame the original conflict, thus promoting more anxiety. Alone in the dark, you find that anger and frustration sometimes assume outsized proportions, which then, like Sam's, are projected outside your mind onto the quiet of the surrounding space.

Smoking dope won't help you keep the lid on those fright fantasies of people in the basement or strangers behind the door; to the contrary, marijuana is not geared to keep you in fighting shape. Once you're stoned, you simply cannot move fast enough to defend against the night-stalkers and will end up feeling uncomfortably out of control.

Keeping the telephone wires burning is yet another scheme for warding off the aloneness terrorist, but the potency of this method quickly wanes when your friends begin to rudely yawn and abruptly cut the chatter short. At this point, you've come back full swing to those loyal companions of the electronic revolution—lights, radios, televisions, air-conditioners, Sony Walkmans, and tape recorders—which dutifully provide you with an immediate means for quelling the nighttime quakes.

Perhaps it would be expedient for the nocturnally nervous to keep a written account of the feelings, thoughts, images, and fantasies that emerge in the dark. We live in an age when it's commonplace to record dreams upon awakening. Writing down your darkness fear fantasies would serve the same purpose. In time, a pattern should emerge which can then be used to identify the drift of the "awful feelings." You may find that your darkness fears are camouflaging a bottom-line anger at the world for denying you omnipotent status. Feeling powerless to "see" or "hear" in the darkened silence could be triggering another root anxiety—the inability to control not only your own personal constellation, but also the entire universe, including the natural laws of day and night. Then, again, while writing, you may find that persons from the past are still psychically "beating you up," and that the conflict has created a mental pocket of unresolved torment. Or, that circumstances in your personal or professional life are generating a goodly amount of needling guilt. Unable to admit that what you are feeling is genuine, raw resentment, you may unconsciously use the dark when you're alone and vulnerable to punish the wrong person—and, of course, that person is yourself.

Sometimes, darkness fears actually act as cover for feelings of joy and success: a fear of unworthiness and subsequent retaliation lies hidden within the recesses of your psyche. Ironically, the anxiety seems to protect you from these deeper conflicts and has become so much a part of your life that you may have cleverly adopted it as a companion. Ask yourself this question: If you dropped the anxiety as a steady friend and ceased hurting yourself, would you mourn its loss? And, what would you have to replace it?

Along with keeping a journal, you may want to start a program to desensitize yourself from the dark places, silent spaces fears. Pick a target date. On that first night, turn on as many lights as are usually needed, and leave the door to the room open. Be aware of exactly how many lights are required and where they're located. Try to avoid dwelling on the anxiety this first night: begin to modify your thinking—summon up thoughts, memories, or reminiscences which are pleasant and happy, or exciting and hopeful. On the second night, turn out the lights in all the rooms but the bedroom, and take food that you dearly love into the room with you, "home" food which has always given you a sense of security, be it ice cream, fried chicken, or a piece of chocolate cake and a glass of milk. Then return again to the pleasant images you summoned up the night before. On night three, leave only a night light on in the bedroom, close the door, and repeat the food and thought process. Night four, move the night light from one corner to another where it's less visible; and, on the subsequent night, move it again to a part of the room where you will be only aware of the glow. You might also use music, the radio, or the television for this desensitization process. Each night, reduce the sound before falling asleep until you're finally able to shut it off. You may also want to tape-record a conversation with a close friend and play it back in the dark for comfort and solace, shortening the amount of replay time each night. Over a period of time, you should begin to experience the space in your room as a secure, safe place, which triggers a series of pleasant thoughts, associations, and the ability to sleep in peace without the internal terrorist knocking at your door.

For those who have recently moved into a new home, you might ask a friend to sleep over on the first night. Bring that person into the darkened room and, sitting on the bed, hold a normal conversation. You might even prepare a snack. You may want to repeat this event on several nights to accustom yourself to the new location. This technique has been most successful with those who feel disoriented by the new rooms, sounds, and spacial dimensions. It helps to bring a kindly presence into the space, a spirit of good will, if you will, and totally alter the strange dark and silent experience.

It's important for the darkly anxious to understand that the degree of the anxiety terrorist's intensity is usually in direct proportion to what is or is not happening in their life. For this reason, nighttime aloneness anxiety is a situational event. There are particular times when the terrors of aloneness are starkly palpable; there are others when you almost forget you're prey to their assaults and realize, perhaps sometime the next day, that you slept in peace without the lullaby of the lights.

There is yet another hour in the day—four o'clock—when, for those who live by themselves, the "awful feeling" of aloneness usually rears its head. This is the time when the hurly-burly of late-afternoon activities begins to ebb, when consciousness needs replenishing, when the spirit asks for nourishment, when the body is shifting its internal balance and requires time out from its metabolic tasks. At four o'clock on a summer afternoon, the sun has taken a position in the west and now casts a quiet haze on the desks and files: the office complexities and social interactions are slowing down for the five o'clock halt. This is the hour when the evening is anticipated, when last-minute decisions are made and plans firmed up for a game of tennis, a film, drinks with friends, or dinner, but for many, "something's just not right."

For some of those people, anticipating an empty home fills them with dread. When no one can be found with whom to share the evening hours, they might head for the local watering holes —the bars or restaurants—where others, perhaps just as alone, gather to while away the time and order drinks they don't really desire. Others head for the department stores or shopping malls, where they kill those evening hours overspending on clothes or cosmetics to avoid the hollowness of home. Then there are those who pray their aloneness won't "get them," but when four o'clock sounds, they find themselves vaguely surprised that it still does.

SITUATION #4
Four O'Clock Music—The Late Afternoon Lament

The hour is ushered in like the overtone of a single French horn alone in the world. The plaintive lament begins quite softly, almost at a whisper, then slowly grows in volume. Its poignant tone hastens the feeling of displacement in life and augments notions of what your choices have wrought on this evening of aloneness.

While much of the office attention has been focused on you during the workday, when five o'clock has passed and you have begun the pedestrian's dance on the crowded streets, the music of the solitary follows your trail. Once you've arrived home, there's no way you can bring the day you've spent or the people you've seen with you through that door. "Well, I *could* have made plans—I'm not exactly the people's pariah—but I didn't . . . I *chose* to be alone this evening." You also did a bang-up job today convincing yourself as well as a few colleagues that you "*must* clean the apartment tonight," that you're "really looking forward to balancing the checkbook," "appraising that financial report," "rinsing out a few things," or "whipping up a batch of something," yet, as you ascend in the elevator, walk up the driveway, or climb the stairs, you are once again struck by your "sole reality," and you now enter your home conscious that "something is off."

What you enter has nothing to do with the day you've just left or the way you've just lived it, and after tossing your briefcase or bag aside, for thirty or forty minutes you're vaguely disoriented. Somewhere between the office and home interest in your previous intentions deflated—"how did that happen?" And, where's that challenging motive to pull you through the room? What happened to your *sense of purpose?* "I seem to have left it back at the office, most likely in the word-processing room," you may think, and with that perception you hasten to make some swift and lasting decisions for this precarious half hour—quick decisions which will muffle the increasing volume of the solitary French horn in the distance.

So, what's it to be? "Well, the phone machine was a washout —nobody called. Maybe I'll look at the 'occupant' mail again and read the subscription promos—you just never know—turn on the television and catch the news, or perhaps take the sheets to the laundry before it closes. What's to eat? The breakfast dish should be washed, and, Eureka! my nail polish has chipped, which means I can kill a good hour with a manicure—save that for later. Mush with the cat, romp with the dog, or maybe walk him to the park? Go for a run. How about a long nap instead, I am a little fatigued. What's to eat? No, turn on the stereo, light a cigarette, pluck a wild chin hair, pour a glass of wine—change that to Perrier. What time is dinner? First read the newspaper, dial my horoscope (throw in the Good Looks line while I'm at it)," or, for the verbally clever, call a friend to whom you've already spoken today and fabricate a fascinating incident sure to keep him or her nailed to the phone for a good ten minutes before definitively deciding "what's to eat."

You know that what you choose at this point has literally nothing to do with anything significant—in itself it is meaningless. You know that whether you watch the news at six or eleven, read the paper or use it to wrap fish scales, eat dinner on the bed, in the bathtub, or do not eat dinner at all, makes little difference. But you also know that what does become weighty here is choosing the routine itself—a piece of structured time that begs to delay or hopefully vanquish the onslaught of aloneness. Decidedly crucial at this time is making a commitment to a specified format that will blitzkrieg the anxiety enemy with an arsenal of busy bombs.

Crossing that threshold from a well-coordinated day to an unstructured evening alone is a bit like experiencing serious jet lag: although you're physically here, you're psychically still there and your inner rhythms are out of whack, disgruntled, and in revolt. Unable to "reach out" and give yourself more of the same, you're suddenly stuck with the experience of yourself, plus the uneasy notion of, "Oh, no, it's just me again." While at the

office you were competent, quick, on top of the case, soaring
with possibility, ". . . and I thought, I really believed, that that
person was the authentic me." So what happened to that
efficient, high-spirited professional who functioned with lightning speed in the office today? And, why do you feel suspiciously as if you've been abandoned?

Anyone who has ever had a love-affair-gone-wrong recognizes
the hollow, empty feeling that accompanies the attempt to
rebuild a life without—a life alone. Being surrounded by an
office family for the majority of the day offers the same sense of
security and importance that your lover did when the two of you
were still as one. The sudden severing of either relationship
(work or love) usually triggers anxiety based upon a feeling
much older than that job or that person. There's good reason to
believe that you've probably always handled emotional jolts to
the system in much the same way as you now handle coming
home to an empty house, and that your arsenal of busy bombs is
a modus operandi steeped in a tradition of avoiding the "awful
feeling."

Between the office and home your good intentions for the evening were mysteriously flattened and then appropriated by a
vague sense of longing that you now can't quite place. Perhaps
it's a reminiscence of a time in your life when you felt protected
by a safe place, secured by caring people, sheltered by warm
circumstance. Over the years you've denied the significance of
this memory in your life and now believe that by filling yourself
up on frenzied activity you'll force yourself into feeling "fine."
However, continuing the race against remembrance is one surefire method for becoming a candidate for burn-out: ceaselessly
bombarding yourself with the ammunition of the anxious is ultimately exhausting and self-defeating.

One good way to bring your "jet lag" rhythms back into synch
is to begin thinking of the evening alone as *privacy* instead of
pain. Perhaps some of your time would be well spent connecting
with the particulars of the past. By exhuming the haunting re-
frains from your own history, you may just discover the clue to
what you seek, and begin to alter your sense of the future.

It's also important to remember that, returning home after a
busy day, you must have something to look forward to, an activ-

ity that is anticipated. *Most alone people do not plan ahead.* What is dreaded is the sense of nothingness, the psychic tabula rasa or blank slate of the mind, which is frightening in its emptiness. In order to fill that vacant space, it's crucial to begin to constitute a life for yourself that includes a *future*. This doesn't mean ten years from now, or even five, but tonight, tomorrow, the weekend, and the week after.

A great many people have found that by ordering their lives, initially shaping small plans to enhance their living conditions or fulfill a creative need, eventually reveals the larger aspects of their personal ambitions. For instance, moving the furniture around the room to give yourself a new perspective might lead to refinishing a table, then painting the walls, rearranging bookcases, and planning to save money for a new sofa. Or, doing macrame could lead to creating wall designs, then drawing and painting. While these projects may sound simplistic, they're not —what they ultimately offer is an occupation with a part of the self that, at the present, is probably lying fallow. People who have depended upon the kindness of the work environment to provide them with their identities are often stunned when they discover the intensity with which they approach a "just-found" project that is tangibly constructive. Their lives become enlarged, enriched, and they look forward to the joy of an ongoing, ever-ripening process.

Along with netting in your creative aspects, planning social events also helps to assuage the "awful feelings." When your calendar tells you that you have a dinner date on Thursday night with a friend, you're not alone. When you're saving money for a trip, perhaps to visit a friend or family member in another city, or even a vacation come summer with a group, you're not alone. And, closer to home, when you've introduced yourself to neighbors and can invite them in for a time-circumscribed cup of coffee or drink, you are not . . .

There are those people, however, who require the company of another living entity in their homes to tame the rather severe feelings of isolation and alienation. If this is the case, it might be very gratifying to get yourself a pet. Dogs require attention, love, and play—they need to be fed, walked, and cared for, and can offer in return a warm, unconditional attachment for which the very alone in this world yearn. Dogs, cats, birds, or turtles can provide a connection with life that may be the first step you'll need to take—they can offer an essential, life-saving bridge between feeling hollow and feeling needed and loved. That special bond between people and their pets is often a cherished, invaluable relationship.

However, whether you choose to record your thoughts, images, and longings in a journal, commence a creative project, arrange a trip, or select a pet, once you've embarked upon a plan that includes the *future,* you'll probably find that returning home in the evening is no longer a dreaded experience. You also may discover that you're no longer living alone, but with someone—yourself, and could successfully muffle the lingering overtone of that lone French horn mourning in the distance.

Like its plaintive cousin, the Late Afternoon Lament, yet another bout with aloneness anxiety often strikes the heart—the insomniac's medley, which breaks up the night at 4:00 A.M. like the staccato bursts of a brass band. While the illuminated digital clock ticks off another half hour of sleeplessness, the brass ensemble in the head plays a morning floor show—an agitated allegretto in fugue form. Variations on a multidimensional theme issue forth in the ragged mind and, with all your defenses lowered and while the rest of the world seems to slumber in unadorned peace, you lay awake listening to the varied voice-parts—a litany of unresolved conflicts: question; no answer; requestion; blank; question again; stop!

SITUATION #5
Four O'Clock Music Redux—the Fugue of the Situational Insomniac

Of course, there is agitation here, restlessness, a toss, a turn, a fluffed-up pillow, a twisted sheet, a spread that falls to the floor; a squirm to the right and then the left . . . Then, startled by the nagging, resolute voices in your head, you may sit up in a sudden

fit of pique and try to banish them with a show of noiseless
temper. But they are vocally relentless:

"Money, money, bills, loans, raises, promotions, loans, debt—
add, subtract, resolve, the dentist! Weight, diet, heart, exercise,
eighteen pounds, perfect life . . . Take her to dinner, new suit,
be impressive, sex, potency, prove, money, money, better office,
prestige, power, smooth presentation, courting clients, fame,
love, sex, sex. Why did I blow the affair? Maybe I should have
hung in . . . what was so terrible about me that made him vanish? I don't want to sleep alone, I like sleeping alone, money,
power, work, sex . . ."

Since insomnia is no respecter of bodies, you may have a
sleeping companion next to you whose presence in your anxious
state is suddenly a perplexing problem. As you stare at this form
reclining on the bed, innovative perceptions begin to form:
There's this woman laying next to me and she wants money."
"There's this man sleeping peacefully and he wants sex."
"There's this body snoring here who doesn't want a thing, what's
wrong with me?" "This person is taking up too much space and
that's just like him." "There's this woman curled up and I can't
remember her name." "Why am I in bed with this peculiar-look-
ing man?"

The four o'clock fugue grows in volume, recapitulating main
themes, introducing episodes, and then, with the subtlest shift in
direction, new themes are sniffed out. Old angers are summoned
up, ancient quarrels are dramatized, frustration looms large, and
dialogues in the darkness draw on the dramatis personae of the
distant past. And then the tempo speeds up—anger changes into
guilt and guilt into shame as the gleeful anxiety mugger dances
on the ceiling, near your bed, keeping a perfect pace with the
metronome in your mind. Robbed of your defenses, ravaged by
doubt, you look to the moon for aid.

It's here that the television sets come alive, that the refrigerator sings with late-night possibility, that brandy snifters are
lifted containing amber liquids to calm the speedy mind. "This is
ridiculous!" you exclaim out loud to nothing in particular. "I
can't deal with it . . ." As you pace and brood around the living
room, you may quite suddenly be compelled to locate a quote
you read in a book years ago—a piece of wisdom certain to

quell the heebie-jeebies of the allegretto in your mind. It's all quite clear now! If you can simply find that quote, why, for sure, then you'll be able to sleep and even feel richer for it in the morning, which is slowly making its way from the east. Blocking out the predawn light, you ravage the bookcases, your old journals, desk drawers, tattered college notes. Exhilarated with triumph, you discover the significant piece of brilliance—but, alas, it no longer holds the potency of its first reading: the high-voltage shock of its uniqueness experienced years ago now proves to be a cruel disappointment. You forcibly crack the book shut, which discharges but a fragment of your pent-up dissatisfaction, yet you are somewhat pleased to note that this little interval of activity did kill some of the time you would otherwise have spent gasping over your own anxiety.

Righting old wrongs is especially popular for the insomniac, but when the righteous impasse is met, when shaking an angry finger at the grave or pulling off imaginary but deliciously wicked vendettas has run its course, the rhythm shifts once again and you're face to face with guilt, the undertone of defensive anger.

"Why did I lie to her?" "Did he believe my deception?" "What if they find out?" "I should have kept in touch, I could have called, I should have dropped a note, I could have told the truth." "I should have, I could have, I wish I'd said, I didn't do, I'm wrong, off, twisted, bent, no-good, worthless, sorry and . . . I cannot get to sleep!"

At this predawn juncture, many people whip off the typewriter cover or grab a felt-tipped pen and begin the momentous note which will vanquish the demons of guilt and no-goodness that plague the early dawn. Hastily scribbled notes composed in a burst of determination are addressed to an individual vividly real in your zonked-out mind and propped up in clear view waiting to be mailed to that same person who has probably long forgotten the incident of your insomniac distress. The mea culpa letter written in this sleepless frenzy usually has little to do with the reality of the present, and will probably be scrunched up and thrown away in the morning, but that's not the point. The anxiety-riddled insomniac, swept away by the four o'clock music of the early morning, has done away with yet another piece of

emotional debris from the past, and whether it clears up who
struck John in nineteen-aught-one, or not, in the classic words
of Mae West, you may find yourself finally drifting off "in the
arms of Morpheus."

"Insomnia is a gross feeder," wrote Clifton Fadiman. "It will
nourish itself on any kind of thinking, including thinking about
not thinking." Anyone who has ever spent an hour or more
thrashing around the bed, tricking their minds and bodies into
believing that "now, ah, I've got it, I'm finally asleep," only to lie
there sharply focused on yet a new parade of mental topics,
knows the truth of those words. When situational insomnia
strikes, it comes with the accompanying feeling of betrayal, for
most of us believe that once we've hit the sack, our troubles,
burdens, and doubts will be drowned in the forthcoming slumber. Sleep itself is viewed as a way out, a respite from the mind
twists and anxieties that plague the day. However, the mind itself never stops working; it's continually renovating, repairing,
and rehearsing, and is busy awake or asleep. When insomnia
rears its head, we're stuck with an intense experience of ourselves from inside out and it seems like we'll never get free.

Situational anxiety is, of course, one of the prime causes of insomnia and, sooner or later, most everyone experiences a colli-
sion with it which can be directly linked to a stressful event
from daily lives. Conscious unresolved conflicts—fear of losing a
job, financial concerns, loss of a lover, office pressures, an illness
in the family—can trigger disrupted sleep, as can emotionally
charged unfinished business from the past—arguments, humilia-
tions, guilt, shame, and the vendetta fantasies that plague the
anxious mind. Further, once you perceive that you are definitely
in a struggle for sleep, the mind seems to rev up even more, and
then presents you with a new floor show of torments—who is
and who might be angry at you, what to wear to the meeting,
should you get your hair cut or permed, what should you do
about these extra pounds, to say nothing of sex, power, fame,
and a zillion other worries that perpetuate themselves in the
thinking and could be called the "snakes and garbage" of the
mind.

Many people who have incurred serious bouts with situational insomnia, and are aware of the twists and turns of their meandering minds, schedule their evening hours to include a period of time set aside strictly for "worrying." Should you choose to adopt this technique, during that hour write down all the stresses, tensions, "snakes and garbage," then take a look at the topics you've listed which might be disposed of on the spot. Since it will still be early, you may want to make a phone call, write a letter, pay a bill, balance a checkbook, or sew a button on the outfit you must wear for tomorrow's meeting; in short, resolve a few of the simpler problems which haunt your nights. However, even if you choose not to take any action, pouring out the pent-up dissatisfactions on paper will discharge some of the excess energy and act to keep a few of the minor anxieties in the other room out of your bed.

Another one of situational insomnia's problems is a bit more tricky. After a few nights of sleeplessness, the bedroom and the bed itself sometimes become associated with nonsleep—torment and tension. The target for anxiety then switches to an obsession over the inability to sleep plus the attendant worries over dragging your body through the day, feeling dulled out, at a loss for the appropriate responses at your job, and irritability. This concern takes precedence over the situation itself and a vicious cycle is created: you cannot sleep because you're too worried about the inability to sleep.

When you wake at four in the morning, instead of fighting your responses, try to cooperate with the insomnia for its duration. The more pressure you exert trying to fall asleep, the less sleepy you'll become. This would be a good time to give in to the disruption, get out of bed, take yourself into another room, and commit yourself to something relaxing. By working in concert with the insomnia, you may find that your mind will ultimately achieve some peace.

Interestingly, many creative people—writers, scientists and inventors, artists and performers—find that this is a most productive time for their unconscious creative processes. Many of them "use" their sleepless hours gathering the wild thoughts and notions that creep into their conscious minds, and they find that their clarity of vision is at peak performance. Other types of people use these hours to sort out the old emotional debris: they write that mea culpa letter to someone from the past, locate the old quote with that fragment of wisdom, or simply pinpoint the topics and subtopics which are consuming their minds. The information you receive during sleep-disturbed hours is important for your conscious mind to register: it's as significant as your dreams—and easier to interpret. Don't let these messages escape your scrutiny.

Depression is yet another factor which encourages sleeplessness. That fallen feeling of despondency doesn't always find an easy escape-hatch through sleep: when feelings are bruised and painful or swollen and impacted, the body often will not respond to the conscious mind's need for rest. If you've been in a depression for some time now and cannot lift yourself from its bind, you might want to plumb the underlying problem through professional counseling and alleviate this disturbing condition. In the meantime, be assured that depression is often a great sleep-disrupter.

Another issue provoking insomnia could be quite easy to remedy. Most of us were taught from childhood that we need eight good hours of sleep. This is not necessarily the case for everyone. Each of us has our own particular and unique biological timeclock which regulates the body's rest requirements. There are some people who simply do not require that much sleep and may be going to bed too early! If you usually retire at 10:30 and find yourself awake and ready for action at 4:00 A.M., switch your schedule around for a few weeks. Try retiring at 12:00 or 1:00 A.M. and check what time you wake. If you begin to sleep later in the morning, you'll understand that your internal biological clock is at odds with the "eight hours" wisdom, and you'll be able to make the necessary adjustments.

On the very practical side, you might check out the environment in which you sleep—the morning light, the curtains, the penetrating sounds. If you are a city dweller, you may be plagued by the garbage trucks, honking horns, or newspaper vendors. It might be wise to invest in ear stopples, calk the windows, soundproof the room, or use the "white noise" of the air-conditioner to block out the sounds. Then again, your bed and even your pillow could be inappropriate to your sleep needs.

Your body may be uncomfortable on that particular mattress, and your head may be too high on that firm Dacron pillow.

It goes without saying, foodstuffs containing caffeine are verboten to the insomniac. Coffee, tea, colas, and chocolate can play major roles in sleep disruption, as can alcohol. It's common practice for many people to take a drink to relax themselves before going to bed. Unfortunately, while you may immediately fall into a deep sleep, it will be short-lived: you may wake up and remain in that state till dawn, or you may be subject to frequent awakenings throughout the night.

It would be more productive to start an exercise program—not just before retiring, but earlier in the day, when you can discharge your energy, use your muscles, and prepare your mind and body for a night's rest.

Whatever techniques you choose, it's important to bear in mind that insomnia is a situational event. There will come a time when it will end—the inner conflict will be flooded by fatigue and flow away into a peaceful sleep. In the meantime, you may want to use the underlying messages of your anxious mind as information and begin to listen well to the varied voice-parts of your sleepless four o'clock fugue.

SITUATION #6
Sunday, Empty Sunday—and Anticipation of Monday Morning

The light and the sounds are different on Sunday. Perhaps this phenomenon is the result of the reduced street traffic, or perhaps it's caused by the late hour of awakening. Whatever the reason, the atmosphere on Sunday morning makes this day consummately different from other days and the restless anxiety mugger haunts the distance with a hungry, unnerving howl. Isolation hovers like a storm cloud and aloneness lurks menacingly just around the turn from the kitchen sink to the unmade bed, where a single coffee cup and special Sunday newspaper sections shroud the tousled sheets.

For Marilyn Braval, on Sunday, even the cat roams the rooms with misgivings, darting her head suspiciously toward the random flutterings of motion. The house reeks of stillness; it seems to highlight the near-panicky conviction that "something is not right." It used to be a family day—the mornings were filled with the smell of warm toast, schoolbooks littered the couch, single socks plagued the dryer, and someone could be heard yelling, "Hey, turn it down up there!" Then something happened. An irrevocable severing split up husband and wife, the children grew and traveled to schools across the country, and the three-bedroom home went on the market. Now Marilyn awakens on this mid-May day in a small condominium in Sherman Oaks where, like a host of other post-crisis people, she lies in bed reading the papers, hoping to be captivated by the crossword puzzle as she nervously plays out the game of surviving Sunday.

"I hate Sunday," Marilyn has heatedly remarked to friends, colleagues, and other teachers like herself; interestingly, they all seem to know exactly what she means. She views her life on this day through a prism of dread and yearning, and is keenly aware of her desire to outmaneuver the tentacles of anxiety which are grabbing at her gut—a feeling she, herself, often refers to as the mounting trip of the "octopus." What she unequivocally needs to do, she thinks, is to commit herself to a flurry of activities all geared to quell that scaremonger in her mind. But she didn't make any plans for the day and she feels so anxious right now that all she can hear is the voice of Sunday chattering in her head:

"I'd do anything to get rid of this feeling . . . maybe curl up in a knot and cover my head until it's over . . . I'd like to find an old movie on television that would sweep me away from myself; I wish I hadn't finished reading that novel, I'd like to re-lose myself in the story; I wish I could lose myself in something! If I was *with* someone, *had* someone, could *meet* someone . . . then again, my anxiety level is so high, if an interesting person popped up, given my luck, I wouldn't recognize him because I'm too filled up with the "octopus" to fit anything else in. Am I going to sit hunched over on the side of this bed with my face in my

hands all day? Get up and do something constructive, wash
something out, dust, vacuum, don't sit around doing nothing
—it's a waste! (I sound just like my mother . . . this is ridiculous!)

"There's something I've left unfinished—I wish I could
pinpoint what it is . . . something is wrong, something's
going to happen, I just know it! Maybe I'm getting my period, maybe I'll turn on the television; that's about all the
energy I can summon up right now because the "octopus"
has me all tied up, and I know this is stupid, but nothing
went wrong this week (that I know of yet), and I don't
trust it.

"Maybe I'll go shopping at the Galleria mall—no, for sure
I'll run into one of my students and have to act cheerful.
(Must grade last week's compositions today!) The phone
. . . don't want to answer it. Just let it ring. Don't want anyone to hear me sounding so off. But what if it's important
. . . then again, what if it's someone who wants to talk
about their problems? I'll have to act very helpful and then
afterward feel resentful and angry . . . I'll say I'm sleeping
and must call back. NO! That would make me look lazy and
peculiar . . . how about saying I have a guest? No, better
fake it . . . hello. Hi! Oh, just sitting here absorbed with the
Book Review section. Never better. No, don't mind at all
. . . sure. No kidding, is that so, terrific. What did he say,
what did she say, how did that make you feel? Drinks, tonight? No, thanks though, I'm watching a rerun of *Upstairs,
Downstairs*. Yeah, but thanks for calling, bye.

"He drives me nuts! Never asks about me and when he
does he doesn't listen. So narcissistic! So self-involved . . . I
need a whole new group of friends. People who are *doing*
things in the world, barbecuing steaks, floating camellias in
their pools, swapping sparkling stories of New York/Holly-
wood deals, dripping haute couture in their Rodeo Drive
cabana wear, planning Palm Springs weekends . . .

"I must stop picking at my nails, they look awful. I should
call my mother. Don't want to. If I don't sound perky she'll
press me for what's wrong and I don't know yet. Then she'll
hark back to my ex-husband and his new live-in lover (num-

ber three!), neither of whom I care one iota about . . .
then she'll get hysterical and I'll end up feeling guilty
and take care of her. (I wish I hadn't thought that
thought.) I should return Addie's call, but then I'll have to
hear how her life is infinitely more painful than anyone
else's in all of Southern California . . . and I might miss my
daughter's call, who may or may not call. Damn, I wish I'd
planned this day.

"All right. Turn on the television, get some sound in here.
Could you believe it? There's a woman in a mouse suit
selling cheese! Is this *Meet Me in St. Louis?* Whom didn't I
call back? I know there's someone I forgot . . . someone
who's sure to be angry with me. Judy Garland was such a
tenuous person . . . probably lived with the octopus too.
Maybe I'll eat something now and grade papers later . . .

"I wish I knew what was off. I need to have an affair. A
real old-fashioned romance with someone who kisses well
. . . someone I can dress up for again . . . a conscious,
worked-out man. (Did I pay my MasterCard bill? I know I
missed something.) Don't want to get married, just have a
full, sexual, loving relationship. Both of us very independent. Can't go out and meet anyone feeling this way . . .
did I feel like this when I was married? I was too busy putting roasts in ovens to know if I did or didn't, but then I do
vaguely remember feeling rotten, mainly on Sundays . . ."

Marilyn spends the remainder of this day of rest careening
back and forth on her complex emotional shuttle. Intermittently,
she stops and fervently prays this day be done, yet understands
that beneath that wish lies yet another, perhaps stronger truth:
the slower it moves, the longer it takes for Monday morning to
arrive. Therefore, although she thinks she just may be bored, she
is almost loath to change the scenario and speed things up.

After two films, watering plants, much foot-wagging and
finger-drumming, Marilyn "catches" herself staring into space
conjuring up the worst of what her colleagues may or may not
say and do if and when she encounters them tomorrow morning.
At this crucial point, agitated, irritated, and seething with self-
doubt, she flings off her sleeping garment, rapidly dresses, and

lunges out the front door to her car, then speeds around the neighborhood streets, wildly wondering where the hell she's going. On Van Nuys Boulevard, she makes a sudden turn and pulls into Bob's Big Boy, where (in case she should meet any students) she dons sunglasses and a scarf and races inside. Then (in case the counterboy should think she's alone at 6:00 on Sunday evening), she orders two Big Boy hamburgers, two portions of French fries, and *two* containers of coffee—to go. Driving home, she feels better because now at least she's "tasted" the day and cannot say she never saw the sun.

At 7:00 she bites into the second hamburger and loses herself in 60 *Minutes*, which nips a good hour in the bud. At 8:00, while keeping her attention riveted on *Archie Bunker's Place,* she dials Addie and hears why her class is worse than any class since they set up classes in Attica. At 9:00, that opiate hour for the Sunday sufferer, she switches to *Masterpiece Theatre,* which ties up the whole horrifying day and holds that other demon of astronomical proportions at bay—the anxiety of anticipating Monday.

At 10:15, grinding her teeth to the rhythms of the "Fanfare" theme, "Da-da dum dum dum dum diddle diddle dum . . ." Marilyn's "octopus" begins its ascent. "What did I leave undone on Friday? Did I lock my desk . . . did I lock up the rollbook? What if someone riffled through my drawer and found those tests stashed in back? Where did I leave my journal! Checkbook —is it in my bag?" She runs a bath, washes her hair, shaves her legs, and feels the dread seeping through her thighs. "Da-da dum dum dum dum . . ." her teeth repeat. "What am I going to do about that parent conference? They sounded hostile . . . should I ask the principal to sit in? How will that make me look . . . Oh, God, Monday—hold back the dawn!"

While fussing with her clothing selection for the morning, Marilyn experiences the full impact of Sunday's anxiety, which has been gradually building up to a bed-time crescendo. This particular aloneness anxiety is well known to those who spend almost every Sunday revving up in anticipation of Monday. Perhaps this most distressing feeling is often described yet rarely defined because of its confounding quality. It would seem that those who dislike their work or simply find it unchallenging would be the main focus of its attack. But that's not the case. People of all work persuasions suffer from Sunday Empty Sunday and Anticipation of Monday Morning anxiety—from those who are high corporate achievers to those engaged in professions, small business practices, and routine jobs.

Sunday itself is especially emotionally loaded for people like Marilyn Braval who, in the past, viewed this day as a "family" day. Many families use Sunday to mutually participate in the chores—to fix a piece of furniture, mend or wash clothes, clean up the house or yard. When that Sunday tradition is truncated, when those responsibilities are no longer in demand, the new freedom can become a disorienting experience, saturated with emptiness, plus the driving need to fill up the space with "something constructive." There is an obvious irony in retaining the name "a day of rest," when an acutely agitated feeling persists which dictates that you are entitled to neither peace nor pleasure. With no set structure to provide boundaries or goals, it can be a very frightening day, especially for those who, during the week, are intensely and constantly involved with their work. The emptiness of Sunday throws these people into a whirlwind of worry, discomfort, fear and, above all, guilt.

What does everyone feel so guilty about on this day? Not working, doing, watching the clock, going to, coming from, producing, promoting, or performing. In fact, with no concrete expectations flowing in from an outside authority, there is the tendency to fabricate false demands. For Marilyn, her mother's voice permeates her mind, filling in for the absent authority, and when that voice is shut up, she substitutes the sound for that of her own badgering requisitions which dictate that she be "helpful" on the phone, a good listener to whining friends, a perfect daughter, plus jam the day with grading work to ensure she won't be left with idleness. Driven by the need to appear busy, useful, and "going somewhere," Marilyn succeeds in intensifying her already flourishing "nothing-went-wrong anxiety," as well as making herself into a sterling candidate for burn-out, which manifests itself in her desire to "lose herself" in something or someone.

While Saturday is relatively free from this agonizing phenomenon (Saturday is okay, it's one day removed from Monday), on

Sunday the concerns for tomorrow creep stealthily in. Something has been left unfinished, wrong or undone, and someone is sure to be angry, onto your act, or filled with a change of attitude because over the weekend they thought things over and saw the light, had a dream that you were incompetent, broke into your desk and found your unanswered mail, talked to the supplier whom you listed on your expense account and found that he took *you* to lunch, figured out you are a threat, decided you are disposable, reread your report and discovered the flaws, and, tomorrow, all of this will come thundering down on your guilty head. Unless you worry excessively, rehearse your answers, prepare your defense and memorize your files, you may be out of a job, or worse, humiliated in front of your peers. However, there is a good chance that if you wear yourself down to a nub by being "helpful" and "good" on Sunday, those deeds will somehow make themselves known to those who control your destiny, and on this particular Monday morning you just may miraculously slip by.

There is yet another angle on the Sunday-Monday anxiety index which focuses directly on unadulterated resentment. It may sound ludicrous right here to point out that Sunday, for better or worse, is a day that brings you closer to your real self. Underneath the mind chatter, taut nerves, and growing dread, lies a stubborn rejection of the shift from "being yourself" to "being someone other"—a personality custom-made to meet the demands of tomorrow's workday. Resentment at being forced out of the safety of the nest ripples through the foundations of your being. No longer able to fret or frolic in abandon to the self's demands, you must prepare for the jarring experience of switching mindsets. With the sound of the Monday morning alarm clock, a "new you" becomes triggered and you must steel yourself to enter a socialized world of power plays, confrontations, expectations, discipline, authority, rules, regulations, scheduling, and performing like a pro.

"But, I don't want to," is the body's message, yet your behavior, by necessity, must change. For this reason, many people arrive at the office on Monday morning wearing startled smiles, false cheer, and, to buoy up the spirits, sometimes new clothes.

Is there anything reasonable that can be done about this ex-

hausting and depleting weekend experience? The answer is unequivocally, yes! You can begin by planning out the day in advance. Since you already know your proclivities for excessive
worry and self-doubt, try to fashion a bill of fare that includes
activities that will capture your attention. By no means create an
agenda filled with busyness—this is a day for self-renewal, rest,
relaxation, and pleasure.

Since the "nothingness" of Sunday may fill you with dread, try
to avoid "sleeping" the day away in order to escape yourself. If
that's your particular pattern, make a brunch date, plan on preparing a special breakfast for yourself, or ask a friend over for
dinner. The better you treat yourself on this day, the less
deprivation you'll feel.

To minimize the feeling of neglect, you might act as if you're
a family to yourself and do some cooking. Buy groceries on Saturday, and on Sunday prepare meals and snacks for the week.
Peel carrots, slice celery, bake chicken, make lasagna, prepare a
pot of soup or a casserole, bake, try out a new recipe—put your
kitchen in order.

If you enjoy reading, buy a few books that whet your literary
appetite and keep them on hand for Sundays. Listen to the
music you can never find time to appreciate during the week, or
go to a concert. Bicycle to the park, drive to the beach or the
mountains, watch a football game, visit a museum or gallery, ask
a neighbor in for coffee, go to the gym, meet a friend, or sit on
the stoop and feel the sun—anything that breaks the intense
concentration and frantic involvement of the routine work week.

Try to relinquish the awful hold that your feelings of paranoia
promote. If you are genuinely concerned over a terrible blunder
you may or may not have committed last Friday, plan on arriving at the office a half hour early Monday morning and check it
out. But once you've firmly decided to proceed with this measure, note it, plan it, and for the rest of the day try to forget it.

If you need uninterrupted blocks of time to free yourself from
the demands of your mother, brother, cousins, or colleagues, and
you cannot tolerate the incessant ring of an unanswered phone,
you might try purchasing a phone machine. You can turn off the
sound, resting assured that the message will be received, and re-

turn the calls at your own convenience, preferably after you've given yourself some leisure time and space.

Sunday is experienced as an anxious, lonely, and guilt-provoking day for many people. Like Marilyn Braval, the chattering voice of Sunday can relentlessly nag at your psyche, begging you to heed its multiple messages. If you listen carefully to what that inner voice is saying, the babble can be translated into a coherent and uncluttered communication. The voice will tell you certain truths about yourself: you'll learn what it is you genuinely worry about; of whom you are afraid; and invaluable information concerning what the "awful feeling" of aloneness anxiety is really all about.

FOUR

Public Aloneness Anxiety

*"Private faces in public places / Are wiser and nicer /
Than public faces in private places."*
W. H. AUDEN

STRUGGLING AGAINST ALONENESS ANXIETY IN THE PRIVACY OF YOUR
home, in a room where no one can see your pulse, is one matter
to consider—but what about showing yourself to the rest of the
world, alone, without a companion to act as a banister or baffle?
This is a public aloneness problem—a situational anxiety of a
different color. Out in a crowd, you must not only finesse the
self-consciousness which threatens to obliterate your carefully
prepared profile, but also work to disguise the visible symptoms
of your discomfort as well. But how can you keep your image intact when your smile is shaky? And what do you do with the
pounding of your heart and the knocking of your knees?

In truth, our society places heavy emphasis on doubles, couples, crowds, and groups. Therefore, it becomes embarrassing to
display genuine pleasure or sorrow alone in public places. Are
you really able to weep with abandon in a melancholy movie, or
exclaim with delight over a savory French quiche in a restaurant? Can you actually pull this off without a little squirm after
the fact; without giving a quick apologetic shrug-of-the-
shoulders to whoever may be glancing your way?

That apology is quite significant. It indicates that by revealing
your wanton emotion in the absence of a companion, you have
dared to defy the unwritten code and could just fall from public

grace! It's simply not socially smart to be both spontaneous *and* alone: those who "catch" you in the act are sure to offer a knowing snort, convinced you are something of a character who couldn't find a friend to go with you. Therefore, we learn to skillfully orchestrate our public emotional displays, hoping to pass as "regular" as we lick our ice cream cones alone on the street, posing as though deep in weighty thought, dependent, for sure, on no one.

The bad reputation of aloneness carries much of the burden for these exercises in false bravado. "What did you do on Saturday night?" "I stayed home alone." That particular answer, for some, carries a stigma tainted with shame. When ultimately translated it seems to imply: "Nobody wanted me and I'm a little odd." Therefore, for many people it is almost inconceivable to feel happy, whole, and desirable when publically alone (especially on a weekend). We have been too thoroughly programmed that to be alone is wrong!

The ramifications of this insidious notion are vast and unruly. They seep into every facet of our living and tend to turn this experience into a personal *bête noire*. The dependency upon friends to act as escorts becomes monumental and eventually begins to alter your decision of whether to be or not to be more often than you'd like to recall. If no one is available to join you for dinner, you'll probably slither home with a slice of pizza and a paper plate; and, if no one's around to meet you at the movies, you might just put off your desire to see that film, plop yourself in front of the TV and watch a boring rerun which is something better than nothing to do. Ultimately the scope of your external vision becomes minuscule, and your ability to take yourself out alone, a proposition of slow, alarmingly diminishing returns.

Underneath all the quaking and quivering, what is so terrible about showing yourself in public places and partaking of society's pleasures when alone? Assuming that your habits are not gross—that you haven't been ostracized from certain sectors for obscenity, you haven't been arrested for "flashing," and you haven't achieved a reputation as a "masher"—what horrors could those people out there discover that could . . . might . . . maybe . . . fling you into a public aloneness panic?

SITUATION #1
Dinner Out!—for One

Carol Matterton, forty-one-year-old business-woman-in-the-world, slim, blond mother of two, never eats in restaurants alone. Fast-food take-out stands create minor quiverings in her blood; a coffee shop is pushing it (even though she can pass as a "busy person on-the-run"), but a *nice* restaurant, an *expensive* restaurant, a *good* restaurant—that's an anxious ordeal of major dimensions.

Nonetheless, on this particular cold Saturday night, having just had an excellent haircut, and having dropped the kids off at their respective parties, she has shakily opted to treat herself to a delicious dinner at a new restaurant—the one with the fresh pasta (green and white) hanging in the window. Conscious of the alarm this decision has provoked throughout her entire body, she nears the restaurant. To prevent any unpredictable awkwardness on her part, she studies the outside menu in advance, then, as though propelled by the sound of a distant storm, pushes herself inside the ROOM.

The maître d' smiles cordially—*didn't he look behind me for my date, or did I just think that?* "Good evening," he whispers, "would you like to check your coat?" "No, no," answers Carol Matterton much too quickly. "I'm still a little chilled." "How many in your party?" he inquires. "Just me . . . ," she replies, and notices that her voice has ascended a full octave. "Dinner," she continues, lowering the pitch, ". . . for one." The host surveys the field for the appropriate table, which appears to be the one in the back of the room where the swinging kitchen doors connect with the dining area. He beckons her over to a small hideaway table for two. She tucks her bulky winter coat securely beneath her bottom, sits on it, then slides off the sleeves and arranges it carefully over the back of the chair—*because it would be just like me to knock a glass off the table or whack a cuff into a waiter with a loaded tray, and this guy knows I'm that type!*

She prepares herself for the waiter, who is taking no notice of her and whom she can easily see is not that busy since the restaurant is only half-filled. A bus boy fills her water glass. She overthanks him, and then overthanks him again for the butter pats. She smiles disarmingly at the approaching waiter *who got stuck with my single table,* and momentarily forgets what she drinks until she looks to the ceiling for an answer. "A glass of red wine, please," she says, then feels immediately inadequate for not requesting a half bottle of something dry and lazy, *but then a half bottle will look like I'm a tippler, and, well, I didn't ask what the house wine was, but, what the hell* . . .

Assuming the pose of what seems to be a perfectly centered, well-adjusted, normal human being, she casts her now sublimely arrogant eyes on the OTHERS, careful not to stare too long, dart away too quickly, yet simultaneously provide an important piece of busywork for herself. Donning an expression of intense purpose, she lights a cigarette, drags deeply, and blows out the smoke through rounded lips which, to her horror, might possibly be construed as an invitation to kiss!

Her face is quite hot; there is as yet no bread with which to stuff down the lingering image of her lewd blunder; those people who came in after her are being served; and, she is most uncomfortable sitting on the thick folds of her coat, which are surely causing an ugly bruise to form on her thigh. She squirms sparingly and spends what seems an era analyzing the menu (which she has already thoroughly examined in the window), registering nothing except the blinding idea of herself as a *woman who couldn't get anyone to go with her out to dinner on Saturday night.* She orders "Spaghetti alla Carbonara with Special Roman Sauce," and seems stunned when the waiter removes the menu from her hands. She's now stuck with nothing to look at but the lace cloth, a bayberry candle, and—the OTHERS.

There's a reason why they didn't bring me bread! She wishes she could gracefully sweep out of this snake pit, but, thank God, the glass of wine arrives. After a winning smile at the waiter's back, she sips and decides to land her eyes on a safe place, something neutral like a wall. With the air of an effete connoisseur, she visually disdains the decor, the watercolors, and the photographs, then suddenly becomes acutely aware of the chatter around her—happy people sharing life, involved, interested, alive, normal, while she is . . . *wait a minute!*

Her life is pretty good! And she's only in here because, like the normals, she became hungry! So what's happening here? She is then stricken with the desire to bellow out through an outsized bullhorn: "I'm a successful management consultant! People pay me for my advice and counsel! I've been married, have lovers, am desirable, have children, and . . . and *I'm a Phi Beta Kappa!*"

None of these accomplishments is significant, however, for right now the only vitally interesting aspect of her is that she is alone in this *good* restaurant, that her outfit may be wrong, that there is something missing, lacking, and peculiar about her. She cannot remember what her new haircut looks like, she's forgotten how to breathe, and she's vaguely dizzy. Carol Matterton lands her eyes on a safe space, a three-by-five area of peach-painted wall, and plans on staying there pretending she's invisible until she can behave like a regular person.

Young Sandra Carson-Orsini, with frozen smile and trembling knees, has just entered the restaurant. Charged by her therapist to take herself out to dinner alone (an assignment geared to prepare her for her incipient role as a divorced yet independent woman), she is reluctantly here but with definite purpose. She likes good food, yet her fears concerning this miserable business of eating alone are near phobic. As the twenty-six-year-old, dark-haired woman waits for the host to seat her, she spots Carol Matterton at the far end of the room near the swinging kitchen doors and decides she's the one to use as a role model for this ordeal. The willowy blonde is attractive, older, cool, poised, and obviously knows her way around the haughty maître d' who has just asked the young woman how many in her party and received her answer. "A table for one!" he yells to the ROOM, and Sandra almost faints.

Through her paralyzed haze, Carol Matterton hears this command and looks up in Sandra's direction. Carol immediately experiences a pang of envy over Sandra Carson-Orsini's spritely know-how—*if only I had been that conscious and self-possessed at her age. Why, the maître d' is even seating her at a preferred table near the front!* She watches the young woman select the chair facing the ROOM and, quite by accident, the two women catch each other's eye.

Sandra Carson-Orsini, having decided this is the woman to watch, offers a somewhat timid half-smile and nod, which throws Carol Matterton into a whirlwind of panic. She doesn't know if the dark-haired woman knows her from the past, is feeling sorry for her, or trying to pick her up! Caught in the grip of the anxiety vise, Carol Matterton lifts her chin a dignified inch and passes over the young woman's eyes as if she'd never seen them. She returns her gaze to the peach-painted wall and poses as one deep in thought.

Sandra is flattened. She has just performed a *faux pas* of mythical proportions and has been totally rejected! Maniacally twirling a short, dark curl—*did anybody see me?*—she arranges her face to meet the ROOM. She quickly decides to evermore avoid the older blonde's table, but, of course, she doesn't and after a fast once-over is convinced that Carol Matterton is wearing a Rolex watch, which supplies her with an important clue as to why she, Sandra, with her common Timex was so precisely shunned. As she fantasizes the size of the diamond studs in the older woman's ears, she toys with her own silver hoops and tries to quell the humiliation rising in her thighs.

She gruffly orders a double gin martini straight up, after which she wonders how she will handle hard liquor, which she never drinks. *Well, screw you,* she thinks pointedly at everyone in the ROOM and, to justify her presence in this restaurant, takes out a pad of paper and begins to write: "For Thursday appointment—Went to restaurant alone. Crashed. Something about me that women don't like (must get to this). Dressed all wrong. Everyone staring at me. My deodorant failed. Notes for myself: I excel in my classes. I have good friends. I will pass the bar exam. I will be a lawyer. I will . . ."

Carol Matterton, weak from hunger and holding herself rigid, sneaks a look at Sandra and decides that the young brunette must do something terribly creative, as she's so engrossed in her writing. But before she can continue this line of thought, her pasta dish arrives. She forgoes the fresh pepper (the long mill might make a scene), accepts the Parmesan cheese, and takes a bite. *Truly delicious—you could die!* she thinks, but her pleasure is short-lived, as the two couples at the next table have burst into animated laughter and Carol is certain it's directed at her.

Sandra, too, stops writing, but she is too far away to make that judgment, besides, she is more concerned with the two men across from her table who are obviously sharing confidences and, she's not sure, but she suspects they are bad-mouthing her.

I wish I'd dressed better tonight, worn a skirt, bought new shoes . . . wasn't so deficient, lacking, really odd . . . no, that's not it . . . But before Sandra can complete her thought, one of the two men looks at her, nods, then returns to his scampi, and she understands in a flash what he is thinking: *that poor, pathetic, lonely woman is trying to pick me up!* The restaurant is now a nightmare of horrors and, by the time Sandra's fried calamari arrives, she believes that even her food is sad and wrong—that the happy, right people would never order pieces of breaded squid.

Carol Matterton finishes her "Spaghetti alla Carbonara" and, before catching the waiter's eye, fishes in her wallet for her American Express Card. "We only take Diner's," he quietly hisses and races off to seat a normal lively couple. Horrified by her error and scared she may not have enough cash, she accidentally drops the card to the floor. She has to remove herself from her seat to pick it up, which, she is certain, is the motive behind the fresh outburst of laughter from that table for four. She retrieves the card, gives her hair a "beautiful woman" shake, sits down, and counts her cash. It will just make the amount of the check, plus an adequate but not generous tip, and, of course, will verify this waiter's perception that single women don't tip well.

Sandra Carson-Orsini cannot finish her food and is having trouble signaling her snotty waiter, who is presently exuding happiness while taking the order at a table for three. She waits, noiselessly pulling on her coat, until finally the waiter drops her check on a small plate. Drawing a crisp twenty from her wallet, she hears roaring laughter from across the room.

"I know they're laughing at me," Sandra muses darkly as she puts the money on the plate and makes for the door.

"I hope I'm not the butt of that joke, too," Carol Matterton says to herself as she lifts her head and imperiously moves toward the exit.

Concluding their last witty exchange, the two couples at the happy, normal table wipe their eyes, dab their mouths, and breathe deeply. "Did you see those two women who were eating here by themselves?" one of the women asks of her friend across the table, and receives a decidedly firm nod. "Don't you wish you could do that alone?"

There are people everywhere who staunchly refuse to eat dinner out alone in a good restaurant—the emotional price is too prohibitive. Those whom are least suspect have been known to forgo "Spaghetti alla Carbonara" for canned Spaghetti-O's, a frozen Morton's pot pie, or a ham and cheese on rye wrapped in white deli paper with a pickle. Yet, many others, like Carol and Sandra, summon up their courage and struggle against the perceptual debris blocking their entry to the good restaurant arena. They pray they will successfully pass, as journalist Mary Peacock puts it, "just like someone who is eating with companions, only the companions aren't there."

Much of the anxiety surrounding this problem is culturally inseminated, and while men, too, suffer the apprehensions of eating out alone and do experience the same stage fright of inner doubt, the public cost is not quite as dear to their self-image. For women, not all the anxiety is based in pure self-consciousness. A woman dining alone may be construed by some men as an open opportunity for advances; they refuse to accept the idea that she may prefer her solitude to his uninvited intimacy. As a consequence, women are then forced to muster the strength and poise necessary to nip that misguided notion in the bud, *and* deal with their own personal interpretations of who they are in relation to the others in the dining room, *plus* gird themselves to sit, eat, and digest without appearing too spontaneous or too depressed. A substantial order for anyone.

Cloaking the heart of this issue is how you perceive yourself in the situation. Eleanor Roosevelt once said, "No one can make you feel inferior without your consent," and it's in this regard that perception and interpretation can render you potentially at war or at peace with yourself. Being thrust into a situation where you are neither recognized nor admired can cue off a need to prove your worth to that mass of strangers who are all seemingly waiting to judge your act. What we all need to ask ourselves directly in these situations is: "What value is being threatened?" This is not easy to do when you're sitting at a table staring at breadsticks, but it is something that can be explored for the future. Although each of us has a repertoire of unspecified clues, you still may have to grope about blindly for a while. A good portion of the conflict is firmly rooted in wanting to be regarded as valuable and important, and even though your life may be steeped in testimony to support those needs, when the security base is threatened, that evidence is obscured.

When you walk into a restaurant, you carry not only the heavy emotional baggage from the past, but also the old labyrinthine dialogue which mercilessly insists, "If I'm thinking it, then they're thinking it." If the thought exchange is one of, "Thank God, I'm not one of those," then you've tapped the worst of yourself and have given the okay to those faceless people in the room to reduce you to the stature of an ant. Unfortunately, you can neither control nor manipulate the thoughts of others from afar, but you can alter your own thought processes and in time upgrade your self-image.

Of course, for the dinner out alone, there are multiple poses and contrived eccentricities from which to select to ward off the bad news from across the room. When chewing becomes stilted and thus open to question as to whether it's being executed with the proper decorum; when mouth-wiping becomes compulsive, for you are convinced that bits of corn decorate the lips; when tonguing the front teeth becomes mandatory as a guarantee against broccoli that might grace the smile—these stances come in handy. Women like Carol opt for the imperious "beautiful woman" demeanor—cool, distant, with just a dash of Catherine Deneuve. Some women assume the journalist pose, placing themselves at one remove from the situation by archly observing from a lofty perch; others choose the compliant young girl, helpless and therefore unassailable. Feigning vagueness, otherworldliness, and absentminded confidence is yet another popular item, while blandness seems to help some feel secure in the knowledge that no one would be interested enough to look, much less to judge. Busyness, however, is the winner in the anxiety poll—reading newspapers, books, magazines or, when really stuck, old letters, bills, or matchbooks rummaged from the bottoms of handbags.

There is the argument that many women feel they don't deserve to give themselves a dinner out at a good restaurant, but this popular notion is a bit tricky. Most people genuinely do believe that they have the right, but their deeply buried emotional life is in heated conflict with their beliefs. Carol Matterton is a perfect example of a woman caught in this scenario: she *believes* she deserves this treat, yet her netherworld of anxieties has worked its way up into her consciousness and placed her in a mild panic. Since her accomplishments, at this point, are incompatible with her image of herself, they cannot help to sustain her, and while she's in the panic, her perceptions can do nothing but distort. Sandra, however, is a different case. She too believes she deserves to dine out alone, but understands that in the past she has been dependent upon her "couple" status as an entree into society. As she seeks to explore this experience from the inside out, her mounting anxiety will undoubtedly serve her well, as she will "use" it to provide her with the information she needs to clean up this issue.

For those who are imprisoned by public places aloneness anxiety, from the mildly self-conscious to the uncomfortable agoraphobic, there are a few behavioral techniques which can be immediately employed to begin desensitizing this situation.

The first time out, do not overwhelm yourself by choosing a large or expensive "good" restaurant. Start with a coffee shop, an establishment that's less populated, close to your home, and do bring reading material. Sit at the counter, preferably on a seat near the end, not a table or booth, and order a cup of coffee, tea, or a soda, something quickly prepared and fast-served. Be sure to pick a week day—not a Friday or Saturday night—and try to avoid the rush hours with the breakfast, lunch, or dinner crowds: choose a mid-morning, mid-afternoon, or mid-evening hour. Push yourself to exchange a few words with the waiter or waitress. During these slack hours they won't be as pressed for time.

The next two or three outings, return to the same place, at the same time, and move up a step. Order a doughnut, roll, or muffin, and make yourself known to the waiters through short conversations. After two or three visits, you may want to sit at a table or booth, but one that's not too conspicuous: pick a spot in a corner or near the door. This time you may want to order a sandwich, preferably one that does not take time for grilling.

When you've begun to feel a sense of comfort and safety in this particular establishment, you may want to move on and select another restaurant in the neighborhood, perhaps a small family operation. Once again, don't go on a weekend or during the mealtime rushes. Find a table that feels safe—against the wall or over in a corner—a location that will alleviate the feeling of being "stared" at. Opening up a conversation with the waiter, perhaps concerning the house specialties, could act to diminish some of the self-conscious anxiety or even the feeling of panic in a strange place. After you've ordered, try to place yourself in the restaurant—look around the room, get a feel of the others, how they're behaving, especially those who are eating alone. If you become "spooked" out, you can turn to your reading matter and try to relax. Remember: if you find yourself overwhelmed, you can always leave food on your plate, ask for a check, and leave. However, you may want to return to the same restaurant a few more times and then move up to the next level.

TIPS FOR THE AGORAPHOBIC

If you are agoraphobic, you may find this technique most difficult. What you will be fighting is the fear of the fear of going into the restaurant, the anxiety of perceiving you *might* be thrown into a panic. Therefore, it might be wise to spend more time than suggested simply walking into that first coffee shop, allowing the panic to wash over you, through you, and then flow out. This condition is most alarming to those who endure its attacks. However, most agoraphobic people tend to slowly withdraw from the world, reducing their fields of mobility, sometimes to the point of being homebound. It's vital to remain in contact with the world, to maintain a connection with external, outside life. The panic you feel doesn't kill—it only scares—and its symptoms, palpitations, shaky legs, blurred vision, the feeling you will lose total control, or hot flashes, are directly linked to *fighting against* the panic, tensing the muscles, constricting the breath, holding oneself rigid. If you haven't already started a program to desensitize this condition, you may want to begin by employing some of the above techniques. Go slowly with yourself. If you find you cannot make it through the door, that's fine. You can try it again later, or tomorrow, having learned, not that this is a phobic pressure point, but that you did not "let go," allow the panic to run its course, and understand that there is a point of peace beyond it. *Agoraphobia is not incurable!* However, if you are very frightened by this condition and feel you cannot make headway by yourself, by all means do contact the local referral service within your city and find out if an Agoraphobia Treatment Center is nearby. You do not have to suffer it alone.

For those who are simply anxious and self-conscious over showing up in a restaurant alone, do remember: while you're undertaking the above process, a number of false notions may be lurking beneath the anxiety. You may be bent on perpetrating an image of yourself that is unreal, perhaps grandiose, but unequivocably fixable.

Ultimately, a dinner companion does provide refuge from a variety of skewed perceptions. If you believe that happy foursome at the table to your left is laughing at you; if you are convinced the waiter dislikes your face; or, if you think that couple walking in is bad-mouthing your dress, then you have but to turn to your companion to base yourself back in reality. What is significant here is the idea that if you did have someone with whom to share this event, you probably would never have bumped headlong into those false, unnerving perceptions.

In truth, those other people scattered about the room have probably given you a cursory once-over and gone back to their espresso. One diner may think for a moment that you look just like his sister in Dallas; another that your mauve blouse is the color of her new couch; and, someone else, that your haircut reminds her she needs a trim. At the bottom is the very strong possibility that the others are a bit awed, not only by your ability to carry this event off alone, but also that you were brave enough to venture out where they would dare not tread.

In line with eating out alone is the miserable business of simply going out alone, especially on a Saturday night. Once again, both men and women suffer this occasion, and the genesis of the reluctance is much the same: the emotional price is too high. The fear that you will be seen, not be seen, make a scene, or end up bored and unsatisfied is sure to call up a quorum of anxieties to bear.

SITUATION #2
At the Movies—Alone

Jeffry has been through this routine before and does not like how it feels. He spent two hours on the phone trying to find someone to go with him to the film, but since it was Saturday evening, everyone had already made elaborate plans *that didn't include me,* and the one person who was free, wanted to spend the evening alone, *or so she said.* Approaching the theater, Jeffry Saurau is not happy. There is a rapidly forming line, which means he cannot slink inside the theater unnoticed, and there is a brutish guard of mammoth proportions with a mocking smile who seems to instinctively know that Jeffry couldn't find a friend. Breathing fast—*there won't be room for me!*—he hastens his pace and slips in line seconds before a smart-looking couple (*God, she must be a model!*) take their place behind him.

He has every right to be here alone on Saturday night; after all, he works hard, is a more than generous tipper, and receives glowing printouts from the Con Ed, Visa, and MasterCard computers on his monthly bills. Furthermore, Jeffry Saurau is not your average, simpleminded moviegoer *like these others who had nothing else to do on Saturday night:* films provide him with important information which he uses for his job as an advertising space salesman. Indeed, he has a reputation among his clients as a keen trend-spotter in these weighty matters of popular culture and jealously seeks to protect it (he could make it to management level within the year).

Having now justified his entire existence, as well as his placement in line in front of the patrician woman whose face is swathed in cheekbones, he immediately decides that her Ralph Lauren boyfriend is much too old for her and, although he secretly believes the guy is probably a terrific stud, that it's his studied rough-wear clothes that fascinate her. Jeffry shoves his hands in his pockets, strikes a pose of infinite macho cavalier, and inches backward so as to better catch their conversation. However, via his acute peripheral vision, he inadvertently witnesses her arms draped around her companion's neck and her full lips whispering words in his ear which he instantly construes as a lusty request for hot unnatural sex.

He turns face front. A duo of young women decked in designer jeans, Hawaiian shirts, and running shoes are heatedly discussing summer employment, a conversation interspersed with the relative merits of each other's lip gloss. Jeffry sneers with subtlety and nuance. Although they're not really worthy of dominating his interest, he is nonetheless certain that both young women know he's just been through a two-hour ordeal *to get someone to go with me and failed.* This perception dizzies him.

Oblivious to his previously well-defined existence, the two women continue to chat, which means, of course, that they not only find him significantly unattractive, they just may construe his aloneness in this line *as the thinly veiled cover of a street pervert! What made me think that?*, he wonders, and offers himself an audible chuckle geared to throw off any psychics who may be standing in line and hooked into his mind. He strongly suspects he is now being regarded as an unbalanced crazy—a person to move away from.

Attempting to deny the presence of Lauren Hutton & Company behind him, Jeffry thinks he sees Judy Quill (*she said she wanted to be alone tonight!*) near the front of the line with what

looks like a real simp. Rather than becoming angry, Jeffry is
stricken by a peculiar sense of humiliation and prays fiercely
that she will not see him! He presses his neck down into his shirt
and stares wildly at the cracked sidewalk.

*Wait! . . . I forgot to get the ticket! Jesus . . . what a jerk!
How did I manage that one? Maybe I'll ask these two women to
hold my place, but, no, they'll think I'm a dolt . . . well, how
about the prince and princess behind me? No, they're already
hostile . . .* Jeffry decides to feign a ticket loss. He begins to
curse in well-aimed whispers, rapidly sifts through his wallet, his
back pockets, and then, in a gesture of resignation, complete
with much serious nodding of head, combs his fingers through
his hair, which is sure to confirm to the psychics in the line that
his loss is authentic. While he's at it, he takes a good look at the
international entrepreneur behind him who doesn't give Jeffry
any recognition . . . *because he doesn't think I'm any real competition!* He then becomes violently enraged at all of the auda-
cious powerbrokers in this hard society who don't know from
world hunger! Having relegated this completely alien man to
flagrant strip-miner, killer of whales, poisoner of the environment, Jeffry turns to him and meekly asks: "Ah, would you mind
saving my place in line while I get another ticket—you see, I
somehow lost my original one and can't seem to find it, and . . ."

"Tickets," the dazzling beauty on his arm exclaims, laughing
and shining in her stardust jumpsuit, and her escort, the Aya-
tollah of world pain, blushes and with some embarrassment
croaks out, "Isn't this the ticket line?" Visibly brightening, Jeffry
nobly offers to purchase their tickets while he replaces "the one
he lost"; money is exchanged and he springs happily to the front
of the line, passing Judy Quill who is hiding her face in her pe-
tite Evan-Picone blazer lapel. When Jeffry returns, however, his
aspirations are shattered. Instead of being welcomed as a real
contender, perhaps joining their party for a late, exotic *ménage à
trois,* the fancy jet-setters merely thank him and return to some
absorbing idle chatter revolving around what seems to be pa-
prika futures.

As the line moves forward, Jeffry lingers close to the beautiful
couple, hoping that any passing clients will believe him to be an

integral part of their intimacy, thereby circumventing the possibility that he will be collared as a weird and unpopular guy. Once inside the foyer, however, the duo swiftly disappears, leaving Jeffry alone with the hot buttered popcorn concession, whose smells make him gulp. Consequently he hurries away from the stand, for to publicly reveal his abnormal passion for popcorn, *alone and friendless,* could prove to be of paralyzing proportions.

He locates an unobtrusive seat near the back. As the lights dim and the movie begins, he finds himself wedged between a tall dark man waving a container of hot buttered popcorn under his chin and a short elderly gentleman smelling vaguely of a Big Mac. He perceives that he is diminishing his shoulder breadth, that his elbows are pressed uncomfortably close to his ribs, and agitation begins to emerge. *There's something about the armrest protocol that seems to suggest I am without turf here,* and that thought makes his groin shudder with anger. Inching his elbow onto the armrest to his right, he takes pleasurable note of the surrendering elbow of his opponent. Triumphing on that side, he begins his campaign on the left—*which should be a snap with this old man*—and has just gingerly edged the elderly arm nearly off its rest, when the doddering hand slams itself down on top of Jeffry's wrist, which instantly retreats to his lap.

Frozen with embarrassment—*this guy thinks I'm gay!*—Jeffry pretends he is invisible and stares at the screen, hoping to get caught up in the story, which he heard is fraught with emotion and pathos. But his cells, now alarmingly alert to all extraneous threats, have signaled the voice sounds from the dark man to his right, who is busily explaining the themes and philosophical symbols of the film to his munching partner. Jeffry is enraged. Virtually incapable of concentrating on the visual before him, he begins another critical campaign—this time to shut them up. Darting his head viciously toward their faces, he shoots them his most deadly glare. Venturing further, he proceeds to cluck his tongue, wildly clear his throat, and exhale with furious and noisy abandon. Yet he only manages to receive a mass of narrow-eyed, lethal looks from the row in front, which happens to include the gorgeous couple who have apparently forgotten his earlier goodwill.

Jeffry quakes with his wrath and longs for a Rolaid. Unable to follow the film, he runs his own script of withering *bon mots* through his head. *"We all paid to hear THE FILM, not you!"* *"Ah, could you save it till later?"* *"Could you keep it down, PLEASE?"* *"HEY, cool it, will you?"* In reality (which is mercilessly slipping away), all he can manage is shortness of breath, heart palpitations, and the fervent desire to maniacally lash out.

Quite suddenly, as if inhabited by yet another personality, Jeffry Saurau, throwing caution, character, and anxiety to the wind, turns to the offending party, pokes his shoulder with a pointed index finger, and, in a loud, definitive voice, carefully articulates each of the following six syllables: "Will you shut the _____ up!"

Stunned by his outburst, he prepares to expire and waits for the ax of God to descend upon his head. Yet, although the mortification in his thighs sets them quivering, to his total amazement, somewhere inside his head he registers the sound of applause, and as he regains his composure he realizes that the section in the back of the theater is making him into a regional hero! People are clapping, an isolated "That goes for me too!" rings out, and he's getting the nod of thanks from the glitterati in front of him.

He noiselessly pays homage to the foreign personality who momentarily possessed him and now tries to get back to the film, which suddenly is of no particular importance. *Where are we? Damn it, I missed the crucial scenes.* He'd like to ask someone what transpired but doesn't dare now; he desperately has to urinate but wouldn't think of it; and so, for the remainder of the reel, Jeffry Saurau fills in his own story line, feels quite strong, and patiently holds it in.

When the lights come up, he modestly nods at the preferred couple now in the aisle, and makes his way to the foyer. Here he arranges his face in studied nonchalance to meet the eyes of the people in the newly formed line. Once safely out of sight, he zips uptown in a taxi where he secures himself in his studio apartment and gives in to his bursting bladder.

Relieved on all counts, Jeffry grabs a beer from the refrigerator and attempts to formulate the trend he should have spotted during this evening's critical culture search. But he's much too taken with his show of backbone and bravado . . . and he only wishes there had been someone important there to see him.

As there are multitudes of people who would rather open up a can of tuna than eat out alone at a restaurant, there are just as many who would rather watch a "Gilligan's Island" rerun than be caught alone at the movies on Saturday night, and Jeffry Saurau's situation is only one of many confronting people under the bright marquees of first-run films. Once again, perception and interpretation are the responsible parties here for either settling down or stirring up the onslaught of the anxiety.

Jeffry just happens to be one of the many young and single who use their job descriptions as an internal press card for entry into the external world at large. Justifying his existence in terms of his professional position, by necessity, leaves a significant void within him—one that can only be filled by outside verification. That common error was probably promoted by important people from his past to whom he still must prove he is *someone*, and every time he is confronted by an attractive couple, he shifts his frail power base over to them, reenacting his childhood and perpetuating the scenario of his original anxiety.

Since Jeffry perceives himself as a small guy in the world of big people, he could easily fail to achieve the adult recognition he desires. And worse, if he continues to abdicate to strangers, he just may not become a major influence on the twentieth century (a position he secretly hopes to achieve) . . . not even a footnote. As long as he interprets his public position from a bird's-eye view, he will be forced to conjure up acts of infinite macho, which will then keep the curtain down on his private self-image, which is teeming with perceptions of himself as inadequate and wanting. By trying to appear as more, when he basically views himself as less, he feeds the conflict and inflates the anxiety. Further, he compounds his dilemma by insisting that he *must* act appropriately at all times, for if he should inadvertently slip into impulsive or even vaguely spontaneous behavior, "the ax of God" will descend, which means that punishment for any untoward conduct is lurking just around the corner, possibly in the next aisle.

Fear that his anger may emerge is yet another tool for stirring up the pot of simmering anxiety. To secure the lid on that possibility, he taunts himself with the notion that he may just be a maniac on the loose, which keeps him in total check, works to inhibit all of his pent-up feelings, and prepares another pot of fertile stock for yet another serving of self-doubt.

Much of the discomfort experienced when "on display" is rooted in the conflict of serving two gods—society and the self. Constantly juggling those allegiances does nothing to dispel the ambivalence toward going out in public alone. One god is always abandoned, and even if it is only momentary, the incident is often felt as though there were a slow leak in the rear tire—very threatening and possibly dangerous. Yet, it may seem impossible to bring these two into synch. For the person who decides to risk incurring public disdain and for the moment honor the god of the self, the results can be surprisingly happy.

Initially Jeffry avoided the responsibility for his assertive self: he treated this new piece of behavior as though "inhabited by another personality," which permitted him to lash out at the offending talkers in the theater. Viewing this situation from the outside, his behavior seems excessive yet ultimately reasonable: as a result, he received the deserved approbation. But what about viewing it from inside out, through Jeffry's eyes? Scary stuff for a man who feels he must always be appropriate.

The risk did pan out, however, and he was successful in his mission. Perhaps this experience will leave him with a more positive regard for his otherwise stifled self. It would be most advantageous if he could interpret this breakthrough as the work of a truly authentic trend-setter, for he pioneered a new pattern for himself (as well as for the others in the theater who, interestingly, waited for him to do the dirty deed).

As with eating out alone in a restaurant, you can learn to desensitize yourself from the anxiety of going to the movies alone. Once again, don't step out your first time on Friday or Saturday night! Pick a week day; go early in the afternoon or evening. Select a familiar theater in your neighborhood and, after buying the ticket, check out where the restrooms are located, then pick a seat *on the aisle!* Don't hem yourself in the middle of a row where you'll feel trapped.

If you must wait on a line, you might try to speak to the people in front or in back to alleviate the feeling of being quite so alone. You could chat about the film reviews, the performers, or offer information you've picked up about the director, plot, period—just to start a conversation off.

It's also most important to *select the film carefully!* If you've recently undergone a painful divorce, don't run out by yourself and sit through a rerun of *Kramer vs. Kramer*. If you're feeling isolated, alienated, and somewhat depressed, avoid making a debut solo flight to films like *Ordinary People*. And, just to be on the safe side, avoid the horror thrillers—à la *Psycho, Halloween,* or *Ghost Story*. It would be prudent to select a film with subject matter slightly removed from your own life's circumstances, a film which will minimize your feelings of aloneness in this situation—perhaps a comedy?

There are, of course, many different angles on this same situation. Other people—men and women—perhaps older than Jeffry, possibly married or recently divorced, gay, straight, or androgynous, tackle this aloneness problem with a variety of fascinating twists. A major piece of this particular anxiety puzzle emanates from the fact that many of these people arrive at public places, like movie theaters, at point zero in internal resources. Having brought nothing with them but faulty and/or empty perceptions about themselves, they interpret the event through a hollow echo chamber of emotional longing and thus become an open season not only for the imagined ill will of others, but also for their own destructive systems of thinking.

It might be wise to begin collecting a repertoire of solid insights about yourself; not the old ones you've been loyally lugging around from the past (those are obsolete and probably boring even to you), but a new, realistic version of both your human capability and your accomplishments, unfettered by the noisy systems of childhood. Once you've established a network of viable conceptions concerning yourself and your life, you may discover just who is starring in the film and what the story is all about.

FIVE

Lateness and Waiting Anxiety

"He who is late may gnaw the bones."
YUGOSLAV PROVERB

"It is always those who are ready who suffer in delays."
DANTE

IF THERE BE AN ACTUAL KING OF THE HILL ON THE SITUATIONAL anxiety index of paralyzing attacks, Being Late could just be the one to appropriate that crown. Lateness hits the consciousness with the impact of a sudden cyclone on a quiet coastal town. Its fast-spiraling winds whip you into a rising current of roaring guilt which mercilessly intensifies as the minutes dash by. Buffeted about by the swirling pressure of time, you are stricken by unrelieved alarm, and your body becomes glutted by anxiety most foul.

Knowing that you are expected by an angry individual who is, right now, pacing in front of the theater, stalling the business lunch, or crossing you off the list of promising applicants is indeed a nerve-mangling experience. Working hard to beat the traffic, as well as the clock, you expend enormous amounts of vital energy performing the emotional acrobatics of the anxious, and later, when the emergency has subsided and the winds are calm, you're left feeling much like a dark puddle at the end of a major storm.

Fending off attacks from both the ongoing anxiety alert, plus the riled one-who-waits, forces you to think fast, talk faster, and do a lot of fancy footwork. What you're basically after in this maelstrom of panic is a safe place to land, a shelter that will protect you from the shrill voice of devouring authority who is over there somewhere, waiting, silently ticking off your roster of high crimes and seething with rueful plans of renunciating your worth. How do you know for sure this is happening? Because you, yourself, behave in much the same manner when left in a similar lurch. Therefore, from the moment your lateness is perceived, to the moment arrival is achieved, you must survey the devastated terrain and scramble for the highest, driest rooftop, which happens to be the best and most believable excuse you can possibly create.

Both the occasionally late and the chronically late often come unhinged by these charged battles against time and guilt. Yet, trapped by circumstance, they both quite swiftly become contenders for award-winning "fight or flight" fabrications. However, with so many chronically late verbal dazzlers continually mouthing brilliant lies and alibis, the occasionally late individual is forced to muster all of his or her imaginative resources to succeed in exuding even a modicum of credibility for that single delinquent offense.

It's important to understand that while authentic accidents and acts of God do occur, no one wants to hear them—they lack the appropriate panache. Lateness offenders must learn the art of garnishing drab excuses with colorful details of catastrophe. The starch has simply worn out of such off-the-cuff excuses as "my car broke down." They must learn to accessorize that statement with glamorous frills such as "Vandals poured sugar in the gas tank," "The steering wheel was stolen," or, "The new parking regulations took effect at midnight, and, in a municipal crackdown, the car was towed away."

If details cramp your style, you may learn to depend on the understatement, that one cryptic comment that tells worlds of what your eyes have seen, as in a weary shrug of the shoulders ("It happened"), followed by a heavy sigh ("What can I say?"). This stance can be varied the next time by simply altering the gesture to a pathetic nod, and the words to "Don't ask." Anger also works well as it usurps the irate prerogative and steals the drama from the one-who-waits, as in "I've had it with those damned trains! Do I have to deal with you now, too?"

It would be prudent to remember that the selected excuse and accompanying behavior must offer just enough factual basis (when possible, a piece of corroborative evidence will do the trick) and fictional magnetism to thoroughly attract or repel the one-who-waits, plus render him or her hopelessly guilty for having entertained even a flash-frame of doubt concerning your good honor.

Nine Topics for the Latecomer in Alarm

One way to arrest the lateness anxiety in its early sweat stage is to prepare your story in advance and, while flinging yourself from wall to wall, edit and refine it. These topics may offer you the assistance you require in a crunch:

1. *The Broken Body:* Includes anything from headaches to heartburn, kidney stones to cramps. However, a wise dissembler knows that if you've selected a sprained elbow, it would be expedient to inform your employer that you "called the doctor at the crack of dawn, he had to come in early, and that's why I'm only twenty-five minutes late." Corroborative evidence: an Ace bandage.

2. *Transportation and Municipal Inefficiency:* Provides latitude for engaging sagas of poor city planning, faulty scheduling, archaic machinery, government indifference, and long, arduous waits for buses, trains, or trolleys. However, can be shortened to a simple "Goddamned subways . . ." Corroborative evidence: a rumpled suit.

3. *Inclement Weather:* Includes all contingencies, from morning dew to snowstorms, heavy overcast, rains, hurricane threats, or high winds. Master manipulators have been known to dampen their hair and speak of the "flash flood which swept over my part of the city, then moved on to yet another state."

4. *Good Neighboring:* Wide open to poetic license. For instance: "My neighbor's wife was about to give birth and I had to drive them to the hospital, took the wrong cutoff, and if it wasn't

for that cop who stopped me for speeding, then provided us with an escort, I probably wouldn't have been here till noon."

5. *Housing Disasters:* Big-city dwellers may opt for the arrival of the exterminator who "brought the wrong chemicals," or "a message was slipped under our door last night informing us that the landlord is planning to co-op the building and that an emergency tenant meeting was being called at 8:00 this morning *in my apartment!*" Also good: "No heat last night," "no hot water," "no water at all." Corroborative evidence: "Booklet of Tenant's Rights."

6. *Family Problems:* The sudden appearance of a long-lost uncle works well here, especially if he's famous. "My husband was sick all night and I stayed up with him," makes it in a pinch, but it also implies you must remain bleary-eyed and disheveled all day.

7. *Criminal Assault:* Gold chain grabbers are currently in vogue, as are purse snatchers and minor terrorists. Here the perpetrators can be awarded great descriptive detail. However, witnessing a robbery provides the perfect arena for suspense and high drama.

8. *You'll Never Believe It, but . . . :* A grab bag of inspired excuses, ranging from "I ran into an old college friend who was ambling down the street, deep in conversation with Diane Keaton . . ." to "They were shooting a commercial in front of my building and wanted my face in the crowd." If you're willing to lie low for a few days, you might call up the office and leave a message stating you've been rushed to the Mayo Clinic. No reason.

9. *Mental Anguish:* Not recommended for work situations: otherwise, to be used sparingly. "I'm terribly sorry, I know this is a problem with me; I've been talking just recently to my therapist about the whole issue of lateness."

While these topics may provide you with the safe place you seek, there's still no guarantee against going through a morning like that of Susan Constant, a woman who was ill-prepared for the red alert of lateness anxiety.

SITUATION #1
Late for Work!

She had no idea that her supervisors at Flood Advertising, Inc.,
had been drawing straws to ascertain who would tell her about
her lateness. Alice Sterne got the short end of the stick and yesterday called Susan into her pale, understated office. "Your evaluation's coming up," said Alice Sterne. "Don't put me in a
compromising position." Susan Constant was stunned. As a popular favorite among colleagues and clients, she was not used to
this treatment. And, although she received the admonishment
like a consummate pro, she was injured, angry, and viciously
mused, "You want prompt? I'll show you prompt!"

This morning she wakes up startled! For one mad moment she
believes it's Sunday, but then with the foggy dreams and harsh
sun doing battle with her senses, nothing in her mind is meshing
precisely. The clock reads 8:35, and she does vaguely perceive
something pressing . . . *8:45!* Dark horror gushes through her
consciousness. Her pulse rate accelerates and her veins fill with
panic. The piercing realization of who she is and where she is
expected to be in *fifteen minutes* descends. Susan Constant
stares at the clock as though witnessing a massacre. She turns it
upside down, backside up, tests the alarm button, sits up, stands
up and, still in shock, picks up the phone and dials TIME. "8:47
and thirteen seconds . . ." She fears for her heart.

Nibbling on her thumbnail, she begins a silent litany: *The
alarm broke. The alarm was stolen while I slept. I do have a terrible cold, strep throat, intense cramps, conjunctivitus, diarrhea,
constipation, a thundering migraine, slipped disc, hemorrhoids,
meningitis* . . .

Pinned to the receiver, she feels cold sweat forming on her
palms. She suddenly remembers she was supposed to prepare
the agenda for the client from Houston who will be arriving for
a major meeting at 10:00 and she's the only one who knows not
only which reports, correspondence, and research materials are

needed, but also where they are filed away. A heavy wave of anxiety undulates through her stomach, moistening her underarms, and preparing what seems a permanent crick in her neck.

Pulling at separate hanks of her hair and staring wildly into space, Susan begins a mechanical walk into the kitchen. "Deny this is happening." She boils water, heads for the bathroom, sits. "There are other jobs in this city. Jobs where they'll recognize what they've got." Employing a meditation technique she read in a book last year, she consciously avoids all other thought. Unconsciously she strongly suspects she will not survive what feels like a certain brush with death.

With shoulder muscles stiffening, Susan jumps into the shower, triggering a violent outburst of oaths, all aimed at the coursing water which drenches her hair, adding another ten minutes of drying time to her already ample police blotter of lateness offenses. *The plumber arrived at 8:30 to fix a rotting riser; the exterminator rang my bell then never showed; the super came by to fix the backed-up toilet; my neighbor was mugged in the hall by a man who looked amazingly like her own son . . .*

In a crazed stupor, Susan mistakenly loads her toothbrush with Prell, drops Jean Naté bath powder on the scale, closes her eyes, opens them and, as she methodically applies a slate-gray eye shadow to the bridge of her nose, she begins to hum the Diet Pepsi commercial. She mascaras her lashes as well as her bangs, and emerges from the bathroom with a jagged lip line of coral color. Forging a trail of powder prints on the hall carpet, she storms the bedroom, flings open drawers and closets and, while visually leaping from belts to blouses, grabs the first available pair of panty hose. With shaking hands, she runs the first pair on the left foot, discards them on the floor, tears the cardboard package off a new pair, carefully works the right foot up, the left, stands, smooths and kneads both legs up, on, in place, done.

"These are not sandalfoot," she says aloud to her armoire, "and I'm wearing open-toed shoes!" At the risk of being jeered by the hidden toe critics at the office, she dives for the pair on the floor, but they were totally ruined, so now she must switch outfits, which seems an insurmountable task given the fact that it's now 9:16. She didn't take her pumps to the shoe repair and the heels are run down, so it's last year's pumps, which are out of style, or, wait . . . what about the black suit skirt, the black silk blouse, the camel jacket, and the new taupe sling-straps which pinch her toes and which she was planning to return to Lord & Taylor, but with a limp, *I could pass as ailing and if pressed say that I took a nasty spill last night, sprained my ankle, and this morning had to spend an hour soaking it in Epsom salts. Do I have a cane?*

The black skirt has a spot, but if she tosses a damp cloth into her bag she can clean it in the taxi where she will also attach her gold studs, and, My God! she has to change bags—it's 9:22 and *I don't know who I am!* She tucks her blouse inside her skirt, dons her jacket and her gold watch . . . *What are you talking about? My Piaget says 9:02. Stopped? Impossible! Well, what do you know? I'm just as surprised as you are!* It's a thought. She grabs the dryer and as the blast of hot air hits her head, she furiously wags her crossed leg.

My mother called and told me I'm adopted, my brother's young son was taken to the hospital with what appears to be a jungle rash, I had to walk here from my aunt's house in Scarsdale . . . With her hair still damp (*It was raining on my side of town*), she begins a thigh-paralyzing search for her house keys, races out the door, down the elevator, and crazily hails every occupied taxi in sight. *A garbage truck blocked the cross-town street, the taxi driver turned rabid—Well, I almost didn't make it in at all!*

Running into the building, she can feel her entire body vibrate but cannot stop now to give it a pep talk. *Late! Never mind that . . . we may just grab up the Ford account because I ran into a guy early this morning on my way here who happens to be the Vice President in Charge of Advertising and he said* . . . She races off the elevator, past the receptionist, into her office, slips into her chair, spreads papers all around the desk top, and throws together the agenda.

With unusual confidence and professional aplomb, Susan Con-

stant walks down the corridor. "Morning, Sue," a young colleague yells out to her from behind a giant production schedule.
"Good morning," Susan replies with grounded authority, then
coolly inquires, "Is everyone seated in the conference room?"
"No," says her friend, peeling the tip of a grease pencil. "Alice
tried to reach you this morning; the meeting's been postponed
until tomorrow and she won't be in till noon. By the way, have
you got a minute?"

If this scenario taps a raw nerve of recognition, then you probably have indeed experienced the anxious lateness alert. But even
if you do sharpen your dissembling tools and, even further, find
your way to the center of the cyclone and tap the calm techniques for feigning sublime indignance or indifference, the red
anxiety alert will not easily be muffled, muted, or lied away.
There's something much larger lurking beneath the offense
which only you can define.

While hurry and worry, fret and fear are the glaring symptoms of lateness anxiety, how you *feel about the situation* is the
basic rub. If you've been supoenaed to testify against your
closest friend at a pretrial hearing, have scheduled cocktails to
inform your husband you're filing for divorce, or are late for
your first dental appointment in six years, the feeling doesn't
need a lot of probing. But if you're late to a friendly dinner
party, a fascinating job, or a first-run film premiere, you may
begin to view your behavior with appropriate suspicion.

TEN UNCONSCIOUS IMPULSES TO
FIT THE LATENESS DEED

There are as many sly motivations for lateness as there are slick
excuses. When you swear you'll never put yourself through the
lateness situational cyclone again, but the menacing winds rage
on, it might be wise to stop hurtling yourself through space and
check out a few of the possible motivations. The following list
attempts to identify a worthy selection of unconscious impulses
that beset the best of us at the worst of times:

1. *Avoidance Amnesia:* A memory quirk which allows you to selectively forget the arrival time of any function at which you are expected but do not want to attend. Provides a sound outlet for mocking the punctuality ritual, plus an extra twenty minutes for profound procrastination.
2. *Grandiose Thinking:* Popular with consistent over-bookers as well as over-extenders. Here you believe you can squash sixty appointments, including two lunch dates, three dinner engagements, a cocktail party, and forty-six phone calls into one day, plus pick up and return the baby-sitter, and catch the "Tomorrow" show.
3. *Cold War with Authority or One-Upmanship:* Lateness acts here as a divine act of defiance aimed against all of those whom for all of your life have told you what to do, when to do it, and how much time it will take. Also a singularly perverse method for demonstrating not only that your life and schedule are infinitely more significant, but that you, yourself, are far more important and powerful than the low-end one-who-waits.
4. *Masochism:* Seeking punishment to keep life's ebb and flow consistent, familiar, and hurting. Not surprisingly, this rates high on the motivation index, for the benefits provide immediate gratification, are self-damaging, destructive, and include the very real possibility of actually being fired.
5. *Sadism:* Lashing out at men or women from a quietly festering vendetta which you've been carrying around since someone significant hurt you in the distant past. At this point the focus of the anger has become blurred, and everyone, including totally innocent parties, gets it.
6. *Attention-Hustling:* A not-so-hidden inducement for arriving late, especially to the theater or to a film where your competition is formidable. Most prevalent at dinner parties.
7. *Learned Lateness:* An acquired skill, usually inculcated by a role model from the past who was also virtually incapable of judging time or consequences. You now emulate that same lack of reality judgment.
8. *Terminal Dawdling:* Carried over from childhood when meandering was fashionable. Then, all issues, situations, and people held equal fascination for easy distraction. Now, there

is an unwillingness to be a responsible mature adult and make distinctions between the important and the unimportant.

9. *Situationally Ambivalent:* Inability to make a decision. Well, you do think you may want to be there, but then again, maybe you don't . . . but you should at least try to be on time, unless on the way you change your mind . . . it's difficult to know . . .

10. *Hate to Wait:* An ironic twist in the lateness game. Here you arrive late in order to circumvent the traumatic tensions of having to wait if the other person happens to be late. It also provides the perfect way to avoid being alone, and goes on to prove an inability to suffer a moment's pain.

These motivations are rarely distinguished or defined by late-comers because defensive posturing usually jumps the motivational gun, and all you do know for sure is that you're in a race for time and fiercely hope to stave off the anger of the other, who is fast becoming your basic executioner. Therefore, don't plan on getting an emotional grip on yourself until after you've dodged the ax.

However, it could prove interesting for you to begin to perceive just how many areas of your life lateness intrudes upon—appointments may be only one area for concern. This problem may also show up in issues of self-neglect: not paying bills on time—the rent, department stores, the telephone company; you may even be someone who regularly receives dunning letters threatening collection procedures because you "put it off." Not tending to dental or medical problems, postponing return phone calls to business associates or friends, leaving the grocery shopping until the markets are closed, or simply procrastinating over having your shoes resoled are all issues that tie directly into the inability to be on time.

While it would ultimately be gratifying to explore your own landscape of situational lateness, it might also be expedient to take some practical steps for your next series of appointments. Chronic oversleepers have reported satisfying results using simple timepiece procedures. One survivor tells of setting the snooze alarm a half hour early and placing it on the floor, approximately three yards beyond the bottom of the bed. By the third or fourth go-round with the alarm, he becomes thoroughly annoyed and stumbles from the clock to the bathroom, where he gets it all going. Another speaks of setting two snooze alarms, slightly out of time synch with each other, and placing them on the floor at the foot of the bed on opposite sides, thus achieving the obvious effect. A clock radio set at full volume and tuned to the grating voice of an early morning disc jockey should do the trick, providing, once again, that the radio is beyond arm's reach. Of course, if you have a mate, you could ask for some help or, in a real bind, place the telephone across the room and have a friend ring you.

For those of you who are untroubled by the early morning malaise, but find your daily appointments consistently running late, you might try wearing a beeper watch which signals the hour and the half hour with both single and double beeps. It's a sound you can't ignore, and while *you* may tend to deny the noise, others won't. They'll inquire into the source of the beeps, thereby activating your own memory center. With luck, they'll take the cue and excuse themselves, enabling you to make a dash for your next meeting.

Prepare for the unpredictable by making allowances for such contingencies as traffic jams at rush hour, clogged freeway exits, an absence of taxis, late trains, a low gas gauge, stormy weather, or other uncontrollable events. And, while you're at it, you could lay out your clothes in advance as well. Nothing can throw a schedule into chaos like a run in the last pair of hose, or the only tie that works with the suit emerging from the rack with a spot of taco grease. If these mundane particulars can be anticipated before the crisis hits, you stand a better chance of devoting your precious time to life's more significant tasks, and just may completely avoid the red alert of lateness anxiety.

If lateness hits the consciousness like a sudden cyclone, waiting approaches like the threatening sound of the wind whistling down the river. The notion that "something is wrong" mounts in the mind, a peculiar sense of foreboding begins to grow, and the anxiety begins its restless ascent.

SITUATION #2
Waiting, Waiting—at the Restaurant

Charles Hunter met Dana Land this past Friday at an uptown art gallery opening. On Sunday he called and asked her to join him for dinner during the week. "Sounds terrific," she responded enthusiastically, "I'm game." They settled for Tuesday night at 8:30 and planned to meet at Le Lit Chaud, which, they both agreed, makes an amazing cassoulet and an interesting bouillabaisse.

Charles arrives ten minutes early to establish his base on the restaurant turf. He pays his respects to Armand, the cool maître d', arranges for a discreet corner table, then sits at the polished oak, six-stool bar, orders a very dry martini, and strikes up a friendly chat with John, the bartender. In the mirror behind the amber bottles, his image reflects his new coarse-tweed jacket, smoky mauve shirt with the soft collar, and the hand-made European silk tie. The ensemble exudes impeccable taste—casual, but playful, with just a subtle clash of color. It works well with his short graying beard and, from this vantage point, his hazel eyes seem to pick up the autumn shades of the tweed.

He shifts his position on the red leather stool and half-faces the attractive woman with the full body and wry humor in her eyes who is sitting to his right toying with a kir. As they idly chat—both comment on the sudden change of season—Charles notices that the stool to her right is empty: if he can prolong this convivial interlude for three more minutes, he will be able to impress Dana as a man thoroughly at home in the company of charming, worldly women, thus giving himself the sexual edge. At 8:30, however, it's the attractive woman's husband who appears, and at 8:33, while staring at a serving cart of colorfully wrapped cheeses, Charles begins to doubt his judgment.

Did he say Fifty-seventh Street or Fifty-second? She may have misunderstood. Then there was the confusion over the day: they did agree on Tuesday, but then Thursday was discussed first

. . . Maybe he should check his calendar—no, he left it sitting on the antique desk at home. Well, this is foolish because they even joked about the darkness of the room, but then, there is a restaurant on Fifty-seventh Street which is just as dark and the names are vaguely similar—at least they're both French. If he could think of the name, he'd call the other place and have her paged (just in case), but that's being compulsive as it's only 8:37, hardly cause for alarm. Yet, there must be some slipup because he remembers she wears a good watch . . . but that doesn't mean anything, does it? What did she say on the phone when they spoke? He said, "How would you like to have dinner one night this week?" and she said, "Sounds terrific, I'm game." At least he thinks that's what she said. Maybe she actually said, "Zounds, horrific, how inane."

Charles shifts in his seat and lands his eyes on a dessert cart filled with strawberries, pastries, and mousse. Perhaps he should call her at her office and find out if she's been held up, although the minute he leaves his seat she'll probably appear. If she's unable to spot him she'll think he's stood her up and leave—so, he'd better stay put. (Did he say 7:30 or 8:30?) No, they both agreed the former was too early—or did she? What if she was already here, waited around, and left? He really should call her home, but it's impossible to keep an eye on the door from the location of the phone, and he's not certain she remembers his last name, so how will she find him? Maybe she was in an accident? That does happen. Does she have a car . . . ? It's either 8:41 or 8:40 by his watch; hard to tell in this light.

He feels uncomfortably warm, begins to tug at his collar and loosen his tie, which has quite suddenly become too tight for easy breathing. Perhaps he'll have another drink, he's a bit on edge, a trifle restless, but maybe he won't: he knows what that will do to him on an empty stomach and he should wait for her. As he reaches in his jacket pocket for a small tin of Brasil Dannenman's, Armand appears discreetly at his side and whispers, "Your table is ready any time you are, Mr. Hunter." Charles nods, slips him a five, and tells him to hold it "oh, another ten minutes." He orders a second martini and rolls the thin cigar between his fingers.

There was something slightly off about her—he remembers now with surprising clarity. Her outfit at that opening was a little overstated, something ostentatious about it, too flashy, almost as if she was wearing a sign stating, "Look! I'm current, even ahead of my time." Obvious. And her laugh—he didn't want to acknowledge it before, but it was grating, slightly forced, a shade too loud. While he's at it, he may as well admit that he does prefer brunettes to blondes, and, yes, he vividly remembers that while expressing his interest in the photorealists, she interrupted him! And then, again (this is not definite), but wasn't there yet another moment when he was commenting on the demise of the minimalist movement that she cut him off? (That bodes ill—he may have made a major cultural error. Are they or are they not still active?) "Excuse me, John! What time do you have? 8:45? Thanks."

Startled by the sudden boisterousness of the couple coming through the door, Charles jerks his head around and watches their interplay of lighthearted intimacy. He turns back to his glass and folds both hands around the stem. The pit of his stomach is steadily sinking; he's beginning to feel ungrounded, a bit hollow. Maybe his remarks at the gallery *were* pretentious . . . Did she cut him off to save him from embarrassing himself further? Or is she just trigger-happy? He secretly acknowledges that he's uninformed about the current art scene, and could have made a complete ass out of himself . . . that's probably it. She had second thoughts about him, reconstructed that evening, and then told her friends she made a date with this guy who's a bummer and wishes she hadn't . . . how does she get out of it? . . . One of them said, "Just don't show; you won't run into him again," and Charles feels his breath constrict. He has been accused before of being too somber, even—God, who said this to him? . . . Nancy Giles—"rigid and withholding." She said it at the very end.

Charles leans over and loosens the zippers on his Italian boots. He's perspiring—is there anyone else in here who's feeling the heat? He'd like to take off his jacket, but . . . well, maybe he'll fondle this swizzle stick. He looks at himself in the mirror and decides to shave off his beard. He should start running again, playing squash; his muscle tone is shot. He's not wonder boy anymore and he did go through that depressing period of time when he couldn't quite make it . . . Something made her change her mind. He combs his fingers through his beard. There are a lot of people he suspects don't like him—the subtle avoidances, the lack of invitations . . . "John, excuse me . . . Did anyone leave a message for me? Charles Hunter. No? Okay, thanks."

Seven minutes to nine! This is really outrageous, insulting, and rude! What a miserable bitch! At this point there's no excuse she can fabricate that will offset the basic thoughtlessness of this inhumane act. This is totally unacceptable behavior. He's had it with the male-female thing that's happening these days. And (it's all coming clear now), she's just another one of those hypocritical feminists—pushy, aggressive, critical and, underneath it all, afraid of real men! All that sensitive understanding is just a cover for insecurity and he's glad he's seeing through those soft manipulative trappings now and not later. He knows he's attracted to strong, assertive women, but he doesn't know what the hell they want and, further, they're so damned busy becoming the men they want men to be, they've left no margin for reality—much less romance. And, if she does appear now, he'll be totally stuck because if he expresses his rage he'll be labeled a controlling chauvinist and if he doesn't, she'll accuse him of having no balls. So, he's left, like most men, trying to find a line that's acceptable to them and, goddamn it! he's sick of feeling punched in the gut. Screw her! It's 8:56. He downs the remaining liquid in his glass and digs into his pants pocket for cash.

"Charles! Oh, I'm terribly sorry to be so late," says the lovely blond woman as she races toward his seat at the bar. She smooths down the hair near her pale cheek, then reaches out and tentatively touches his hand. "Hello . . ." Charles murmurs through stiffened, smiling lips, and while drawing his hand away from hers tersely adds, "You look wonderful, Dana." "Thanks, look could I order a drink?" Raising a single, halting finger, Charles motions to the bartender. "I think I owe you an apology," she goes on, "at least an explanation . . . you must be in a rage." "No . . . not really," Charles answers, lighting up his cigar. "These things don't bother me. Besides," he adds, blowing out a thin screen of smoke, "the little interval gave me a good chance to catch my breath. By the way, what are you drinking?"

It's difficult for most of us to adjust our waiting behavior to fit the province of civility and self-control, especially when a battery of bad feelings is violating all known social codes. Waiting for a person who doesn't arrive forces the emotions to shift and twist, and often it takes but a matter of minutes before the storm that's heretofore been only threatening to break loose, sweeping calmness and composure away in its wake.

The Five-Part Waiting Process

There seem to be five parts involved in this business of waiting, and while the content of the anxiety varies in differing situations, the style most often remains the same.

One to four minutes seems to be the approximate length of time most of us can endure waiting before the reservoir of doubt is tapped. At that point, a subtle rise on the anxiety scale summons up questions concerning your own memory and judgment. Usually lasting four to eight minutes, issues of self-skepticism skirt the mind and, like Charles Hunter, you begin to suspect that the date, time, place, street, or week may have been mistakenly noted on your calendar. At its most bizarre extreme, you sometimes wonder if you ever made the appointment at all!

The second level commences after approximately eight minutes have elapsed. During the next four, fleeting notions of the latecomer's safety are entertained but quickly discarded, for a sense of physical discomfort—tension, agitation, and restlessness—follows hot on its heels. It's either too warm or cold, noisy or quiet, dark or light, and you wish you had worn something else a bit more comfortable, at least a different pair of shoes.

Around the twelve-minute mark, level number three descends—an interval of another three to four minutes—often experienced as lengthy on the anxiety clock. Unable to tolerate the growing conflict, you begin a serious search for the latecomer's defects and imperfections. It gains momentum. Being hell-bent to find the fatal flaw that will render him or her worthless, shallow, and undeserving keeps your line of defenses well pampered, but after this strategy peaks, it has nowhere to go but downhill. As your feelings plummet, you painfully crash into level number four—the meat and potatoes of the process.

This is the bad-news portion of the waiting game. When the big hand hits the sixteen-minute mark, a five-minute chasm follows which catapults you into feelings you've probably been wrestling with since you were back in the crib looking up, batting at your mobile, desperately trying to win some recognition. These are the all-too-familiar snake-bite feelings of worthlessness which challenge your otherwise rational sense of self-esteem. Here the anxiety sneaks right through those sturdy foundations and metamorphoses into a dull ache. At this point, having completely personalized the actions of the latecomer and turned them against yourself, you have thus succeeded in procuring yet another affidavit proving you're a grand loser. It is no longer he or she is worthless, shallow, and undeserving, it is yourself, for if you had been a truly valuable person, he or she would not have been late. And if you had not allowed yourself to be viewed as a patsy and a pushover, this incident would never have come to pass.

The tension and pitch of this level cannot be long sustained, however, for the mind is a fierce protector of life and leaps back into the fray rearmed with fighting spirit. After around twenty-one minutes of waiting, you do experience a new awakening. Here, in level number five, anger and self-righteousness rally to your aid. No longer the passive victim, you become the arch aggressor in the waiting war, and with new eyes begin to see the late offender as just one of the many thoughtless, monstrous human beings who people this entire society. The anger does serve you well here—it gives you the strength and energy to rise to the occasion and, if feasible, head for the restroom to regroup.

But when outrage and fury have nowhere else to go, they get stuck like sludge in your system. What can you do next but chew your hand, mutter oaths into your martini, and worry over whether this whole episode will boomerang back on yourself, if

—and *just if*—you're wrong. What if something serious actually did happen to the person who still hasn't arrived?

Beneath the anger there is the lingering doubt that you just may be overreacting, a notion which is rapidly pushing up against the lingering hope that you are very wrong about his or her motivation for standing you up—if, indeed, that is what is happening. If you are right, and this person is a thoughtless, selfish creep, you'll not only be disappointed, but will still suspect that his or her offense has something to do with you and your desirability. If you are wrong, and this person was actually helping a hit-and-run victim to the local hospital, then you'll turn the hate back onto yourself and cringe when you think of your misguided animosity. It's a no-win situation.

An important aspect to the waiting war concerns the qualitative difference between waiting for a friend and waiting for a lover. With a friend there is trust in the possibility that he or she is being slightly inconsiderate—probably got stuck in a lengthy conversation, is simply running late, had a flat tire. It's an unnerving experience, but later, or even tomorrow, hopefully, the two of you will discuss the issue and hash it out.

Not so with a lover—especially if you're in the throes of a new and uncertain romance. Here, faith quickly flies out the window, for you have given him or her the power to fling you directly back to the depths of your worst and most insecure feelings about yourself. While he or she is the most important person in your constellation, you, quite obviously, do not hold a place of equal distinction with him. And, if last Friday, you touched his shoulder but he didn't touch yours (a sure sign of his waning affection), tonight, when he's late for the film, he's not simply running late, he's out charming his new interest the same way he charmed you when you and he first began charming each other. If he does show up now, at this late point, although you're smarting and pained and swear you are through, whatever he tells you you'll believe. There is also the good possibility that you will express your rage at quarter volume and even excuse yourself for being angry because, really, it's very uncomfortable for a woman to hang around on the streets alone . . . it makes you feel, well, anxious.

There is an issue lurking behind the waiting dilemma that would serve you well to explore. As with those who are late to avoid the possibility of being alone, the inability to tolerate the tensions of waiting could be attributed to the same cause. The aloneness is experienced as devastating and traumatic. You may feel that you've had your share of mistreatment in the past, and at this point in your life deserve the respect that can only be proved by immediate gratifications. "I don't want anyone in my life ever again," the thinking goes, "who will hurt me in any way." Therefore, being kept waiting is equated with being hurt or humiliated, and you cannot allow yourself to give an inch on this issue. This just could be a distorted sense of injustice that has become rigid and unyielding.

What can be done about the waiting anxiety? It's difficult to make any hard-and-fast rules about how long one should wait and still remain a certifiable, well-adjusted human being. Above and beyond the kaleidoscopic changes to which your emotions are prey, you must handle the general frustration generic to the waiting bind. As an unwilling participant in this tangled web, you must find the thread to let you out.

Perhaps you could set up a time frame which will suggest to yourself how long you are willing to wait before putting your own dignity in jeopardy. Since each situation has its own particular colorations, you may want to assess your appointments individually. If you're waiting for a business associate in a crowded restaurant at lunch time, you may decide, after fifteen minutes, to order and eat. Professionals are usually aware of busy schedules and will have to catch up with you as they can. This applies to both the person who is in the power position and the one who is seeking the trade.

Friends, acquaintances, and even those involved in new love affairs could start by setting a few ground rules for the relationship. By informing your date that waiting is most disturbing to you, you may avoid some of the problem. Of course, the chronically late will not adjust smoothly to your demands, and, if that person is waging a deep-seated, long-standing cold war with authority, don't anticipate positive results. You may have to enlist ever more creative attacks on his or her failing.

For instance, if he is chronically late and she is a stickler for punctuality, there is an interesting arrangement that can be worked out. She anticipates his lateness, therefore tells him that the party, film, dinner date, reservation, or departure time is a half hour earlier than the actual time. Although he suspects she's lying (they've been living together for over two years), he's just not sure, and even though he has caught her in the act and she has sworn to never trick him again, she continues and he's not clear as to what he should believe. Therefore, tops, he's five minutes late.

Another couple, married for seven years, have mutually worked out a method for her chronic lateness. He is given five minutes to rake her over the coals, freely expressing his outrage at her thoughtlessness, and she has agreed to endure the storm. When he has vented his anger, she is given five minutes to explain, which is followed by ten minutes of discussion wherein they explore her hidden motivations.

Of course, all of these machinations can be circumvented by simply acting as if you are alone and continuing with the prearranged plans. After you've waited for a half hour, go shopping by yourself. If the movie starts at 8:00 and she's not there at 7:59 leave her ticket at the box office, perhaps with a note attached, and file in. If you don't want to eat alone at the restaurant, give a message to the host or cashier, and leave. It might be wise to inform your date in advance of these contingency plans. It won't stop the sparks from igniting, but it will cover your tracks and possibly make him or her think twice the next time an attempt is made to engage you in the waiting war.

Interestingly, there are many in our midst of a seemingly mutant breed who float late through life's appointments with neither care nor qualm, happily validating Jimmy Walker's leisurely view on this important issue: "If you're there before it's over, you're on time." Most of us, however, subscribe to the more salient sentiment of Shakespeare, who wisely cautioned: "Delays have dangerous ends."

Dinner Party and
Social Anxiety

*"No one walks into a party without having a far better party
going on inside his head."*
JULES FEIFFER

SITUATIONAL ANXIETY FREQUENTLY EMERGES UNINVITED AT THE
Party—a word literally defined as "a social gathering, usually of
invited guests"—often interpreted by the socially anxious as a
nerve-frazzling event approximating living-room theater.

From the moment an invitation has been delivered or received, hosts, hostesses, and guests alike assess the significance
of this situation and begin to anticipate the success or failure of
their performances. The other guests often loom as formidable
figures with which to contend, therefore rehearsals in the head
are commenced. Dialogues and pieces of business are fantasized,
costumes chosen, and, most important, a definitive role must be
selected. Whom do you want to play at this party? Certainly not
yourself—you may be too anxious to come as you are—and, further, if you felt competent enough to play yourself, why would
you take a deep breath at the door before ringing the bell, then
enter laughing?

Walking into a party as a guest is a difficult part to play: anxiety tends to flatten your feelings about yourself and elevate the
stature of the others who may or may not be known before arriving. Guests do worry about how they will be perceived by

other guests. Will they be dressed appropriately and in like kind? Will they fit in socially? Will they hold their own intellectually and follow the conversation that takes an esoteric drift? Then there's the problem of *what to say*. Anxious people tend to mumble and hesitate, gaining time to ascertain if the substance of their remarks will be judged pertinent and enlightening or foolish and dull. Often, they must also measure their opinions against those at the table with the boldest views, and sometimes, if other guests are forceful and speak in a loud voice, they will retreat to safe ground and live out the situation in silence.

Protocol is another issue for the situationally anxious guest to consider. Should you take the chance of introducing your new lover at this particular party? Would it be wise to bring a date? If so, who would prove to be the greatest asset? And, if you've been fighting with your mate, can you call a trustworthy truce for that evening, or should you even consider attending at all? Etiquette and manners are great problems for many guests. It matters little how many books you may have read, there is always the chance that you'll fail to use the proper fork or inadvertently slurp your soup. Further, whether you leave some food on your plate or ask for seconds, as an anxious guest you could construe either as a blunder and for the remainder of the evening bludgeon yourself in secret, in spite of the fact that no one cared.

To the person who is throwing the party, the areas of responsibility differ from those of the guests who are catching it. The host or hostess must maintain directorial control: they must be fastidious about the comfort, mixture, and balance of the invited guests, plus worry about the feelings of the uninvited. Menu selection and the excellence of the food are primary issues, but more important to the anxious hostess is the question of whether there will or will not be enough! Then there are the problems of how one's home will be judged, what to wear, and how to keep the conversations smoothly functioning at all times, yet not become unhinged when the cat jumps on the table during the fish course.

It seldom matters how many lists and schedules have been meticulously set down on paper, the party in your head—the lively one in which all the guests are very busy laughing, swapping anecdotes, interrupting and asking for second helpings—can never quite be achieved. Therefore, it becomes replaced with the other party—the deadly affair, where the guests are idle, uncomfortable, polite, and play with their food and their watches. The anxious host or hostess anticipates the worst. His or her identity becomes precariously balanced on the outcome, and, of course, on the critical reviews which will roll off the press come the dawn.

SITUATION #1
The Dinner Party—Hostess/Host

THE DRESS REHEARSAL

Here's Linda, the director of this event. She's a competent, articulate, well-liked divorcée in a high-powered job. Linda is successful and respected, and at this moment wishes she'd never thought of giving a dinner party. Her major concern is for everyone who enters her home to be *comfortable,* but because she's an inveterate flirt with Failure, she's never convinced they are.

For a week she'd been fretting over the mixture of guests and, after much deliberation, pruning, and prudent planning, she picked up the phone and began inviting. The list became unwieldy. One of her guests, Mary Appleton, is a professional acquaintance (who could prove to be a good future connection!), and is bringing her husband—an unknown quantity. Another guest is Jonathan, a man she met at a business lunch, and she can't remember if he is or isn't bringing a date. Her friend Alec is bringing someone she hasn't met, and her other friend, Sarah, asked if she could come with her brother, Jack, who's in town for the weekend. Her plans are in chaos. Observed from an aerial view, the players seem implausible; in cross section, the casting is clearly catastrophic.

Shortly after the last call, Failure moistened her palms and, simultaneously, it occurred to her that, as a group, these people were totally wrong! "They're bound to take an instant dislike to each other." As a result, she'll be seen in a new and unflattering light, *found out!* and revealed to be a fraud. "My God, I wanted to impress Mary Appleton, and now Sarah is bringing Jack, whom I've never met, but didn't she say he's a political radical and a picky eater? And Jonathan, I think, is conservative, and if he brings a date, I don't have any extra chairs—can I borrow one? Then, Alec never said whether the person he's bringing is a friend or a lover (Oh, my God, what if he brings a lover!)." While lighting her third cigarette in fifteen minutes, Failure begins to stiffen her neck and place her forehead in a vise.

Compounding her apprehensions over the guests she did invite is a growing misgiving over those whom she did not! "If Stephanie finds out, she'll be hurt and want to confront me, and I owe Nan and Bill an invitation, and both Jimmy and Arlene asked me to throw a party, and do I go through a series of elaborate explanations, or should I say nothing and wait for the awful reprisals?" While mulling this over, Failure bites on her nails. "Of course," she thinks, checking out her nibbled cuticle, "any one of them could call during the party and what will I say? They'll hear the voices! Well, I could bluff my way through —wait! . . . turn on the Record-A-Call and get the messages later! But then, where will I say I've been?" These particular mind twists are now becoming a complex network of nattering voices, steadily gaining in volume.

As she taps out the half-smoked cigarette, it occurs to her that she has no date for herself, but then that's probably appropriate because if she invites Daniel, the man she's dated a few times, he might not be eager to help with the hosting, and then "I'd have to worry about taking care of him, make sure he's comfortable and easy, otherwise he'll feel rejected and withdraw and then I'll feel abandoned and hurt . . . no. I've already got too much to worry about, really. There's this peculiar group of people coming to my home, half of whom I don't know . . ." and she is swiftly turning them into an ominous cult of ill-wishers. This dinner party proposition was much easier when she was married. Back then she only worried about whether, after a few drinks, she and her husband would begin to publicly snipe at one another, or whether they'd keep their anger bolted down.

However, right now she sees the old days as a proverbial piece of cake—she's suddenly stuck with the discomfort of her own convictions and wishes she had a wife!

Along with her augmenting apprehension over the mix of invitees, she is faced with the menacing choice of menu. If she doesn't make something *difficult*, it won't look as if she *cares*, so she may prepare something chic and current, perhaps nouvelle cuisine. "But I'm not sure what that means," and she's not certain she knows where to buy morels and girolles, "or even how to pronounce them!" But, rack of lamb sounds elegant, even though she's never made it, and if she serves cold cucumber, dill, and yogurt soup, tossed salad with fresh basil and crumblings of feta cheese, rice pilaf, and sweet-spiced carrot cake, it will not only look like a complex dinner, she'll have made the evening worth their while.

But after purchasing all the ingredients, on the day of the dinner party, her sense of proportion takes a dive and she becomes obsessed with not having enough! "What if someone eats a lot and someone else wants thirds . . . What if there's *nothing left to eat?*" she exclaims out loud to the minced dill, and as she ponders this new crisis, Failure drags out her coat and runs her up the block to the specialty shop where she overspends on more assorted cheeses, homemade hommus, and a pound of baba-ganush "just in case."

As she recleans the bathroom sink, Failure performs a slide show of vicious little scenarios which continue to pop up and haunt her. Click: stiff smiles through stilted introductions; click: empty chatter from the colorfully articulate; click, click: lukewarm soup and wilted lettuce; CLICK: her most prominent guest proclaiming an utter dislike for garlic, with which the lamb is thoroughly stuffed! Each image augments her tension, and as her anxiety unfurls, resentment begins to smolder against the "critics and judges" who will shortly appear at the door.

After frantically changing outfits—a long skirt, to silk pants, to a wool dress—she races to the living room picking remnants of invisible lint off the carpet, then to the dining area where she rearranges the two odd chairs around the table to obscure the fact that only six of them match. Back in the bedroom, she changes

into the long skirt and a bell-sleeved blouse, and a half hour before their arrival she is so thoroughly agitated that she breaks a
wineglass, destroying an otherwise perfect table setting. "It looks
terrible! There's a wrinkle in the middle of the cloth, and a tiny
stain noticeable to the discerning eye, which I can hide under
the trivet—but should this be ironed?" Deciding that would be
truly compulsive behavior, she races back into the bedroom and
changes into olive culottes, but while pulling a hand-knit
sweater over her head, her mother's voice starts its haunting refrain: "A good hostess always sets a 'nice' table." Running into
the bathroom, she accidentally whacks her hip against the sink,
blackens her left temple with a trembling mascara wand, and is
horrified by her hair, which looks to her like a haystack.

While checking the refrigerator to be certain the salad has not
fled, Failure grabs this opportunity to pursue some questions:
"How should I introduce Mary to Jonathan and give each an appropriate handle to generate a good conversation?" "Is Mary's
husband a talker?" "What if Alec overdrinks, and who is this
person he's bringing?" "What if Jack gets rambunctious and
takes over the conversation . . . how will I shift the focus elsewhere?" "What if Sarah doesn't like Jonathan when I've told her
he's single? If she's attracted to him she may totally avoid him!"
"But then, what if Jonathan brings a date and she doesn't talk?"
("Did he say he was bringing someone?!") "Shall I serve the
salad after the main course or simultaneously or before . . ."
"Where shall I put the coats—what about cat hair?" "Do I offer
a lint brush? Why didn't I alert them against wearing black?"
"Someone recently told me they hated yogurt . . . who was it?"
"Should I have music?" "What if a blaring silence descends upon
the table?" "What if all I hear is the sound of forks scraping
plates?" "What if the evening resounds with a dull hum . . . ?"
("I'm not going to think about that!")

The only aspect of the evening with which Linda is not
obsessed is whom to seat at the head—fortunately her table is
round. But that's no real safety net, and as she checks her forks
again for any unseen crusty particles, the doorbell rings. Linda
takes a deep breath and opens it to find Jonathan, alone, holding
a bottle of wine. "Who is this man?" she thinks with alarm, as he

kisses her cheek, but that thought is truncated by the arrival of
Alec with his new lover, David, and within twenty minutes all of
her guests have arrived.

ACT I: THE PRELIMINARIES

During drinks and hors d'oeuvre, Linda floats among her guests
refilling glasses that aren't empty, dumping ashtrays that aren't
filled, offering cheeses and dips, napkins and ice. "Who's for
more hommus?" she overinquires, then dips pita bread in the
babaganush and thrusts it at Jack, who is holding a drink in one
hand, a cheese wedge in the other, and discussing Solidarity
with his mouth. "Who needs a refill?" she cries out buoyantly,
and a chorus of "Not for me!" assails her ears, none of which she
believes. "Is it too hot in here?" she asks Mary. "You may be sitting in a draft," she tells David. "Is that chair comfortable?" she
inquires of Alec, who has sat on that exact seat on too many occasions to recall. "Sarah, did you meet Mary? Oh, yes, of course
you did, I was just so anxious for you two to meet . . . Mary I'm
really glad you could come, I've been wanting to do this for a
long— The pilaf!" In the kitchen she misplaces the hotpad,
burns her thumb on the lamb rack, and as she crumbles feta
over the salad, it occurs to her she has heard nothing but one
crucial piece of information: *Ed Appleton is a gourmet cook!*

ACT II: THE TABLE

"Please sit down, everything's ready," Linda exclaims, downing
her gin and tonic. "Can I give you some help?" ask Sarah and
David in unison. "No, no, everything's under control," she assures, using her hostess voice, "I just want you all to relax," and,
carrying the soup tureen through the kitchen door, trips on the
carpet, experiencing a near miss with an unspeakable incident.

After the guests have been served, Linda eyes them with
hawklike precision, especially Ed Appleton, who she is certain is
disdaining her choice of herbs! The noise level is just right; however, Linda can't be certain that everyone is speaking, and this is
paramount, for she must be sure *everyone's involved and no one*

is idle! Circling her gaze around the table, she makes the following important observations:

> Jonathan is too quiet, which means he's bored and wishes he
> hadn't come.
> Mary is speaking only to Alec, a sure sign she hates the other
> guests.
> Ed didn't finish his lamb and is now telling Jack about restau-
> rants specializing in nouvelle cuisine, conclusive evidence my
> menu is gauche.
> Jack has not once directed his attention toward me, which
> verifies my suspicion that I'm being abrasive.
> Sarah is looking at Jonathan through narrowed eyes, validat-
> ing my earlier notion that they are a poor match.
> David is fidgeting in his chair and twirling his wineglass, mak-
> ing me feel thoroughly ungracious!
> Alec, however, is talking to everyone, regaling the guests, sep-
> arately and together, with his wit and style, which worries me
> because the spotlight was supposed to shine on Mary.

Further, even though everyone has complimented her on the
food, since she could not taste any of it, she is experiencing the
comments as untrustworthy, even condescending, and is still
offering up little inappropriate apologies, which no one completely understands.

At 11:45, Ed Appleton glances at his watch, a gesture Linda
observes, and she experiences her stomach sink. At 12:10, David
yawns, and at 12:30, her guests begin to take their leave.

At 1:00, alone in her kitchen, Linda begins to wash the pots.
"Be honest with yourself," she thinks as she moistens the Brillo.
"If the party had been a success, they wouldn't have left so
early."

Throwing a dinner party is no simple matter, especially if you're
given to flirting with Failure and ultimately allow its power to
rule your thoughts. Once you've attached yourself to the notion
of failing, it's hard to shake yourself free: very much like a
dead-end love affair, your intellect may strongly advise you to

disengage, but your emotions are too hooked to heed the wisdom of those words. Failure, that spector of doom, is a stern taskmaster; it ironically demands that the individual thwart its power, yet it is always one step ahead.

The dinner party situation can easily become a compost heap for all the smoldering insecurities—those tiny messages of doubt —that leap up unexpectedly during any given day of our anxious lives. Having invited people into your home, you have opened yourself up to judgments and critical assessments of not only your personal social capabilities, but also your standard of living and your values. When these aspects of your life are threatened, Failure begins its seduction number and it takes a fairly well-balanced and centered person to resist.

Of course, every dinner party is not so loaded with imminent disaster. There are as many reasons for giving one as there are guests you may invite. Many people circumvent the intimate gathering of folk and collect a handful of reciprocal obligations: at that point, they throw a large cocktail party, put out the wine and cheese, and leave the crowd to their own devices. Others give structure to the event by planning a celebration—a birthday, a congratulatory occasion, or a holiday—and work their menus and dialogues around the particular festivity. Some people give a dinner party to force themselves out of isolation and to broaden their social arena, while others use this affair as a professional aid—a coming together of acquaintances with whom to increase their network of connections. And, of course, there's that person who's the only one with a home large enough to accommodate a group of guests—the one who gets pressed into service by other anxious friends.

In Linda's case, what started out as a semiprofessional dinner party ended up with a mélange of types, and to someone who is anxious, mixing people from different aspects of your life is more revealing than showing them your soiled underwear. A single hostess or host has to be fairly secure in their own worth to gracefully entertain a collection of hybrids. One person is bound to dislike someone else, and even if they don't, it's very risky business to display your own variety of tastes in people. If you've passed yourself off as a free-thinker, and a born-again

Christian is one of your guests, there's a good chance that your radical friends will view you henceforth as untrustworthy, or at least a little odd. In any event, whether your food's not up to par, your home is not what was expected, or your friends are a disappointment, the worst fear is that you will be seen as a fraud.

THE DOUBLE EDGE OF
THE FRAUD SYNDROME

Since social anxiety is intimately linked with a threat to one's self-esteem, the fear of being *found out* and labeled a fraud goads the imagination and stokes the adrenaline. What it is that will be discovered is usually based on a misguided self-perception of who you authentically are in your internal life, as opposed to who you are presenting externally. If you secretly perceive yourself as a social rube, you then double up your efforts to conceal that ineptness in a flurry of activity—overserving, overtalking, overlaughing, and sometimes making more of a pest out of yourself than a comfort.

Here's where the fraud syndrome becomes very tricky. While you privately harbor suspicions that you are indeed one kind of fraud—someone who is substandard to the perfection you are presenting—you may, in fact, be a fraud of a totally different color: a person who is deluding yourself into believing you are inferior in order to maintain a familiar system of belief.

One way to break your own specific fraud code is to stop for a moment and consider your own wild thoughts, those tiny flash frames of ideas that come and go, usually regarded as pieces of mental frivolity. Your wild thoughts are not simply momentary lapses into whimsical sport; they're as important to your inner schemata as are your dreams, and are usually much easier to decipher. Wild thoughts emerge out of your private psychic framework and contain messages regarding those aspects of yourself and your perceptions of the outside world that are rarely given serious consideration. So, think for a moment of the wild thoughts you've noted then discarded which flashed a picture of yourself as competent and even wise. Those thoughts are ulti-

mately of more authentic value than all the self-abusive natter-
ings you've collected over a lifetime. Try to hold on to those
quick hit-and-run flash frames. Over a period of time, you may
begin to view yourself more objectively. When, like Linda,
you're about to entertain a group of guests and the fraud
syndrome begins its weary tirade of insults, look to the underbelly of that assault. You may be reminded that the only impostor here is your own insistence on worthlessness. At that point
you may cease berating yourself for those anticipated but unspecified transgressions and peel the potatoes in peace.

Above and beyond the psychological implications for easing
the anxieties of hosting a dinner party, there are the practical
measures you can employ to ease the burden of this event.

If you're still unsure of your ability to pull this off solo, why
make it difficult for yourself? When you plan your next party,
simply don't do it alone! Of course, social occasions are much
easier to juggle for those who have mates with whom to share
the responsibilities, but if you are a single person, you can still
invite one friend with whom you feel intimate and whose perceptions you trust. Linda might easily have asked either Sarah
or Alec to help her out, but her anxiety had already bush-
whacked her and held such thinking in check. Before you're
ambushed by your apprehensions, press your friend into service.
Spend some time discussing your fears, your doubts, and all
your anxieties concerning the affair. Define your goals for the
party, which could be anything from establishing a professional
connection to providing an entree for a romantic liaison. Be
specific in your discussion—air your anxieties over the two or
three invitees you're sure will mix like oil and water. Verbally
exploit the worst possibility that could occur, then analyze just
what real damage might ensue as opposed to the catastrophic
but imagined expectations.

Ask your friend to arrive early that evening and give a taste
test to the food, as well as an objective eye to your home. Anxiety has a way of numbing the senses—you lose your capacity to
judge the tastiness of food, and therefore cannot trust any compliments you receive; your vision becomes distorted and the
walls quite suddenly seem gray; you cannot hear what's being

said and you think you're being ridiculed! Therefore, it would be important to further use your selected friend as an emotional shim during the party. Ask him or her to give you a hand with your nerves! Give him or her permission to signal you when you're definitely speeding up, or to give a nod of reassurance when you seem in doubt. Your friend might also help you clear dishes, serve and refill drinks, and jump in when a disturbing lull in conversation descends upon the table.

If you're worried about imposing such tasks upon any one person, pick someone who feels more comfortable when they have a role to fulfill. Many guests welcome the opportunity to be of service during a party; it defines their part in the production and often assuages their own anxiety of just "being there" with nothing to do or say.

As far as menu is concerned, a fabulous gourmet cook once remarked that he is rarely invited into his friends' homes for dinner. "They become intimidated and think I'm judging them in terms of their culinary expertise." He suggests that the person who is not an experienced cook avoid the attempt to compete with Julia Child or Craig Claiborne. "If you make the best tunafish casserole in town, by all means serve that dish. If fried chicken and country gravy is your forte, why not bring it out? And if you only know how to broil a chop, buy the best ones in town and start from there." This advice is most rewarding—gourmet cooks are not out to get anyone (except possibly each other!) and welcome invitations to dinner from steak-and-potatoes people. Like Linda, many hostesses think that if the dish they prepare is not complex, difficult, and calling for exotic ingredients, their graciousness is in question. Logic would dictate that it would be unwise to experiment with new taste thrills at your first dinner party; therefore, prepare a tried-and-true menu, one that has consistently worked well in the past. Guests become uncomfortable and annoyed when the hostess or host runs a litany of apologies for their food.

Another tip which may prove useful is to plan a menu that can, in the main, be prepared in advance. The first and second guests to arrive are usually awkward with one another and need to have you there as a catalyst. Further, no one wants to be the first to mess up the chopped liver design or cut out the first wedge of cheese. If you're not trapped in the kitchen, you can set them at ease by fixing the hors d'oeuvre and setting the party in motion.

Of course, if you're given to perfectionism, you're going to worry excessibly about there being *enough* food. This might be a good time to think about your proclivity for overbuying and losing all sense of rational proportion. Underneath the concern for abundance is an insecurity played out by the anxious hostess or host over her or his inability to sufficiently *nourish* the guests. However, is it in fact a food hunger you're worried about, or is it an emotional malnutrition? If you actually believe that you, yourself, are withholding intimate connections, you may be projecting that fear onto the food and acting out some fancy transference. On the other hand, anxious hosts and hostesses rarely do run out of food. You might try to remember: if there's nothing left, the dinner was a success. If there're left-overs, you're set for another meal. Most guests dislike being pressed to eat more than they can handle. They become uncomfortable, and sometimes even cranky, when an overzealous hostess insists on refilling the plate. The situation can become awkward: if you as the hostess act hurt when refused, the guest might then succumb to your demand but view you as something of a social tyrant.

The clothes issue at a dinner party cannot be dismissed easily either. It would be prudent to remember that as the hostess or host, you set the standard for the evening. You cannot be overdressed or underdressed—it's your party. If you're given to changing outfits five and six times, stop for a moment and try to ascertain what image you're attempting to convey. It might be wise to plan your outfit in advance and try it on. Last-minute confusions over the look you want to achieve keep the anxiety churning. (On the very practical side, remember that bell sleeves act as catch-all nets for foodstuffs, and three-inch heels can be immobilizing as well as dangerous when you're trying to balance a platter.)

Try to plan your time to allow yourself an opportunity to relax after your preparations have been carried out. A hot bath or stimulating shower before your guests arrive could help to wash away some of your body's anxious debris. Give yourself ample time to dress, make up, and do your hair, and try to provide a good fifteen or twenty minutes to sit in your favorite spot and slow down your mounting momentum. You may want to invite your intimate friend to come early, and share a drink with you beforehand. If you've been working on this party alone all day, a friend who arrives early might help to bridge that gap between your private thoughts and your public actions, as well as ease your startle response to the first ring of the bell.

THE GUESTS YOU DIDN'T INVITE

There will always be people whose noses will be out of joint when they learn they were not invited to your party, and this eventuality cannot always be avoided. When one has acquired a tribe of friends whom they look to as a primary or secondary family, choosing one over the other for a particular amalgam of personalities can generate guilt and inner chaos. "I am not confused, I'm just well mixed," wrote Robert Frost, and perhaps you might begin presenting yourself to your friends as a person who entertains variety. The confusion over guest lists and the attendant worry over hurt feelings often causes anxious people to completely cancel their proposed plans. Healthy relationships with friends, however, usually include a knowledge of the others' lives—their social, professional, and personal goals. If you're worried about excluding a dear friend on any particular occasion, you might want to inform him or her that you are throwing a party, discuss the reason for the occasion, and how you arrived at your selection of guests. Depending upon the degree of intimacy, it's often much easier for the overly sensitive person to hear about the party directly from you than hear about it later from a stranger.

There is one person, however, who would be better left uninformed and uninvited. That, of course, is your mother's voice, or any other authoritative critic from the past who continues to plague you with self-doubt. Part of the negative fraud syndrome discussed above is a direct result of judgmental conditioning. At the outset of your party, you might want to reflect on those old voices and begin to regard them as veritable gate-crashers to whom you will ultimately refuse entry.

THE REAL INVITED GUESTS

If you'd like to put you and your guests at ease, you might begin this task as you're inviting them. When you make the call, be certain to give them details concerning the party which will pave the way for a comfortable evening.

Although this may be a dinner party, be sure you tell your guests *it's for dinner!* Don't laugh—often the information of which you are most aware gets lost in the conversation and assumptions are made which guests confuse. "I'm having some people in on Friday night at 7:30" is not sufficient. An anxious guest may be embarrassed to ask if this invitation is for dinner or simply drinks. As a protection, they may gobble a sandwich before arriving, just in case! Then, of course, you'll feel slighted because food was left on the plate, the guest will worry about your feelings, and the anxiety dodge will be in full swing.

You might also inform your guests of the attire—whether this is to be casual, dungarees and T-shirts, "nice but not formal," or "formal but not black tie." This information will circumvent much of their prior concern.

And, as an added aid, perhaps you could mention one or two of the other guests, who they are and what the common denominator might be—similar or connecting professions, mutual interests, or personalities for potential friendships.

Conversely, if your guests are bringing someone with whom you are not acquainted, glean some information for yourself. You might hear that the unknown quantity is a reformed alcoholic and want to stock up on Perrier or soda, that the person has just gone through a traumatizing event and is still a bit shaky, or has an area of expertise that could be of interest to another guest.

Yet, with all the information you may give or gather in advance, there is still no reason that you will or should maintain total control over your group of guests. People may not take to each other. Everyone harbors their own private idiosyncrasies and personal anxieties about which you will probably know nothing! You cannot control the behavior and interaction of seven other people! Try to remember: unpredictability among people is the heart of an interesting evening.

And, finally, think for a moment of the many times you've been a guest in the homes of others. Were you as critical and judgmental as you assume your guests will be? Did you drop your friendship with the host or hostess when you found one of the fellow guests to be a distressing bore? And did you sever your relationship with the host or hostess because the roast was overdone, the pasta was not al dente, you disliked Brussels sprouts, or they ran out of ice? *What were your specific concerns?*

If you can't remember, read on. The next situation may jolt your memory.

SITUATION #2
The Dinner Party—Guests

What Linda doesn't know is that her guests—the players—have all brought their own private anxieties with them to her home, and that underground activities of which she could have no knowledge are separately and psychically brewing in each of them.

Take Jonathan *(". . . too quiet, which means he's bored and wishes he hadn't come")*.

After she phoned and invited him, he couldn't reconstruct whether she said, "Bring a date," "You'll be my date," or, "Don't be late." Placing the receiver on the hook, he doodled madly on a yellow pad, crosshatching margins and drawing scrolls. Ever since his divorce two years ago, Jonathan has been in a state of domestic limbo and avoids parties. When he does submit, it's either for business reasons or for purposes of meeting women. He's actually much more comfortable in one-to-one encounters— he experiences himself in groups as jagged, unnatural, often reverting to monosyllables or silence. When everyone is talking, he begins to feel like a nonperson, unseen, disposable, and un-

able to find an opening. As a consequence, he prefers large cocktail parties where he can lose himself in the crowd and corner
one person in an intimate chat. "So why did I say I'd go?" he
questions himself. "Because the invitation to a party made me
feel desirable," he answers, "and Linda had that warm, silvery
laugh."

Then there're Mary and Ed Appleton (*"Mary is speaking only
to Alec, a sure sign she hates the other guests"*).

When Mary received Linda's call, she was thrown into
conflict. She and Ed were smack in the middle of a cold war,
and although they were still speaking to each other, they had
been acting the distant but polite strangers. He had withdrawn
into silence, and she had been cautiously dancing around him,
taking a wide berth around their incendiary topics. Mary can
enjoy parties; she likes to talk about her job and is quite adept
at relating entertaining office stories, which always include her
own amusing foibles. However, she's never quite sure she's
picked the appropriate story for the particular crowd, and has
been known to completely forget the punch lines. When she's
about to take an anecdotal nose dive, Ed is a champion at jumping in and providing the forgotten closure. They have a reputation for being the "golden couple"—two people who actually
make their marriage *work*. But now she's petrified her peers will
discover they're not so shiny—especially someone like Linda,
whom Mary views as not only a potential friend, but also a person who might be professionally helpful in the future. At the
party she felt frozen and, as a consequence, dashed for a seat
next to Alec, a genuinely funny man, to whom she could safely
relate. But she couldn't avoid glancing at Ed, who was piercing
her remnant poise with icy stares. Overreacting to everything
Alec said, at one point, she laughed boisterously and dribbled
dressing on her wrist.

Of course, there's Ed (" . . . *didn't finish his lamb and is now
telling Jack about restaurants specializing in nouvelle cuisine,
conclusive evidence my menu is gauche"*).

Ed only agreed to attend the party because he was afraid if he
said, "No," he'd push Mary too far. Ever since she got her promotion, he's been feeling overlooked and is beginning to feel like
an unnecessary social adjunct. He has just begun to realize that

he's never known what to say to Mary's friends and is obsessed with his search for a pithy phrase. Although he's never told Mary about this particular stress, he believes she should be perceptive enough to *sense* it. He has now become hypersensitive about being seen as a man who "goes with the territory," and doesn't feel terribly confident about his own presence. Therefore he's begun to drink a lot at parties and hears himself strongly asserting opinions he's only half-formed. As for his expertise on nouvelle cuisine, he's never even picked up a whisk, but he has picked up the language, which makes him feel he's defining himself as someone who might just be in-the-know. Watching Mary doing her razzle-dazzle number over there with Alec totally irked him. He lost his appetite as well as his ability to converse and was ready to go home.

David, of course, was the most distraught (". . . *fidgeting in his chair and twirling his wineglass, making me feel thoroughly ungracious!*").

When Alec informed David they were going to Linda's for a dinner party, David broke out in a freshly minted sweat. "Do you think that's a good idea?" David asked, horrified by the possible ramifications of this soiree. "Sure," Alec said with confidence. "She's one of my oldest friends, she's almost family!" David was not reassured. Along with being thrown into a nest of heterosexuals, he had to pass muster with Alec's friends, and, "That's enough to make a Valium anxious," he said. "What am I supposed to talk about? What are these people into? Will they take me seriously?" he thought. All of these questions were crucial to the longevity of his and Alec's relationship, which had just gotten itself off the ground. Thrown into a thicket of doubt during the party, David first tried to adapt to the mode of the group. He then tried to make himself helpful to Linda, with whom he felt fairly comfortable. But ultimately he felt abandoned and unseen by Alec, who was, as usual, holding court, so he took refuge in the design of the wineglass and tried to pass himself off as mute.

Alec was tense (". . . *talking to everyone, regaling the guests, separately and together, with his wit and style, which worries me because the spotlight was supposed to shine on Mary*").

"Terrific!" he told Linda after she invited him, but as he hung up the phone, he was immediately thrust back into the panic business. Known for being an excellent raconteur, and therefore the life of every party, Alec continually works to polish that reputation. He has learned to cleverly maneuver his anxieties by camouflaging them under a guise of gregarious storytelling and hilarious routines. Very few people actually know Alec—he eludes capture with the cunning of a shadow and is therefore often fatigued and depleted when he returns home. This particular party, however, had his guts tied up in knots, "My God, I didn't tell her I was bringing a lover!" and it was important to him that she approve of David. Yet, even if she did, what if her friends didn't? Then he was afraid he'd oversold Linda to David, and what if he didn't like her? By the time he arrived at the party, he was so jittery he found himself taking over the conversations and concealing his insecurity, as well as David's, in a nonstop blitzkrieg of sparkling repartee. When he left, he still had no idea of Linda's perceptions—he'd done a good job.

Jack was a totally different story (". . . *not once [has he] directed his attention toward me, which verifies my suspicion that I'm being abrasive*").

Jack was not acquainted with anyone at that party, including Linda. He only went at Sarah's insistence—there were a few friends of his own he wanted to contact while in town. Jack is very uncomfortable with himself and only feels easy when he's revved up on politics—current issues which skirt anything remotely concerned with popular culture. He cannot relax in ordinary "social situations"; he needs to discover where everyone stands on the political spectrum and then provoke heated discussions. However, during hors d'oeuvre, he found that no one was buying what he was selling and he was squashed. Without a syllabus to attack his incipient anxiety, he became awkward and edgy. Compounding these issues, he was startlingly attracted to Linda and, as a result, retired to the bathroom, where he smoked a joint. During dinner, he fell silent and pretended to listen and respond to Ed, who was boring him to death with restaurant recommendations. While feigning interest, he became violently hungry and ate three pieces of cake, simultaneously fantasizing how he could manipulate the hostess into bed.

Which brings us to Sarah (". . . *looking at Jonathan through narrowed eyes, validating my earlier notion that they are a poor match"*).

Sarah's stomach tightens when she's invited to a party. She's a very quiet person and much of a loner. Sarah works for herself as a graphics designer and, when she is suddenly thrust into the midst of a crowd, experiences herself as alien and inept. Desperately craving reassurance from others to ground her in the moment, she pressed Jack into acting as her escort and emotional banister. Unlike her brother, however, Sarah feels very much at home when the discussion turns to the art world, literature, or theater. When the conversations turn to specialized topics, she actually blushes and crawls back into herself. Sarah admires Linda. She sees her as well-rounded, busy, involved in everything, and also as a safe, warm hearth. However, the night of the party, Linda was imprisoned in her hostess momentum and Sarah felt ungrounded by the absence of intimate contact. The first part of the evening she remained close to Jack, but during dinner her insular nature took a turn and she began to take note of that quiet man, Jonathan, whom she decided was a soul mate. Unable to think of any interesting opening lines, she stared at him intensely, hoping he'd mystically perceive her silent message. Jonathan, to her dismay, became at one with nothing but his plate.

The next day, however, each guest called Linda at home and, having achieved some distance from their own particular anxieties, were able to give her an overview of the evening:

- "Thanks for inviting me, Linda," Jonathan said. "Your dinner was delicious and you are a lovely hostess. I enjoyed your friends, and, by the way, is Sarah involved with anyone?"
- "Linda! Ed and I had a terrific time. Your friend Alec is incredibly funny and your lamb was perfect," Mary said, "In a few weeks we're going to have a small dinner party to celebrate our fourth anniversary. I hope you'll come, and I hope we'll have a chance to speak alone before then."
- "So, what did you think of David? Well, he was a little intimidated by meeting you for the first time. No, no, you made him very comfortable—you were wonderful! Stop worrying

about everything—look at me, I don't give a damn what anyone thinks. By the way, the soup was gorgeous."

- Linda? This is Jack. What are you doing tonight? No, no, not
with Sarah, with me . . . Well, what if I call you around
5:00? Will you be more rested then? Okay, talk to you at
5:00, and thanks for last night."

- "Did Jack just call you?" Sarah asked. "I thought he would—
he's smitten. I just want you to know that I had a really nice
time. I didn't feel too spooked and . . . ah, I was thinking of
having some people in to my studio . . . you know, just for
drinks. Do you think Jonathan would come?"

As you can see, parties are difficult propositions for guests as
well as for hosts or hostesses. Yet, the guests' concerns at these
affairs do differ—they're not on home ground and must feel their
way around to acquire some familiar markings. Like Linda's
guests, each invitee comes with their own anxieties and then attempts to cover them by presenting a specific profile. Everyone
wants to be seen as sociable and interesting, yet, as Llewellyn
Miller has stated, "It is a sad truth that everyone is a bore to
someone." Therefore, the profiles you prepare don't always work,
and it's not imperative that they do.

Nontalkers like Jonathan fear they will say the *wrong* thing,
and the *thing* in this case means venture an opinion or imply a
judgment that could be held up to ridicule. The truth is, for
every conceivable topic that may emerge at a dinner party, each
person at that table has a fascinating opinion. This even includes
subjects about which you may know absolutely nothing! In that
case, your opinion might be "I find this boring," or, more to the
point, "The subject makes me tense." Obviously you're not going
to blurt out that particular piece of information, but you might
ask a few questions about the topic to obtain a better grasp of
the substance and then extend an opinion. Shy guests usually believe it's better to keep their mouths shut than open them up
and release a social gaffe. However, to present yourself as someone who is without thought is the first lie of the anxious nontalker. When one begins to grow tense, and "feel like a nonperson, unseen, disposable . . ." they are usually withholding

themselves from the proceedings. Relationships are born from verbal interactions, and to remain incognito at a social gathering is to perpetuate the feeling of being invisible.

For someone like Jonathan, it might serve you well to do some homework prior to attending a social function where you're bound to be thrown in with a few frisky talkers. All those people over there who seem to the verbal manner born are probably aware of two important conversational notions: (1) an interesting dialogue is often generated by mutuality of opinion—in that case it's called a discussion; and, (2) opposing viewpoints make for lively interaction and are often referred to as arguments. To venture a question may generate a discussion or an argument, and either will help to assuage that awful feeling of "lonely in a crowd." Therefore, in your day-to-day activities, you might want to begin testing the water by asserting yourself into conversations. Ask a few questions and judge for yourself whether you feel isolated and unseen, or a natural part of the party.

On the other side of the silence coin, however, is the nonstop questioner, the investigative reporter who conceals his or her party anxiety under the guise of an interview. This person rarely offers any information about themselves, but finds everything and everyone "interesting to note." If you're trapped in that particular style, you might want to test your own unknown waters by sharing some of your own notions and ideas about the world and yourself. Try to remember that this stance is one of the many flip-sides to the nontalker, and although you may have managed to capture the attention of the other through such flattery, you have still left yourself outside and will probably go home feeling angry and unrecognized.

Yet another version of the nontalker is the person who walks into the room and immediately heads for the bookcase, where he peruses all the latest novels and psychology books. If books are not in evidence, then a newspaper, magazine, or journal will do. The methods behind this party madness are twofold: first, it allows the anxious guest to delay the awful business of saying hello; and second, it provides an opportunity for another guest to seek him or her out. The party reader hopes that he or she will be seen—that a braver guest will approach with a question pertaining to the book. However, this is most exasperating to hosts and hostesses, and is a generally uncomfortable experience for the other guests. Most people are perceptive enough to realize that the person hidden in reading material is a nervous wreck!

Those who are given to talking may have an easier time but can fall into just as many anxious traps. For instance, if you find you're consumed by your work, you may be the one to instigate office stories or professional monologues which may only be interesting to those in related fields. Many people are so utterly wrapped up in their business lives that they've neglected the entire spectrum of current events. Other guests, like Jack, are only comfortable when they're holding court on their particular area of interest—in his case, politics. When the conversation takes a turn, these people become uneasy and fidgety—they begin to isolate themselves and feel alienated from the crowd. If this is a style you recognize in yourself, you may want to think about becoming a more well-rounded reader. Instead of perusing the newspapers for your specialized interest—the business section, national or international politics, sports, or the entertainment section—provide yourself with the time to read the whole issue. Subscribe to a few national magazines, or those that are geared toward your specific city. Get an idea of what the public is talking about, what issues are hot. Although at the outset this may seem a bit forced and unnatural, ultimately you could find yourself involved in more of the party action, and, as a result, getting a piece for yourself.

Linda's guest Alec was the kind of guest most hosts and hostesses applaud. There's nothing like good raconteur and a lot of laughter to diminish fear levels in a group. However, Alec's particular anxiety that evening could have been assuaged and disposed of earlier. One of the most difficult situations for anxious people is introducing their new lovers to their friends. Everyone is bent on gaining everyone else's approval and the air is charged with anticipation. Perhaps it would be kindlier toward yourself and toward your lover to arrange for a more intimate meeting with close friends prior to a formal event. Instead of thrusting him or her into a den of strangers, set up a date in someone's home where all parties are comfortable and trustworthy. The new person, like David, is filled with apprehension, worried about performance, unsure of how to act, and can quickly misread the intentions of the crowd. Alec could have just as easily arranged for drinks with Linda and a few close friends to make this introduction. However, he chose to launch David's debut at a party where the players were, in the main, unknown to even him.

Most single people mistakenly believe that couples have an easier time in the party situation than those who arrive alone. However, while the couple arrives with an identity intact, the dynamics between those two may be completely out of whack. That's the case with Ed and Mary. When you're fighting with your mate and you are invited out, some people think it's best to decline the invitation. Depending upon the degree of the domestic war, however, it might be wiser to attend. Domestic détentes usually leave one or both of the people feeling either abandoned or unseen. A party could be the right prescription for rediscovering yourself and your particular attributes. When communication breaks down in the home, it often takes a third person, or even a new situation, to provide some new life and light on what seems to be a deadlock. However, do be wary of turning the evening into a sniper's revenge. Often, the need to air your grievances becomes so overwhelming that the repressed anxiety builds and an understated shooting match commences. This can be very harmful to both you and your mate—it augments the hostility and makes you both undesirable guests at any party. If communication between you and your mate is still feasible, you might discuss this particular contingency with him or her in advance. Set up a contract between yourselves for the evening and then try to allow yourself some joy. If something particularly interesting occurs at the party, it might act as a bridge for a more intimate discussion when you arrive back home.

Loners, like Sarah, also have a difficult time adjusting to a party atmosphere. When you work in isolation, propelling yourself into the midst of a crowded environment can be temporarily disorienting. Having lived all week inside of yourself, plunging outside can trigger extraordinary amounts of anxiety and alienation. You may literally feel as though you've arrived from another planet and are unacquainted with the language of the mainstream. People involved in lone creative pursuits usually experience this phenomenon and, unless they are immediately introduced to a like kind, revert to silence and fixed smiles. One way to overcome the culture shock of this event is to ask the host or hostess if you can arrive a little earlier than the rest. Offer to help out with last-minute preparations, or just sit and talk with him or her as a method for easing yourself into the party mode. As the guests arrive, you may introduce yourself and offer some information about your line of work. If you can corner one person for a short while, it will be less difficult to merge with the others and you'll already have set up contact with one other person. Unfortunately you can't always depend upon the hostess to look after you; she's going to be busy with a number of people.

ICEBREAKERS AND ETIQUETTE

If you're still feeling unsure of how to open a conversation and assert yourself in a social gathering, you might remember to be a good listener. Often as the anxiety builds, the ability to focus on what any individual is saying becomes truncated. As the party commences, try to remember the names of the guests to whom you've been introduced or the names which you've overheard. If an awful gap of silence descends upon the table once everyone is seated, you can be sure that they are grappling with their social anxiety and waiting for someone else to break the ice. If Sarah had been prepared, she might have looked to the man who interested her and said, "Jonathan, tell me about your work." Using the person's first name is very reassuring to the one being addressed. It means you listened, remembered, and that he or she is important. A very shy woman once remarked that hearing her name called across the table was like "a ray of sunshine and warmth spread across a glacier." She immediately responded and the conversation commenced.

In terms of etiquette, we strongly suggest that those of you who feel socially inept at the table make a point of buying a book and learning about the various table settings and protocols. However, if you're racing off tonight to a fancy soiree, the only suggestion that will be of use is to follow your hostess's lead. You can also easily learn by example and surreptitiously watch how the other guests handle their manners. Becoming socialized is very closely related to minimizing party anxiety. Once you've learned the basics, all you have to worry about is who you want to be and what you want to say.

But please do not berate yourself if you leave a dinner party feeling less than perfect. ". . . it is always like that at parties," wrote Marcel Proust; "we never see the people, we never say the things we should like to say, but it is the same everywhere in life."

SEVEN

Birthday Anxiety

"How old would you be if you didn't know how old you were?"
SATCHEL PAIGE

BIRTHDAYS ARE VERY DIFFICULT TO FINESSE. IN FACT, THEY CAN raise so many complex and calamitous questions, people have been known to take to a darkened room and quietly molt all day. While shedding the skins of the year gone by, all is not quiet in that singular barricaded space. There are too many birthday bugaboos with which to contend—accounts to settle, memories summoned up, the pangs of the past, the problems of the present, the fears of the future. A special urgency is born on this day, and while you may check your cheeks for a subtly changing shape, then capture a glimpse of a graying hair, one constant persists: how will this day alter the scheme of your life?

It usually doesn't. Yet, characteristically, all of the birthday issues tend to quietly creep up and lead multitudes of people into the thick of situational anxiety. There are two basic methods for approaching this day: if you yearn for perpetual youth, you may deny the birthday, pretend that time has stopped, but ultimately maximize your smoldering anxieties, which are aware of the truth. If you suffer from the want of immediate recognition, however, you may encounter a different problem. Since it is unequivocably your day, only rarely shared with another, the soul seeks to celebrate and yell from the window, "Look, I am born!" It is often hard to understand that this is a regular day for everyone else, and sometimes almost incomprehensible as to why

all those people out there aren't catering not only to your basic
birthday needs, but also to your random whims as well! After
all, it only occurs once a year—it's not as if you need that attention *every day*—so what could be wrong with asking for a little
visibility?

Absolutely nothing—except that you may not like the sound
of that child's voice which keeps nagging at you for more. That
voice gets thrown into direct conflict with the mature adult in
the sensible shoes who understands that this particular day will
test your mettle as a rational being. These two sides of the natal-
day question often become twisted confrontations, and the
harder one tries to repress the inner voice, the louder it sounds.
Take, for example, Robert Stokes, a man who finds Bobby, his
inner kid, at odds with the mature guy and would like nothing
more than to muzzle his mewling child.

SITUATION #1
Attention Please! Birthday!

The moment he waked, he perceived something was wrong.
There were traffic sounds from the street, and *people were going
about their business as if this was a regular day!* "I don't like
this," thought Bobby. "All right, just can all that expectancy
stuff, you're a grown man!" Robert sneered and, having stated
his case, he gave an adult stretch, a mock yawn of maturity, and
rolled out of bed.

Stumbling through the living room, he was startled to find
there was no Porsche parked on the rug, and although Bobby
checked behind the couch for any hidden violinists, Robert repressed him and went into the bathroom to brush his teeth. No
one said anything about it on the "Today" show, and the kettle
didn't sing either, but nonetheless both were gratified to note that
the morning paper had printed the date smack on top of the
front page.

"Why are you wearing that suit?" Bobby asked.

"It's my suit, my one of two!" Robert replied, refusing to submit to the prattling in his head.

"At least wear the vest. I mean, can't you look a little special . . . ? How else will anyone know what's up?"

"You really are a pain," said Robert, and pulled the three-piece Glen plaid off the hanger.

Good Morning America, too, behaved as though nothing was happening, and by 8:30 Robert began to wonder if he was really expected at work. "They must realize what day it is," Bobby thought, then jumped because he thought he heard the phone ring. Passing through the kitchen, Robert found himself thoroughly disappointed in the melon, which was sitting on the table looking exactly like a piece of fruit, and when he stopped in front of the hall mirror, he pressed his face close to the glass and said out loud, "So, you're forty, where's the action . . . ?"

Although no one was hiding in wait outside his door with a banner, when he passed the mailman on the street, the leather bag on his back was clearly filled with cards, and Robert shot him a knowing look.

As he walked into his office, the receptionist said, "Good morning," a phrase obviously loaded with hidden meaning, and as he worked his way down the corridor to his office, he pretended to a natural gait. Just in case anyone was watching, he took off his glasses and rubbed his eyes, a normal response to a normal morning, and a gesture that would ensure they wouldn't know that he knew that they knew it was October 13.

"You're behaving like an ass," thought Robert, sitting in his chair.

But Bobby was tenacious. "So, where's the surprise Danish?" he said, then searched frantically for cards and messages on the desk.

Robert sniffed, then shuffled through his papers. "At my age, you do gain wisdom, insight, and even enlightenment on these occasions," he mused maturely, then picked up an invoice and checked the date. "This should have been handled two days ago!"

"Relax . . ." whispered Bobby. "You're off the hook. No one's supposed to hassle you today. There's a hold on everything bad —no slurs, no extra work, and if you're hiding any correspondence in the back of drawers, this is the time to own up. Everyone's got to be nice to you today."

"If they knew . . ." Robert added quietly.

The first person to enter his office was Tom, a co-worker and peer. "Morning, Bob . . . Say, that suit looks good. How come you're all dressed up?"

"Well, it's my . . . *blubfthy* . . . no reason," said Robert, biting Bobby's tongue, and then experienced an instant wave of self-disgust.

At 10:00 the phone rang, and a familiar voice said, "Happy Birthday, Bobby! How do you feel today?" "Hi, Mom, fine . . . You know, I'm glad you called, I'd almost forgotten what day it was. Yeah . . . so what's new?"

However, that call didn't count, he knew she'd phone, and, further, it only made him a little jumpy. "You were expecting Rosemary," Bobby stated.

"No, no . . . will you stop! I broke off with her, remember? She was getting too attached . . . she's not about to call."

"But you expect her to, in fact, you think she's going to come running back today, don't you? You should have waited to break up after your birthday . . . not very smart. She was always big on these occasions."

On his way to Word Processing, Robert passed a group of people hanging around George's desk and his heart banged. No one actually said anything, but Miriam Benson's smile implied a distinct intimacy which assured him *plans were in the works*.

"Did you tell anyone that today is your birthday?" Bobby asked, somewhat rhetorically.

"No, I don't think so . . . except my personal friends, and, you know, I told them I was busy tonight and that I hate surprise parties so I wouldn't be disappointed when I didn't get one."

Bobby winced. "Did you tell anyone here . . . at the office?"

"Well, no. But Personnel knows," thought Robert, and simultaneously it occurred to him that his boss *was saving this particular day to give him his promotion!* Quite suddenly he felt vindicated, ripened, centered, sage, and hastened back to his office to wait for the call!

At 11:00 the phone rang and he answered with casual professionalism: "Robert Stokes, may I help you?" The party on the other end hung up. "That's it!" cried Bobby. "They're checking to make sure you're in your office! Get ready, look nonchalant, be involved in paper work . . ." Robert grabbed a ledger and, listening for sounds of a gathering crowd outside his door, prepared an expression of astute concentration.

At 11:15, no one had gathered, and at 11:20 the phone rang again. This time it was Paula. "Happy Birthday, Bob!" she said, using her enthusiastically sexy voice. "I've decided I'm going to pick *you* up tonight. How does 7:30 sound?" "Fine," he replied, but after hanging up he went into a spiritual slump and realized that because he was seeing her later, that call didn't count.

At 11:30, it dawned on him that no one was inviting him to lunch, and he began to panic. "For God's sake," yelled Bobby, "go arrange something . . . you can't eat alone!"

"Okay, okay," Robert replied, and sauntered next door to Steve's office, where he found a few people making plans. "Hey, Bob, want to join us? We're all going over to The Net." Crushed by neglect and hating fish, Robert shuffled around the edge of the desk. "Oh, I don't know," he said, eyeing them suspiciously, "I thought I'd eat at my desk, catch up on some reading." But on his way out he pulled down on the points of his vest and, passing Miriam Benson, began to mumble, ". . . just thought I'd see what's up in here . . . it's my birth . . . day . . . today." He then walked head down back to his office.

Miriam ran after him. "Why didn't you say something?" she said, and as though on cue, she became visibly stricken by guilt, then vanished. The phone rang at that exact moment, but it was only his brother, and because it was expected, it simply didn't count.

After hanging up, he sighed and, assuming an air of Solomonic sagacity, tapped the bridge of his glasses. "I grow old . . . I grow old . . ." he stated meaningfully, addressing himself to the stapler, "I shall wear the bottoms of my trousers rolled."

"Cut the drama," said Bobby, "those people should have known . . . they were supposed to divine these things—that's the way it's supposed to go," he murmured, biting his knuckle.

At 12:00, Miriam Benson, clearly breathing with difficulty, raced back into his office. "Here," she proclaimed, smiling broadly, and handed him a small store-wrapped package.

"Miriam, this was really unnecessary," he said, bobbing his head in mock appreciation. ("I could kill you!" he spewed out to the kid jumping around in his head.) With superimposed, false joy, Robert untied the gift and, as he opened the box, it flashed through his mind that this might be his promotion, disguised as ". . . a cat mug! Wow, Miriam, that's just terrific," he said, hoping his face did not betray his total chagrin. "I really love these things . . . and I sure need one . . . the Bob-Cat, huh? . . . very cute," he said, and sat himself on top of the desk to conceal the Italian cup Rosemary had brought back from Florence and given him as one of his many gifts on his last birthday.

At that moment, four people from his department walked in holding a small cake with a blue candle stuck in the middle. "Happy Birthday," they all sang in and out of tune, and while he surreptitiously slid a manila folder over the Florentine cup, he feigned a blush. "Hey, you're in luck," said Lisa Stern, "you're a Libra and your Mercury is in retrograde today . . . lucky your moon isn't in Taurus," she added with relief.

"Well, you gonna eat it all yourself or divide it up?" said Astrid Jones, and everyone joined her in a round of applause. Robert blushed for real. "Thanks a lot," he said. ("On Steve's birthday they got him a Sara Lee . . . how come I only rate a Twinkie?") "Let's go to lunch," said Steve, and on the way down the elevator Robert stared at him, wondering how come Steve was three years younger, yet had a house in the country, two kids, stopped smoking, and got a better cake.

After work he raced home and focused on the mailbox. Although it was stuffed, the contents were inessential—Executive Seminar brochures, *U.S. News & World Report,* and wait, two envelopes! The first was a card from Aunt Ann, which didn't count—she sent everyone cards and kept a vinyl book with birth dates written in next to her niece and nephew's favorite colors. The second was from his dentist and included a reminder for a checkup. "Well, the day's still young," Bobby said hopefully, "and you just never know *what might be waiting in the house.*"

Robert opened the door and began to whistle as he walked inside. "Ah . . . it's GOOD TO BE HOME," he said loudly. "Think I'll GO INTO THE KITCHEN and pour myself a drink!" Nothing happened. "Well, maybe I'll GO INTO THE BEDROOM, and change clothes," he stated, and glanced behind the couch on his way. "I'm going to JUST OPEN THIS CLOSET

DOOR and hang up my jacket," he proclaimed, this time glancing over the bed. And after he'd hung it up, "a nice shower would perk me up, think I'll GO INTO THE BATHROOM NOW." But when he threw back the shower curtain, all he saw was the gold washrag, which had fallen into the tub.

"Check the Phone-Mate," said Bobby, but the red light was not blinking. "God, my shrink didn't even remember! *That's a real bummer*," they both said in unison.

At 7:30 the doorbell rang and Paula sailed in carrying a large package wrapped in silver paper with red plaid ribbon. "Happy Birthday, Bobby," she said, and kissed him generously on the mouth.

"Oh, that's nice," he said, then, pointing to the package, he asked, "What's that?"

"Well, open it up and see!" she said, and for a moment looked just like a tent with a light inside.

"I'm a little embarrassed by all this," Robert said to her, shuffling his feet boyishly. "I just want you to know, I didn't ask you out because of my birthday . . . I mean, I don't really care about birthdays any more . . . don't go in for them . . . So," he said as he ripped off the bow, "I hope you didn't make a big deal." But as he tore into the silver paper, he heard himself inwardly groan, "Please God . . . if I have one wish, let me be a grown-up . . ."

"If one doesn't get birthday presents," wrote Henry Reed, "it can remobilize very painfully the persecutory anxiety which usually follows birth." This proposition is easily understood, for behind the gift you're given rests a symbol far greater than any cat mug or Porsche you may drink from or drive. The gift acts as a palliative to the fear of being forgotten, and that fear is as old as the phrase we've come to know as separation anxiety.

Much of the nail-biting that occurs around the time of your birthday is directly related to an old dream of being united with loved ones—experiencing a reunion with the safe people and places from the past. Since the birthday is the most personal of holidays, the nation does not celebrate with you: department stores do not turn out decorative windows, no one advertises on television, and the cities do not honor the day with parades. You're on your own; the day is purely yours, and the wish to be recognized grows large.

This desire for reunion runs deep and long, and in many anxious people it recontours itself as a bottomless pit of needs. The mewling child finds its way to the tip of your tongue and demands that you recognize its craving to be remembered. Of course, as a wise and rational adult, you may, as was mentioned earlier, hide yourself in a darkened room for the day to muffle its sounds from the world; or you may feel you've matured enough to finesse the kid in public and pacify it with a pat on the head. But those methods don't work—the kid feels abandoned and lonely; it wants attention and it wants it now!

THE JANUS HEAD OF BIRTHDAY ANTICIPATION—HOPE AND FEAR

One of the reasons many people become distraught over an approaching birthday is directly related to their own nervous anticipatory responses. The ability to anticipate makes seers and prophets of us all, however, and like the dual Janus head, one side is viewed through a prism of hope and belief, while the other is viewed through a refractory of fear and dread. The inner child is forever hopeful—it sees possibility in every nuance and subtlety. The adult, on the other hand, is fearful—it has learned that to live in the world, one must make adjustments, one must *fit in*, and becomes irritable when the child inside reflects the needy, hopeful side.

Along comes the approaching birthday, and the neglected child starts kicking up, whispering words like, "You'd better make this right for me!" The adult gets edgy because he or she doesn't know how to make it right—the need is too vast—the adult sometimes feels it's better to ignore it than give it a token gift. Some people play possum on their birthdays and pretend they're asleep for the day; others cope with the situation in silent hope, watching their friends and colleagues pass them by, upping their anger ante by waiting to see just *who* will be sensitive enough to divine that this is their special day. Many people like Robert/Bobby get thrown into a conflict which keeps them hopping in and out of their roles while they anxiously wait for the

proper person, the person "who counts," to make it right for
them on this their natal day. Quite obviously, those who "don't
count" are those who can be relied on, who are expected and
predictable. Those who *do* count are either phantoms, specters
of contrived longings, or simply the one person who isn't there
anymore whom you never got along with anyway, but whom
you now remember as the one from whom unconditional love
was forthcoming.

Of course, the person who will love you unconditionally does
not exist, but that person could show up and surprise you. Now,
this is a bit slippery, because if you're like Robert and afraid in
front that your birthday will be a disappointment, you will tell
all your friends not to surprise you, just to circumvent the possibility of not being surprised. Then you wait to be surprised.
Surprise, in this case, means going beneath your words and making an assumption that you generally speak out of two sides of
your mouth, which in this situation happens to be very genuine.
The adult says, "I hate surprise parties," but the child says,
"Gimme, gimme some," and your friends, colleagues, and loved
ones must learn to decipher the code.

In lieu of being surprised, the child inside can become an ec-
centric despot. Like Bobby he believes that anything you do on
your birthday is "okay"; you're off the hook for any behavior because today is a celebration of me! Anyone who does not understand that rule becomes untrustworthy, whether or not they did
or did not know that on this day you have risen!

Conversely, the adult—like Robert—is a bit humiliated by the
whole event, and the pressure to hold this tyrant firmly under
wraps keeps the anxiety percolating. Further, the adult just may
be harboring the suspicion that he or she does not *deserve* the
attention the child craves. The adult just may have come from a
family where inner needs were considered self-indulgences and,
although the child inside felt and still feels deprived and
neglected, the adult was conditioned to believe that he or she
was not worthy of celebration. In that case, he or she may avoid
their kid all day and ultimately settle for something better than
nothing to do.

Celebrations are basic rituals for any rite of passage, and
there's a reason for these festivities. Not only is the person in
question honored, but the celebration is fashioned to quell the

incipient anxiety. Surrounded by friends and family, one is not forced into a direct confrontation with their personal angst. People divert; many people divert much; a crowd diverts absolutely. Therefore, if you are a person who is given to the ravages of birthday anxiety, it would be an act of self-kindness to attend to that day (it may be only a week away) and start peddling some security systems for yourself.

While on the face of the birthday issue, no one actually wants to spend it alone and miserable, there are those who ironically seem to enjoy feeling bad, for in so doing, they prove to themselves that they are right about the rottenness of life. After informing their intimates that they are well taken care of on that particular day, they then wait to see if anyone will be forthcoming with a celebration, and when no one is, the feeling that life is truly the pits gets a firm endorsement. There is an odd perverse pleasure in feeling drummed out of the human race for these people—one that validates their reasons for maintaining their position as the outsider.

If you find that on your birthday you usually feel like an orphaned saint, or that your inner child will fall into a dead faint, perhaps you should start planning for this occasion with more caution. Before the hour is upon you, remember: aloneness is an anathema to this particular day—it feeds the neglect and nourishes the deprived feelings. You would do well to make contact with one or many friends prior to that day and plan a get-together or an outing. Too many people discover that they're blocked from this route by a barrier of pride which forbids them to ask for attention. However, this is definitely a false notion and one that has probably fed a basic isolation for many years.

If you have no family to call on, or if you would prefer to avoid your family for any number of reasons, it's imperative that you reach out to others. Begin by informing someone in your office or circle of professional colleagues that your birthday is coming up and you'd very much like to plan a lunch that day. If you don't work, talk to a neighbor and plan an outing. You might even invite others into your home and throw yourself a small party. Whatever you choose, the idea is to share this event with another person, and, ideally, someone with whom you can discuss the importance of the day and perhaps hear their birthday anxieties as well.

While you're working yourself up to this new method of behaving, you might give some thought to that neglected kid inside, and just how he or she has been treated on past birthdays. Try to remember what you did on those occasions, and, concomitantly, how you felt. Then try to trace the source of that neglect —reconstruct the value system you learned at home and try to summon up the attitudes of your parents toward birthdays in general. A careful investigation of this issue might illuminate for you just how you've assumed the mantle of your mother or father and, as a result, how you've become that same neglectful parent to yourself. If history is, indeed, repeating itself, it might be time to short-circuit its performance.

At the same time, you may as well dig a little deeper and begin to recognize just how you behave when you receive a present. Now, this is an issue which is reflective of how deserving you feel yourself to be. However, it also will give you a sound idea of just how you behave in the face of what some consider to be an awkward moment.

How you receive a present is very much connected to who is giving it, what you know about that person, and what you feel about their gesture. If you do become tight and tense when that package is handed over, you're not alone. For the uncertain and anxious person, this is sometimes worse than being forgotten. With this information in mind, you may find the following quite useful.

SITUATION #2
Getting a Gift

Yes, it's your birthday, and you've just been handed this object— a Gift. The Giver is sitting on a chair directly in front of you, observing your approach to the object. Both the Giver and the Gift have been elevated to the realm of the sacred, which forces your toes into a tight curl.

The Gift is wrapped in gold foil with bright red ribbon. It is not store-wrapped—it was done up *by the hand of the person in that chair!* How long should you stare at the Gift to ensure the

Giver understands that you understand the significance of that wrapping?

On an unspoken and unexpressed signal, you will perceive that it is now time to *touch the card*. Sliding it out from under the ribbon, you will stare at your name, which has cleverly been written on the face of the envelope, and it may be appropriate here to fondle it. At this point, it is imperative that you look back at the Giver with intense appreciation in your eyes. If the handwriting on the envelope is well scripted, you will understand in a flash that *thought preceded that penmanship,* and you will open the glued edges with delicate care, giving the stock its full mystical importance. You must take time opening the card. However, you are acutely aware of being watched, and a series of calculated responses will leap to your mind, none of which will accurately fit the measure of your gratitude. You will gingerly pull the card out and gaze at the drawing or cartoon as though standing before a treasure at the Louvre. You will look up to the Giver and nod your head, then *open the card* and read the Hallmark message, as well as *what's really being said between the lines.* You will then read the message from the Giver, and although it may simply say, "Love, Ann," you will nod your head, again, with perception that passeth understanding.

You may want to pause here and discuss the nature of friendship, simultaneously proving that you are indeed sensitive to every nuance of the "thought that counts." While conversing, although the package you hold is the precise shape of a regular book, you will act as though it is a nightgown and maintain an expression of profound curiosity, expectancy, and wonder throughout.

"Well, what *is* this?" you might decide to say, which will unnerve you, but you may find those words easier to say than "You shouldn't have done this." The latter might easily be construed as "You *shouldn't* have done this," as opposed to "*You* shouldn't have done this"—in either case you will be wrong. You may take this opportunity to light a cigarette and think it through; if you don't smoke, however, a sip of a drink will not be looked at askance.

This might be the right time to caress the foil and remark how

210

exquisitely the Gift is wrapped. Although you will hate yourself later, do not be dismayed if you hear yourself saying, "Should I save the paper?" This will be a minor misdemeanor in the scheme of the whole process.

As you pull the Scotch tape off the sides, your mind will be filled with anxious prattle concerning the method for expressing your gratitude. You will be prematurely tense. You may have read this particular book, or it may concern a subject on which you are totally bored. In any event, you will continue to act as though it could be a gown and pursue your solicitousness of the paper, which will later be scrunched up and tossed in the trash.

As the Gift is unveiled, your stomach may lurch. If it is indeed a book you have longed to read, you will not be able to sufficiently express your sincere gratitude. If it is a book you've read, you will not be able to sufficiently express your sincere gratitude. If you have, indeed, just finished it off last night, you will pray it's not inscribed. If it is, you must never let on, and read the inscription as though experiencing sex for the first time. For the nonverbal, a moistening of eyes might do well. For the verbal, expressions of deep humility and awe are also in order.

You will overthank the person profusely for his or her thoughtfulness, time, choice, paper, ribbon, card, envelope, as well as "for just being you," and begin to speak rapidly about something else to bridge this awkward gap. However, you will still be stuck with the Gift on your lap and experience an inability to put it aside on a table for fear of being caught acting as if you deserved it.

For the remainder of the evening, you will be aware that the Giver has given you a Gift, and experience your conversation, as well as the special emphasis in your good-bye hug, as unnatural.

Later, when you are alone, you will be haunted by the fact that this Gift might be *setting a precedent*. Will you now be expected to buy the Giver a Gift, and when you do, can you top it? Pondering this thought, you will find yourself assessing the Great Decisions of Western Man, and fall into a deep sleep.

If you do find yourself growing tense when the subject of presents rears its head, you may just be a troubled taker, which is part and parcel of a deeply ingrained belief system which states you do not deserve. People who were raised in troubled families often feel not only that they are being awarded too much privilege in receiving a gift, but that there's a hidden price to be paid behind the gesture. In the past, that was probably accurate. However, now, as an adult, the gift-giving ritual is an accepted part of celebrations and it would be to your advantage to revamp those perceptions. This is not to say, of course, that people have thrown away all their hidden gift-giving agendas, but it does imply that you, as an independent agent, do not have to become a pawn in that plan.

Most people give gifts because they receive joy in the act of bestowing a present on someone they regard as special. While no one enjoys experiencing their gesture being treated cavalierly, at the same time, a friend is rarely lost because the paper was hastily ripped off. If, however, this is a most unnerving experience for you, and you feel inept in your method of receiving, you might start amassing a few role models from your friends and colleagues. Observing the social behavior and protocol of this ritual could be the right prescription for changing your feelings of self-worth. You might even find yourself eventually accepting tokens of esteem as if expected, yet with the appropriate grace.

Receiving a gift is very much akin to receiving a compliment. For many people, before they can assimilate the information, they must first compute the intention, and then apologize for the flaws not seen. In so doing, they destroy the generosity of the thought. While it may take years to learn the fine art of a simple "Thank you," it can and does happen to the most awkward and unskilled of people. You might also try to "see" yourself from the vantage point of the other guy. By behaving overly dramatic and intense, you demean your own importance and could actually end up insulting this person's intelligence and judgment.

Very practically, the next time someone remarks how well you look, work at saying, "Thank you," and then pull the invisible zipper across your lips. You'll probably feel ungrounded, and may even sway, but over a period of time you will have conditioned yourself to respond appropriately and with self-respect. Simultaneously, this lesson will bleed into your ability to receive

a gift with greater poise, and although you may still hear Bee-
thoven's Fifth sounding in the background of your mind, you'll
minimize the gift anxiety and eventually experience yourself as
someone with the right to be esteemed.

However, whether you fondle the ribbons and caress the foil,
or not, there are all those other concerns surrounding the birthday issue that tend to hold fast to the heart. When all the frip-
peries have been flushed away, you're still a year older, and a
new anxiety—tenacious and alarming—looms on the horizon.

FUTURE FEAR—THE SHOPPING BAG LADY ALERT

Someone once wrote, "The past is always tense." To the anxious,
the flip-side of that remark could easily be disposed of by in-
timating that, "Yes, but the future is always perfect." Then
comes the birthday, and suddenly you're thrust into reflections
of not only what your life has wrought, but also where it's going,
and the future takes on new configurations. While hope does
spring proverbially eternal, a creeping uneasiness starts jimmy-
ing your sense of identity.

Those who see themselves as the perpetual *Wunderkind*, the
comer who is still fulfilling his potential, or the debutante who is
always coming out, suddenly give pause to their projected roles
and begin to wonder if they may have been deluding themselves
for a bit too long—if they actually do have all that time to
remain static. They look back upon their years and may be instantly stricken with the insight that the future of then is happening now—"I am my future of ten years ago."

About the same time this enlightenment takes hold, the shopping bag lady, the one who lives out of a tattered suitcase or su-
permarket bags and sleeps in the park, becomes a prime figure
against the ground of your future-fear gestalt. The shopping bag
lady (who finds her counterpart in the Bowery bum or "crazy"
man who wanders the neighborhoods and malls) becomes de-
pressingly fascinating. Who is she? What's she got in her bags?
And, although she's alone, when you spot her spouting a tirade
of words, to whom is she addressing herself? Once you've begun
to question her identity, you're hooked. That lady in the park is

no longer an alien being to be avoided; she shares a common denominator with you, and although it cannot be immediately distinguished, you'd like to know more.

Most of us fear her—she's a vision of a future that was never gracefully resolved or fairly concluded. She and her counterpart trigger an anxiety that is based on semi-reflections—self-neglect and eternal omnipotence—and because she just might tap the raw, undeveloped side of yourself, you'd often like to just wish her away. But she's a very important person, and to banish her from your conscious thoughts is a futile gesture, providing only temporary relief. The shopping bag lady is "unfinished business" made real. Her loud, angry arguments are a dialogue between herself and people with whom she could never make sufficient emotional closure. Now she verbally shadowboxes with the ghosts of the past and lives out of bags stuffed with bits and pieces of slim necessities and dreams. When she does set off a series of unbidden responses in you, it might be wise to back up, assess your own "unfinished business," and look to the ways in which you may have denied the realities of your life.

YOUR PERSONAL FUTURE
FEAR QUOTIENT

Before you begin to deny that you have a denial system in motion, perhaps you might want to take this personal inventory test and use it as a catalyst for confronting just how you do operate in terms of your future fears.

I. Your Work Life

Are you content with your job?

Is it in an area you personally selected, or did you "fall" into it?

Do you feel it's permanent or temporary?

When did you receive your last raise or promotion?

What steps are you taking to change your direction?

Where do you envision yourself one year from now? Five years from now? Ten years from now?

A year ago, when you projected yourself into the future, what was your goal? Are you there now?

II. *Your Personal Life*

Are you steadily involved with one person?

If yes, do you see this person as someone with whom you'd like to grow old?

If no, are you thinking of meeting someone, and if so, what steps are you taking?

What excuses do you use to keep yourself alone?

Where do you envision yourself one year from now? Five years from now? Ten years from now?

A year ago, when you projected yourself into the future, what was your goal? Have you connected yourself to that process?

III. *Your Physical Health*

How often do you go for a physical checkup? A dental checkup?

Are you addicted to habits which are known to be harmful to your health?

How long have you been aware that these habits are self-abusive?

What excuses do you use to avoid change?

How do you envision your physical health a year from now? Five years from now? Ten years from now?

IV. *General Questions*

How much of your time do you spend in self-recriminatory thinking?

How much of your life do you dedicate to procrastination?

Do you honestly perceive of your own personal future?

If this abbreviated quiz makes you a little uncomfortable, there's good reason to believe that you do have a denial system working for you and that it's successfully feeding your future fears, which boldly show themselves come your natal day.

DENIAL AND THE ILLUSION OF STOPPED TIME

Hidden in the outback region of your mind sits the basic anxiety, common to all humanity—the denial of mortality. In order to keep that lion at bay, we construct intermediate denials which act as camouflage for the ultimate fright. You begin to deny that you're getting older and therefore that time does not pass. Since the finiteness of life is too big to engage, like Miss Havisham you set the clocks at a certain hour and refuse to admit to any changes or transfigurations.

Jack Benny remained "thirty-nine" all his life and, conversely, a woman we know was so beset with anxiety concerning her incipient fortieth year, ten months before that birthday, she began to rehearse saying, "I'm forty," and in so doing almost entirely missed her thirty-ninth year. The leap from twenty-nine to thirty, thirty-nine to forty, forty-nine to fifty, and so on, are landmarks, and most people have difficulty making the transition from one stage to another. Those birthdays provoke intense anxiety. However, at forty-five, you may not be in condition to hit the ski slopes with a person who is only twenty-five and been in training all his life, but when denial is at work, that notion is pushed aside. Many people ignore the age discrepancy, jump in for a competition, and throw themselves into life-and-death situations simply to prove that time has stopped. Others may slowly become aging ingenues and maintain girlish attitudes toward responsibilities to the self through the age of forty-two or fifty. They never expect to be thirty or forty, fifty or sixty; they've lived so long watching others of those ages from a safe distance, when that particular birthday approaches, they're genuinely shocked. A basic anxiety here concerns a self-imposed code of behavior for the ages of men and women. Many people authentically believe they must give up certain pleasures at a certain age and that, in the relinquishing, nothing will replace them. They fear change and vilify risk so as to perpetuate the status quo.

However, the fear of risk is the hobgoblin of the anxious, and although they may be counting the candles on the cake with great alarm, once that birthday has passed, they return to their safe places and resolve to make a move in a new direction "next year." In the meantime, they have become by age possessed, and not only refuse to confront those realities, but, like the shopping bag lady, never clean up any of the messiness inherent in significant areas of their lives.

In order to avoid the trauma of "getting older," it's important to begin to constitute a life for yourself that's substantive and nourishing. When one remains twenty-two into their forty-first year, they usually surround themselves with people who are much younger, and shun their peers of age. The practice is disorienting and helps to perpetuate false notions of who you are and where you're headed—there tends to be no balance. If you've ever sat talking with a friend for two or three hours, you may remember the experience of leaving your seat and walking over to a mirror, perhaps to comb your hair. So much time was spent looking and identifying with your friend, that upon looking at yourself in the mirror, there is an eerie moment when you are stunned to perceive that you look exactly like you! This phenomenon is the result of fusing with others, which can result in a mistaken identity. For this reason, among others, generational gaps are important for maintaining perspective on yourself as a growing person. Keeping friends of many different ages provides significant insights into where you've been and where you're going.

The questions, however, remain: Will you begin to risk making the changes necessary to your life, and when will you begin?

Perhaps a starting point would be the making of a resolution to form a peaceful truce with yourself. You might begin by making a list of your realities. "I am X years old." "I understand that I am human and have limitations." "I accept the fact that I have these talents and skills, yet not those." "I do have potential and it rests within this framework." "These are the possibilities which I can anticipate." "I have accomplished these goals." "I would like to broaden my field of friendships and social acquaintances to include and to enhance these aspects of my life." At the end of the list you might jot down those people in your life who are older and who do impress you as role models for the future.

John Barrymore has been quoted as saying, "A man is not old until regrets take the place of dreams." By beginning to alter your future (which is within the next five minutes), re-evaluating your life and adjusting its time frame to fit the facts, you may diminish much of the situational anxiety of birthdays and ultimately grow into fruition with security and grace.

EIGHT

New Job Anxiety

". . . we wise grown-ups here at the company go gliding in and out all day long, scaring each other at our desks and cubicles and water coolers and trying to evade the people who frighten us."

JOE HELLER
Something Happened

TYPICALLY, THE FIRST DAY ON ANY NEW JOB WILL PROVOKE situational anxiety. This particular occasion acts as a very strong catalyst for the emergence of uncomfortable and uneasy feelings. Prior to landing the job, you probably survived two, maybe three, or even four interviews, first with headhunters, and then with the powers at the new office. Further, you actually kept your mouth shut when necessary, stifled the nervous laughter, gracefully straddled the line between modesty and strength, plucked the perfect hero or heroine story from your bag of former job achievements, and listened without interrupting. And then you were hired! A celebration with family or friends followed—you were toasted, wished well, congratulated, and while Upward Mobility danced a crazed boogie with Career Strategy, you ran out and had two suits altered.

Monday morning is nearing, however, and apprehension has begun to snake its way into your career euphoria. A nagging concern follows you on your errands, and as you pick up your newly heeled shoes, it occurs to you in a flash that what you experienced last week as your professional business savvy and dynamic professionalism could be . . . may be . . . might have been . . . merely an *illusion of competence!* Although your new supervisor did seem to display boundless faith in your potential, couldn't he or she have been blinded by your résumé (which you spent six weeks editing)? In retrospect, didn't he or she seem more relieved to "fill the spot" than with your particular gifts? And how many others did they interview before you, who were probably better qualified, but . . . maybe wore the wrong jacket? Skulking down the street, you make a sudden turn and veer into the leather shop, where you overspend on a new attaché case, a purchase that takes on new and profound implications.

The anxiety which accompanies the new job situation is fraught with complications which take unexpected shifts and turns. Not only must you compete with your own résumé and interview expertise, you must gracefully demonstrate during the first three hours that the company has definitely *made the right choice!* Proving you're a real revenue generator between nine and twelve on the first day takes much subtle cunning and delicate maneuvering, especially since, at this point, you're not quite sure where to sit.

The quintessential problem emerges in the desire to appear as if you belong when everyone knows you don't. This issue addresses itself to the clothes you choose to wear the first day, how you walk, with whom you speak, how many sugars you take in your coffee, and if your smile is indeed neutral. Not unlike the situation traced back to youth when you were the new kid on the block, in the new office there are the bullies, the menacers, the ingratiators, the pests, the wrong people with whom to be associated, and the real power brokers who get a big allowance. But, at the outset, you just don't know the political ropes, and you just can't be too sure whom to ask for the bathroom key.

Now, if you've switched jobs within the same industry, you may have an easier time, yet you must prove to know everything and everyone connected therein, including vendors, suppliers, consultants, and clients. (A first-name basis is preferable and a short anecdote wouldn't hurt.) However, if you've transferred to a new industry, you must prove that your skills, insights, and responsibilities are easily translated and transposed into the new language and lingo, and no matter what issue is discussed, you're ready with a proposed solution. But before you can seriously strut your achievement acumen, you must first learn the company code and, further, understand that when you're anxious, you're never really alone.

SITUATION #1
The First Morning on the Job

Attired in a tweed suit, a rose silk blouse, and a self-possessed stance, on the first morning of your new job as Account Manager, you roar into the lobby of the building ready to take charge. But while standing by the bank of elevators, your belly is dive-bombed, and you understand in a flash that Ambition, Perfection, and Fear—that old, familiar triumvirate—intend to hound you all day. Ascending to the thirtieth floor, you tighten your hold on their sounds, but as you step out onto the carpeted corridor, they wrestle their way free.

Did they say Monday morning, October 11? Or was it the eighteenth? whispers Fear, and quite suddenly your memory is corked! *What if no one remembers you,* Fear continues, *what if they changed their minds last week and couldn't reach you by phone?* You clutch your new attaché case in a wet hand and, holding your head uncomfortably high, walk through the glass doors to the polished desk. "Oh, yes . . . good morning, Ms. Best," says the mannered receptionist, "I think Dora Regent is expecting you. Do you know your way to her office?" "Yes, I know my way," you respond with calculated professionalism, ". . . but, thanks."

. . . *Expecting you!* utters Perfection. *I told you to be here five minutes early. Now she's here before you—this bodes ill!* "No, no," you think, "that would have made me seem too eager to please, and . . ." *Bad move, bad move!* says Ambition, cutting you off. *Think of your goals!*

Your new supervisor greets you holding an armful of binders. "Hi, Laura . . . good to see you. Let me show you your desk. I've got to run up to the thirty-fourth floor, so just get comfortable, and . . . there are a few things on your desk to read. I haven't looked at them yet, but, glad you're here . . . we'll talk later." With an almost lifelike smile, you watch her shoot buoyantly down the maze of corridors and then disappear.

Don't just stand there, hisses Perfection, *you've got to look*

BUSY! "I know, I know," you think, "but she did say to make myself comfortable." *That was a test,* Perfection says quickly, *and you never know who's watching you. Within the first three minutes you must prove that you're EARNING YOUR KEEP!* "You're right, okay . . . I'll get to these memos immediately." You sit, arrange the papers neatly in front of you on the desk, forcibly trying to concentrate on the words and not the people who are now taking their positions in the office. (*Don't worry about who's who right now*), says Ambition, parenthetically, (*I've got my awareness focused on each and every one—we'll deal with the politics later*).

"But what the hell am I reading here? These memos are all about mail distribution and supply requisitions! There's nothing here about accounts or current projects!" *What's it to you?* Perfection snaps back. *Read them until you know them by heart; memorize! You have to know everything! You can't be sure when you'll be questioned about these issues!* "Don't I know it," you think. *And wait a minute . . . you can't be sure of when your boss is coming back, either—you don't want to be caught just READING! You must seem as though you're reading AND THINKING! Get out a pad and make notes. Remember: you're intensely involved in thinking, absorbing, analyzing, reinterpreting because they've hired a person WHOSE MIND JUST NEVER STOPS!*

"You're right . . . that's perfect. I'll be solidly prepared with an in-depth understanding to the company's approach to these issues. I'll jot down a few ideas, carefully picking up the subtle ambiguities . . . How about: "Will using the service elevator for mail distribution actually prove to be time-saving?" And let's see . . . "Unless periodic updates are made, printing new supply requisitions could make a nasty bite into projected cost factors . . ."

Well, says Perfection thoughtfully, *it's good, but not exactly like I would have worded it. I'd be leery about saying anything too critical. The notes should be of a "curious" nature. You don't want to seem like you're judging or improving, just that EVERYTHING IS GRIST FOR YOUR MIND'S QUICK MILL OF IDEAS! Elevators and requisitions may be her pet project, you*

just never know. I'd take a safer posture—the journalist's stance,
the distant but keen observer.

"Oh, I'm glad you saw that . . . I'll do it. But, now what? I've
read these memos eight times and I'm getting sleepy. How long
can I continue tapping this pen against my temple? Isn't there
supposed to be an Office Manager? How do I get my supplies?
My God, the phone's lighting up! Should I answer it? Does
someone else answer for me? What's my extension? I need a cup
of coffee, fast! Is there a coffee wagon, or does this office have its
own machine? I see mugs on desks. Should I ask to chip in? Is it
free? I've got to ask someone!"

NO! screams the triumvirate. *You'll look like a goldbricker,*
yells Perfection. *You don't know WHO you're asking yet,* bellows Ambition. *Your face is too frozen,* taunts Fear.

"I've got to do something! I can't just sit here doing nothing—
it looks terrible. I could read my book . . ." *Absolutely not!* says
Perfection. *That will look as though you're reading a book.*
"Even if it's a job-related book?" *A book's the kiss of death.*
You're only allowed to read what looks like company stuff—you
know, material which comes in binders, folders, files, typed
pages, or printouts. "I suppose the newspaper is also out . . .
but what about the Business Section?" *No, it could be construed*
as entertainment—you might be found enjoying it.

"Well, is it all right to go to the bathroom? I'll just wander
around and ask someone where it is." You begin to rise from
your seat but are shoved back down by Ambition. *Who are you*
planning to ask? You don't know the hierarchy yet, so don't
make any premature alliances! "But, it's just the Ladies' Room!"
Very important issue, declares Ambition. *Everyone will be*
watching to see WHOM you choose to query. That woman over
there—the one in the blue scarf . . . she "looks" like a peer, she
seems sympathetic, but is she? "Well, I'd never ask her! She
looks like upper management." *Good,* says Ambition, much
relieved, *it would look as if you're currying favor—brown-nosing*
on your first day. "That person over there looks fairly innocu-
ous." *Forget it—she might not be on the same level, or worse, be*
on her way out, and you'll owe her. REMEMBER YOUR
GOALS. Besides, she might be allied with that guy over there
who's a bit talky. She'll tell him that you asked her, and he'll

repeat the story to two others who could be looking to get the whammy on you, and soon they'll all know that YOU COULDN'T FIND YOUR WAY TO THE BATHROOM!

"All right, give me a break! I'm just going to casually stroll around the office, nod to a few people, get the lay of the land." *That might be a good strategy,* Ambition agrees, *but don't act too footloose, and watch your demeanor—you must appear confident, but not aloof, or as if you're checking up on anyone. And you can't seem nosy. Curious, yes, but nosy, never! Don't forget to smile pleasantly,* adds Perfection, *but don't look scared,* Fear concludes.

You make your way around the edges of the office, with Fear holding your mouth in a particularly bland smile. "I'm dying to stop and chat, but I don't want to look as though I'm looking for someone to talk to when I'm looking for someone to talk to . . ." *And, you're the most junior person here,* Fear says, shortening your breath. *Even those with lower salaries are more important because they've been here longer and know what's going on! You have no context for anything. You don't KNOW THE ROPES!*

"But I must appear to know EVERYTHING, be on top of the case," you think. *Then walk naturally!* Ambition commands. *You have to set a tone of understated authority yet gain no hostility. But, is she dressed right?* Perfection says, butting in. *Is your outfit appropriate to your entry level? Pick up every clue you can! You've got to FIT IN, yet make a statement. How are the other women dressed? (Your shoes may be too sexy . . . they're all wearing medium heels!) Keep observing! (They're all wearing gold studs, why did you wear the silver?) How do the women relate to each other? (They all seem to know each other so well!) How do they relate to men? (You must assess this situation!) Memorize these facts!* "I don't know if this is the right place for me," you think. "There must be other routes up the corporate success ladder!"

That's all well and good, says Ambition, *but you're just letting Fear intimidate you . . . it's an old trick. Let's get down to the nuts-and-bolts of the situation: WHO'S ACTUALLY GOT THE POWER HERE?* "I just don't know yet—it's hard to tell. I sense that clique over there is a power base—none of them has acknowledged me, so they must be important." *Keep your eye on them*, cautions Ambition.

"Hi, there . . ." says a voice from behind you. "You're Laura Best, aren't you?" You whirl around and mechanically extend your hand. "I'm Ted Friendly, we'll be working together on the Jflkmlrt Account . . . Say, you might want to take a look at these figures; those jerks on the thirty-fourth floor really got this ass-backwards . . . see what I mean?" "Hmmmmm," you say, and are so pleased and appreciative of being recognized you almost . . . *Pull yourself together!* shouts Perfection. *You're tipping your hand!* You skim the document in Ted Friendly's hand and, knowing absolutely nothing about the Jflkmlrt Account ("if that's indeed what he said"), pretend to an intimate knowledge. "Very interesting," you begin, but Ambition grabs you in a half nelson and whispers threateningly in your ear—*EASY! Don't agree or disagree, and don't criticize, especially those on the THIRTY-FOURTH FLOOR! Mr. Goodwill over here might be hand-in-glove with the author of that document and word will get around.* "God, this is making me very tense . . . I have to act dead!" *No, present yourself as capable; even "allude" to being an expert in your field (which you are!), but don't tell anyone anything! Bland, bland, bland . . . but personable.* "Okay, I'll try." "Thanks for showing this to me, Ted," you say, not moving your lips, but still perusing the document which is blurring before your eyes. "I'm certain we'll be speaking much more about this particular issue. But right now, well, would you believe it? I've got a hundred things to do before lunch! But it's good to meet you." Walking intrepidly in the direction of your desk, you narrow your eyes as though completely preoccupied with Serious Work.

"She's still not back!" you think. "Well, God, I can't keep roaming—first time around and I've already started dissembling. Was that a bad move? Can he see me from here? Why is this desk empty? *Good thought*, says Perfection. *Who sat at this desk before you? A he or a she? Promoted or fired? Who's out there resenting you for taking that place? What kind of phantom competitor are you up against?* "I'd love to know . . ." *Whoever you're replacing probably generated large revenues their first day*, comments Fear, sliding down to your toes. "I'm really not sure I made the right career choice," you think again. "These people might not be right for me . . . but then I haven't given it a chance. Maybe I'll check out her office and see if there's anything on her desk that would apply to my duties—I can't stand not knowing!" *Just cancel that thought,* says Perfection. *Someone may be watching and think you're gathering information, trying to spy on your supervisor, setting up a whole political coup! They might even think you're burgling,* says Fear, canceling your last thought of first-day initiative.

You're about to risk it and make a personal call when Dora Regent, carrying that same armload of binders, sails toward your desk. "Laura, I'm so terribly sorry to have kept you waiting all morning. I was stuck upstairs . . . oh, come on in." You follow her into her office, but before you can assess the decor—a Chagall poster, some framed cartoons, and a few green plants—she's telling you about Derek Jeoslknl's proposed budget cuts, and Paula Radsirmcw's client schedule—names which are instantly lost and forgotten. "Well, our office manager's out sick today, so you really haven't gotten a preliminary orientation, but how do you like it so far?"

Make it good, threatens Ambition, *you're on!* "I'm delighted to be here, Dora. I think the company will prove to be both challenging and stimulating, and, frankly, I'm anxious to get down to business."

"You'll be handling plenty of that," says your boss, flipping a sheath of printouts. *At last . . .* sighs Ambition, *NOW you can let her know she's hired the Right Person!* "But first," she continues, "let me ask you a question . . ." *Get your Important Feedback and Brilliant Suggestions prepared,* hisses Perfection. Fiddling with her pottery mug, Dora pauses. "Oh, never mind, we'll get to that later. More to the point, are you ready for lunch?"

Now, of course, lunch is a completely separate matter, and although this activity shares many of the same anxieties endemic to the first morning on the job, it focuses more attention on your very personal habits. There are many variations to the first-lunch theme, each one charged with its own bolts of uncertainty and self-doubt. But there is good reason for worry. In the minds of the anxious, nothing is left to chance. What you do with your lips and how you breathe are all being recorded on the Cosmic Ledger of Upward Mobility.

If by chance you should be left to go out alone, you might be relieved. This is an opportunity to let your shoulders sag and to loosen your belt. However, you're still not off the professional hook—you just never know when you may be spotted. Therefore you must choose a restaurant commensurate with your level. You don't want to eat in a "good" restaurant and be seen there alone, and you don't want to be found at a sloppy Joe's burger hole. So, you must locate a "nice" coffee shop where it will be appropriate to sit at the counter. Reading material, again, is important. Novels are out—that displays a frivolous bent; self-help is taboo—it suggests a less than perfect inner life; magazines are okay, as long as they're scientific; and that leaves the newspaper, which is difficult to fold.

Should a few people from your department show up, you could be critically endangered. If they invite you over, you cannot refuse—you'll be pegged as a "loner." When you join them, and you will, they'll ask you personal questions which you'll have to volley and deflect. They'll soon tire of prodding you and turn to their own affairs, which you may not feel ready to hear. You'll want to glean all the information you can, but they'll perceive you're not trading, and then you'll be regarded as a potential threat. Signals will pass and conversation will shift to storm windows and snow tires, subjects on which no one can be personally hung. At this point, you'll be convinced that all those career handbooks you've read were written by monks and that you should have scheduled lunch with your boss.

So, right off, let's clean up the facts. Lunching with your new boss on the First Day has nothing to do with refueling the body —it's a CRITICAL ASSIGNMENT. If, like Laura, you've been invited to join her or him, your startle index will immediately take a giant leap. You cannot refuse this offer! You cannot claim a previous commitment, beg off for a deadline, or take along a friend. Your only avenue of escape is to fall into a dead faint.

SITUATION #2
The First-Day Lunch with the Boss

The restaurant will be chosen for you, and you'll *love* any kind of food that's suggested—you may even express gratitude over the chance to "eat Eskimo" today. After all, you're a person who's wide open to challenge. But once you've arrived and have been seated, your decision-making apparatus will be put to a rigorous test, your awareness will jump to the tenth power, and you may be menaced throughout by harrowing thoughts bearing some resemblance to these:

- You will be trapped at a table across from the *face you fear the most*, which will loom close to your own. You'll be certain your eye makeup has collected in the corners, and that you missed two salient beard hairs while shaving. Are you smiling too much or too little? Are you fulfilling the requisite personnel skills?

- Your boss may order a Campari and soda. You would love a glass of white wine. But is white wine appropriate to your entry level? Should you ask for the year of the house wine to prove you're discerning? Will you seem like a tippler, and *are you being tested?* On the other hand, if you cannot drink at lunch and order a Tab, will you be seen as straightlaced and untrustworthy? Will you be experienced as provincial, or simply lacking executive potential?

- The menu is blurring before your eyes, and you're experiencing an inability to remember what you eat! How much time can you safely spend reading the menu, and how often should you look up to ensure the connection between you and your boss has not been irrevocably severed? Will eye contact ensure corporate visibility?

- Your boss orders a salad. If you order the Salisbury steak, will you be seen as hungry? Will your boss assume you have no regard for salutary foodstuffs? How fast will it get around that you have a "lusty appetite"? And, does Managerial material eat meat?

- Your boss orders steak tartar. If you order a salad, will you be seen as a health food fanatic? Could this be construed as a threat to your boss's position as an arbiter of taste, and is lettuce relevant? Will you be judged as a "false dieter" out to make a favorable impression?

- The order has been taken and your napkin is spread evenly over your lap. You're staring at a stranger who has your career plans by the throat. Is this the time to query her or him on matters of profit sharing, or do you touch upon that during the beverage course?

- Your food has arrived. Can you safely fork the lettuce and place it in your mouth without dribbling dressing, and is this the time for a profound response to the administrative question that's just been presented? Is your boss watching you chew? Are the real shakers and movers prudent chewers, and how many chews should you take before becoming obsessive?

- A napkin-covered bread basket haunts your peripheral vision. Should you eat a piece of bread, and, if so, how big a piece? Will you be asked to attend the Denver convention if you use a lot of butter? Is butter compatible with a sound professional aptitude?

- The waiter removes your plates and inquires about coffee. You'd like a cappuccino. Will you be pegged as capricious and jeopardize your areas of responsibility, or as a person with a canny sense for detail but bent on status-hopping?

- When you get up to leave will you know more than you did when you came in, and will your knack for swallowing without moving your throat prove to be an essential asset come your six-month evaluation?

Of all the helpful information you can gather regarding the issues in these situations, this is the most significant: FIRST-DAY

ANXIETY IS NORMAL! EVERYONE EXPERIENCES IT. You're not ready to be hauled away in a net—you're simply in a new, unfamiliar, unknown environment, and your psychic directional sense cannot locate the street signs. As a consequence, your observations may be raised to the tenth power, but are they focused in or out?

REALITIES OF THE FIRST DAY

Because your vision tends to be myopic the first morning on the job, there are certain facts which are completely disregarded by the anxious employee.

1. On the first day, there is no common ground. You should not expect to fall into easy conversations in either the office or the bathrooms.
2. They don't expect you to be brilliant and knowledgeable by 11:15, and you're not expected to achieve by 12:00.
3. Most companies are aware that it does take a certain amount of time to produce. They make an investment in training personnel, and, depending upon the nature of the work, look at the first few months, even the first year, as a speculative investment in your skills.
4. You are not expected to generate revenue on the first day.
5. You are not expected to know the complete organizational structure, or the specific vendors, suppliers, or clients.
6. No one expects you to know the geography of the office—where the bathrooms are located, the mail, printing, or supply room, as well as the water cooler or coffeepot.

However, there are certain issues which can be cleared up during the interview phase of your employment which can make the first day easier. If you're applying for a secretarial position, find out how many people you'll be working for and the limits of your responsibility. For other positions, find out if you'll inherit a secretary, share a secretary, be able to hire your own, or be using a pool. If it's feasible, it might be wise to ask for a tour of the floor you'll be on and, of course, who to report to on the first day. While these practical matters can be disposed of in advance, you'll still need the first few weeks and even the first month to absorb all of the intricacies of your particular office. This is most definitely—EXPECTED!

FEAR AND FIRST-DAY DISTORTIONS

One of the peculiarities endemic to anxiety is the anticipation of making a complete fool out of yourself and its attendant rebuke. In order to circumvent that occasion, one takes a look around them and seeks out the "sameness" in others, then attempts to emulate that style. In the new job situation, usually there is a gaggle of codes which present themselves at first glance. Once these codes are visually perceived, an internalization process begins which rotates your vision from the "out there" to the "in here." You no longer have the full capacity to assess your surroundings: your surroundings begin to assess you. In short order, you fall into the anxious trap of noticing what you *don't* have rather than what you *do*, and observing what they *do* have, all of which you are without.

This is a painful syndrome, one that's geared to blind you to the realities of your new job. It could even be said that when you become inordinately self-conscious, you have given up your eyes, surrendered them to those you most fear, and become a receptacle for your own projected self-abuse. The first morning on the job is tailor-made for the anxious: frustration levels are pushed to their limits, and the fear of disapproval forces all of the anxious shenanigans to the surface. Since you cannot "see" what's going on around you, you usually find ways of making yourself more comfortable, and can easily fall into traps which in the subsequent weeks can prove to be disastrous.

The following list addresses itself to a handful of pitfalls the anxious employee might mistakenly stumble upon while trying to banish the first-day jitters:

1. *Going dead to avoid interactions with co-workers:* This reaction is experienced by people like Laura, who feel that *any* behavior she displays will be substandard and therefore taken as a mark against her. Paradoxically, it also implies that she must psychically kill herself off to prove she's a worthy investment.

2. *Rapid talking to avoid being seen:* Many people become verbal rattlers and engage co-workers in a maze of words which have little value to either party. In this way, the new employee becomes a visible presence, but his or her performance apprehensions will go unobserved.

3. *Being helpful—the conciliatory stance:* By acting the savior your first day out, you can immediately prove that you are indeed useful, special, and earning your keep, plus circumvent your first-day test anxiety.

4. *Presenting yourself as an eager beaver:* Those who become stuck in dead-end jobs often introduced themselves the first day as people willing to shoulder any and all responsibilities, even those assigned to others. This is geared to shelter the panic within a network of charitable contributions.

5. *Making quick alliances:* Seeking out intimates the first day and instantly trading information, personal or professional, is a system for diminishing the feeling of isolation. By establishing an oral contract, you believe you can quell the anticipated hostility and thus minimize further alienation.

6. *Overresponding to information:* Dramatic responses to written or oral communications is a method for keeping others focused on your desired self-image while blinding them to your very real feelings of self-doubt.

7. *Attention-hustling:* Here, the new employee becomes a dynamo of energetic charisma. Constantly in motion, you introduce yourself to every cubicle and office, dropping amusing anecdotes and witty saws to ensure you will be highly visible and desired. If no one can get enough of you, you may be prevented from feeling inept.

8. *Overextending:* By dropping hints that you will be available at any time for any one, you appeal to the neediness in others and conceal your own first-day fears.

All of these responses ultimately lead to one goal—neutralizing the others to ensure they will use their eyes favorably. However, as can readily be observed, on the first day of a new job, you're setting a tone and writing a script which could take months, even years, to undo.

THE HIGH ACHIEVER—PERFECTION, FEAR, AND AMBITION

Of course, these anxious reactions have everything to do with an inner code of perfection which promotes fear and confuses ambitious goals. To the high-achieving perfectionist, issues of self-worth and marketability are measured against unrelenting standards of excellence which are both unreasonable and self-defeating. Many, many high achievers are guilt-ridden people who need to work harder than the others to prove themselves efficient, capable, and worthy. They are continually striving for success, competing with peers, pushing toward goals, and racing from human weakness. Unable or unwilling to comfortably delegate work or depend on the competence of others, the high-achieving perfectionist takes tremendous amounts of responsibility upon his or her shoulders and, as a result, *must know* every twist and turn on the industry map, plus commit to memory every possible route and junction. He or she has a schedule of appointments and tasks for any given day, either written down or mentally planned, that could easily provide three people with work. Failure is lurking just behind that closed door over there, and judgments are continually being formed to undermine their exacting performance. Therefore, they must strive harder!

Perfectionists never authentically believe they're right, and even when they've been rewarded for their talents, skills, or particular achievements, they become suspicious and begin to question the thoroughness of those in authority. If a project is handed in and complimented, the perfectionist will conclude that his or her supervisor missed the essential flaw in the document and will insist on pointing it out. And if four people accept their work, there's always the fifth to consider.

The perfectionist is also, ironically, bent on being *wrong*, even when all evidence is to the contrary. A man who dresses impeccably on his first day may encounter another newcomer who appears to be disheveled in appearance, perhaps a little unkempt. As a perfectionist the first man will assume that the other newcomer must be far more brilliant, intelligent, and maybe even of genius proportions to have been hired and, as a result, feel demeaned. Someone else will always eclipse his self-esteem.

As a consequence, the perfectionist becomes his or her own worst tyrant—self-deprecating and self-abusing. When they're not worrying about image, they're worrying about performance, and in order to control the anxiety they, by necessity, become inflexible in their behavior and rigid in their thinking. The inner life of the perfectionist is both chaotic and unyielding. They have to be fast on their feet because the external rules can take those unexpected shifts and throw him or her into a panic. In the new job situation, the rules are unknown and reactions are unpredictable: this is like being thrown into an emotional minefield. Not knowing what to say and whom to trust, like Laura, they sometimes resist any disclosures about themselves and write it off as "protectiveness."

PERFECTION, PROTECTION, AND PHOBIAS

It goes without saying, the first day on the job you must be protective about yourself. You want to learn as much as you can without revealing too much, yet resist the impulse to hide. To the perfectionist, being protective takes on exaggerated proportions and can easily slide into phobic behavior. Distinguishing between these two propositions would serve this person well. The protective person resists the tendency to allow the ticker tape of anxieties to be pulled out of their mouths; the phobic person will avoid contact for fear they will "mess up," "make a fatal mistake," or "utterly fail my first day out."

When you find that your protectiveness is becoming compulsive, even phobic, it would serve you well, not only for your future career, but also for all areas of your life, to think about what *mistakes* mean to you. It may become clearer if you write out a dialogue with yourself, or even tape-record your anxieties, and later, after relaxing, listen to a playback of your own voice. The dialogue might go something like this: "If I make a mistake the first day, I will be regarded as a fool. Why? Because only incompetent people are that stupid. How will that alter the behavior of others toward you? They would avoid me. And, how would that make you feel? Miserable and inept. And how will those feelings influence your performance? I'll be terribly insecure and afraid to assert myself again. What does that imply? That I'm basically worthless, will ultimately be found out, and lose my job."

This dialogue (which, of course, will be your version and your specific doubts) will serve not only to break down your hidden thinking process, but also to highlight the importance of becoming a mistake-proof person. Once you've understood how this dynamic rules your thinking and behavior, you might want to list or record the many disadvantages of becoming a patsy to the tyranny of mistakes. Most perfectionists will readily admit that they "wish they weren't this way." Querying them further, they will confess to the fear of their own inner controls. "When I'm scared of making a mistake, I can't add figures and hit the wrong numbers on the calculator," says a bank teller. "My desire to be perfect jams my thinking," reports a network consultant, who then adds, "My passive memory clams up and I confuse my words." Others have responded, "I'm too nervous to take creative risks," "too anxious to assert my opinions," "I agree with everyone and then resent them," "I end up talking out of both sides of my mouth," "my stomach knots up and I become irritable," "I don't want to be confronted by anything new—it's just too anxiety-provoking." These statements should provide you with enough insights into the negative nature of perfectionism to realize that this mode of thinking and feeling is the precursor to a very successful case of burn-out.

PERFECTION AND BURN-OUT

In *Burn-Out: The High Cost of High Achievement,* a definition of this term was suggested which has direct application to the perfectionist's personality: "Burn-Out: To deplete oneself, to exhaust one's physical and mental resources. To wear oneself out by excessively striving to reach some unrealistic expectation imposed by oneself or by the values of society." For those of you who enter a new job situation with an undertone of panicky conviction that you will fail, you could easily find yourself "excessively striving to reach some unrealistic expectation," way before your duties and responsibilities have even been firmly established.

It's difficult for the perfectionist to comprehend that life in this office existed before him or her, and that they've landed in the middle of a continuum. However, this can be attributed to the dual nature of the perfectionist's mind. One voice persistently whispers, "You're off!" "You're doing it wrong," "You're about to kill the whole job," while another voice, just as exacting, declares, "You can do this better than anyone else." Caught in the cross fire of these two suggestions, the perfectionist begins to take sides. One moment he or she will be filled with grandiose illusions about their talents and skill. Comes the next, they're berating themselves for being frauds.

This dichotomy can best be illustrated in the ambivalence of your arrival on the first Monday morning of the new job. On the one hand, you'd like the red carpet treatment—a trumpet blast, and a welcoming committee ready to usher you in. On the other, you'd like to slip in through the side entrance, take a peek around, and run home to change if your clothes are wrong. The desire for instant approval, admiration, and recognition is a powerful force, but the perception of yourself as a fraud is just as tough. Somewhere along the line a demanding, overcritical, judgmental parent went at you about your room, your clothes, your friends, your grades, and now, as an adult, the thirst for unconditional acceptance seems thoroughly unquenchable. Therefore, when you do receive the rewards, you're still looking for the punishment and any attempt to rest on a well-deserved laurel is short-lived.

So, how do you go about relieving this baffling and irksome emotional condition, especially when you're about to enter a new job? Understanding the dynamics is only one part of the process, and while it solves some mental riddles, it doesn't always help to change the feelings. Quite practically, you might begin to set up safe and protected situations where you can rehearse making mistakes, from the minuscule to the whopper. This may sound forced and unrealistic, but think further. If you are a compulsively neat individual, one who cannot tolerate a dust mote on the sill, what would happen if you left it alone for a week and refused to fuss with Fantastick? On a weightier note, when friends are discussing a book or article, what would happen if you admit you have not heard of the book and know nothing of the author? Watch their reactions, follow up the feelings that beset you and try to discern whether the anxiety over this "flaw" was greater than the expected punishment. By allowing yourself small mistakes (which could range from sloppiness to ignorance), you'll probably begin to see yourself more realistically and understand that you are permitted to be human—it may even be desirable.

In conversations with family or friends, offer a piece of information about yourself, something about your doubts or apprehensions, then observe the response. You might even speak of your first-day fears and ask how they resolved the same situation in their jobs. By fostering this kind of inquiry, you will have begun a process of reshaping your awareness, perhaps learn more about the real interplay between people, and could establish a new and nourishing intimacy. Once you've collected a series of adventures in imperfection, you might be more inclined to regard yourself kindly, and even develop a sense of humor over the "errors of your ways," at home and on the job.

THE WORK ENVIRONMENT— ONGOING ANXIETIES

Compounding as well as augmenting your own perfectionist anxieties, there will probably be many more issues with which to contend as the first day rolls into the first week and month. You may find that you're unclear as to authority, the delegation of responsibilities, and the dissemination of information. Who should be receiving what, and in which order? Should X have been the first to receive the data, or Y, and was that a no-no? How does the inner power structure work from inside out?

Then you might overhear disturbing conversations concerning raises given and withheld, promotions achieved and failed, and become uncertain about the monetary rewards attached to this position. If there are a lot of people coming and going, your job security might become threatened—"the turnover in this office is suspiciously fast-paced and key people seem to remain a very short time . . ." How about the evaluation system? What if you've been confiding in and complaining to the wrong person? *"That's* the one who's writing my report!"

What about the hailstorm of memos flying through the interoffice mail? You didn't count on this much writing, but everyone here seems to be intent on "covering his ass" in words. That means that you'll be writing one memo to cover the memo that Y sent last Tuesday, and another to X who needs to be informed (in a totally different style and with a much softer tone), just in case six months later, if either Y or X decides to blame you for the blunder at the meeting which you did not attend (even though you did verbally state yesterday to both of them you would be absent), you'll be off the hook because, yes, you did put it in writing. So you'll write plenty of memos and "cc" as many people as you can quickly summon up to cover every possible contingency. Then you'll be okay—unless, of course, you messed up on the power structure and placed the wrong name on top of the "cc" list.

At this point you may begin to feel a loss of control over what's happening around you. No one seems to be making decisions, and when they are, you aren't informed ahead of time that those decisions will be made or even told after the meeting (that you did not know about!), later in the afternoon, that they were. The intensity of this particular office, however, may be such that it fits your own perfectionism like a glove. When you've worked until 7:00 each evening four nights in a row, and on the fifth someone says, "Leaving early, huh?" you'll hope that no one else has noted your tendency to work "half days," or keep "banker's hours," and, along with taking work home, you'll stay until 7:30 five nights the next week.

These are but a few of the performance/perfectionist anxieties connected with the work environment which can ultimately diminish your life and keep you rooted to and obsessed by the need to prove you can make it, plus do it better each successive day. Unfortunately, after a given period of time, the high-achiever perfectionist soon finds his or her personal relationships falling apart, marriages on the rocks, no time to go out and meet a new man or woman, or even remember to send a birthday card to Dad.

Along with learning to accept yourself as fallible, you may also have to begin to lower your self-expectations. If you've just come into this job as a new marketing expert and they've been consistently losing money, you can't turn the company around in six months. It may take you, along with your new group, at least a year to develop a product. However, if you're riddled with anxiety, you'll probably tell them you'll have this licked in two weeks to a month, then become incredibly overwhelmed with pressure and stress, give up your personal life, suffer insomnia, complain to everyone, and become monomaniacal about this project you assured them you could deliver in twenty-three minutes!

You must learn to answer questions of time by allowing yourself a bit more than you realistically believe you can have it done. If you aren't sure of how long it will take to deliver, ask for twenty-four hours, even a week, to evaluate, assess, and discuss the project. You may not be given that job; the principals might expect the project delivered in twenty-three minutes, but you may land the next one, and your employers may appreciate an honest and realistic assessment of needed time. By hemming yourself in on these issues, the anxiety situation becomes self-perpetuating and, ultimately, it will be you who have worked to promote it.

Learn to listen and to ask for help and clarification. Another anxious reaction concerns the fear of appearing stupid. Therefore, when an assignment is delegated to you, and you miss some essential information, don't pretend you understand, then race around on a secret data-gathering mission. It wastes your time and keeps the anxiety well stoked. This also applies to setting priorities. If you're handed four assignments, find out which is needed immediately, which are important, and which ones can wait. Be sure to ask when each of the assignments is needed, and if the time allowed is too short to possibly complete it, you must learn to say so, and take your chances with the repercussions. However, try to complete the tasks you've begun. Don't let them pile up incomplete and find you're stuffing them in the back of drawers—you'll end up pacing and brooding through another series of sleepless nights.

There are some other anxieties which will demand your attention—those which concern personalities in the office. Many people have found that by keeping a log containing the who, when, where, and why of their anxieties on any given workday, they are able to focus in on the trouble spots. For example, one log may read: "The office manager makes me nervous . . . when he peruses my desk . . . because I'm certain he's displeased with the stacks of files waiting for review." Another example might read: "The vice-president gives me the shakes . . . when she stares at me . . . in her office . . . which makes me feel as if I'm lying . . . because I'm not certain what it is she wants me to say." This log will begin to give you a fairly accurate reading of your personality anxieties and help you to sort out the particulars of your daily dreads. Once you understand precisely which situations trigger your tension, you'll be able to begin to alter your perceptions and perhaps change some of your immediate responses to the people in question.

Additionally, for the high-achiever perfectionist, it would also be most important to learn to detach some from your job. Your work life isn't your entire life—you and your job are not as one, welded together for infinity. Perhaps a little unwinding during the day would give you the needed change of pace to view yourself from a new perspective. Relaxation techniques would be a valuable asset that could be employed several times during the workday. Try to go out for lunch alone once in a while, take a walk, or go to an exercise class (most health clubs, including the local Y's, now offer half-hour classes during the workday lunch hours). If your company has a gym attached to it, swim in the pool during the day, or go for a short run. It would also be to your advantage to begin to set some personal priorities. Decide just how many nights a week you can afford to work late and still maintain a private life (preferably no more than two), and begin to assert your need for evenings away from work. If your new style is incompatible with company policy, you may have to think about making some changes—it could be crucial to your life.

However, you still have that first day with which to contend, so let's return to Laura Best and discover how she could have minimized much of the anxiety in her situation.

If, like Laura, you enter the office on the first morning and are left to your own devices, you might prepare yourself for that contingency by asking your new boss for material to read which will lay the groundwork for a grasp on the current projects. Tell him or her you'd like to be updated and perhaps can save some time by studying any documents pertinent to your responsibilities. If he or she is on the run, ask if you can peruse some of the materials on the desk and, further, who might you introduce yourself to who could show you the ropes, or who might you approach on a peer level who could give you a basic orientation.

Try to remember: everyone who works was once a new employee. This situation is not unique. It's not the first moon landing where there are no role models. Most supervisors will understand and appreciate your concerns.

Most likely, you will *not* leave a trail of petty offenses if you approach a stranger and ask directions to the bathroom or even how to obtain a cup of coffee. The people in your new office are just as curious about you as you are about them and will probably be delighted to offer assistance. Most people thoroughly enjoy being needed, and take pleasure in aiding the new kid.

As for that Friendly guy who stops to complain about the budget—instead of your pretending to know everything he's talking about, this might be a good time to gather information. If he mentions the Jflkmlrt Account, it's okay to be baffled by what he said and to query him further on the client. Find out exactly what he does, his areas of responsibility and, without agreeing or disagreeing with his gripe regarding "those jerks on the thirty-fourth floor," simply demonstrate your interest and concern. By the time your supervisor returns, you'll be that much better equipped to grasp the basic concepts of your job.

It might be enlightening for you to remember that the person who hires you is most eager for you to work out. Since you are a reflection of his or her professional judgment, for at least the first six to nine months you'll be offered as much help, understanding, and assistance as is possible. The people who count are on your side. And, finally, it would be to your advantage to real-

ize that everyone from the new vice-president on down suffers
on the first day of the new job. However, it's temporary—the situational anxiety will pass—you'll survive it and, in a very short
time, probably look back and laugh.

Body and Beauty Image Anxiety

"We are so vain that we even care for the opinions of those we don't care for."
MARIE EBNER VON ESCHENBACH

CAN YOU EVER COME TO GRIPS WITH THE WAY YOU LOOK? MANY people never do and are continually butting up against occasions which trigger heavy doses of situational anxiety. Most image-anxious people spend lifetimes measuring their visual appeal against whoever else is in the room. Potential competitors are everywhere waiting to mock your thighs, ridicule your nose, or render a slur against your subversive split ends. These issues are particularly difficult for women. Society has not as yet provided them with the same visual endorsements as it has for men; therefore, the two sexes often respond to a poor self-image with different attitudes. Women tend to assume an apologetic mode for what they consider unattractive about themselves, while men often outwardly deny their self-consciousness and put on a tougher front.

However, the mental life for both is riddled with threatening scenarios, ranging from the subtle insult to the assaultive confrontation, all revolving around *that one area everyone is staring at!* That area assumes outsized proportions, carries its own spotlight, and obliterates any and all other features. You are no longer a person of many parts: you are a bulging stomach, a skin blemish, an underdeveloped muscle—you are, a FLAW!

This fear of scorn was probably acquired way back in grammar school, when the fifth-grade in-group gratuitously dished out such dandy little appellations as "the pole," "the fatty," "the weasel," or "the pox." Stuffing science books into your open locker, you trembled and prayed that the vicious finger of derision would point its saber at any poor slob but you and, as you prayed, Anxiety gave a roar. Closing the metal door, you probably concretized what in later years would come to be known as your specific Achilles' heel—skin, breasts, or penis size —and Vanity, making itself fully known, fell out of the locker and limped down the hall beside you.

Simultaneously, your uncles and aunts, parents, siblings, and cousins were probably gathering together over dinner tables, dropping scraps of information concerning neighbors (and even other relatives), which only helped to shore up your vision of expectations in the external world of good looks. "Big as a house," "skinny as a rail," "runt of the litter," "Well, his mother ought to watch what she puts on his plate!" resounded as chilling critiques that would haunt you for years, and if by chance your name was indiscriminately bandied about that same table, you spent the next few weeks fixing splints on Vanity's fractured feelings.

It's years later and the splints have now metamorphosed into cosmetic camouflage and earnest regimes—makeup, moustaches, and Clairol dyes; eye tucks, nose jobs, bottom lifts and top extenders; fad diets and fierce exercise—but the fear of being seen as different, odd, peculiar, or simply not good enough, lingers on. People no longer fling verbal affronts in your face, now they only *look*, and in the looking you know for sure that all they see is the Flaw. "Get off my back, chin, hips, thighs!" you long to scream out, but the Flaw is relentless. It shows up in every mirror and is reflected back in the eyes of all the important people-in-the-know.

Body and beauty image anxiety inevitably augments and amplifies the day before a cocktail party, the night before a job interview, and, most specifically and painfully, one week before summer is officially announced. The flat-of-bottom, small-of-chest, or squat-of-leg grow fearful and shy, but the overweight are particularly beset with grief come June. Summer is regarded as "flesh weather," a season when fat cells and flab have no place to hide, when one must rehearse the fifty reasons why they're comfortable wearing that jacket when it's ninety-two in the shade. "Let's go to the beach!" is an invitation so loaded with threat that it starts the anxious biting not only nails, but also wrists and toes. Uncomfortable, uneasy, and convinced the Flaw will be found out, they look to the kaftan for aid. Last year's play clothes are shunted aside, except perhaps for that one pair of shorts "which just might still fit." But as the shorts are pulled up over the hips, a tiny noise emanates from the seam which sends the system into shock and renders it insensible for the next six weeks.

The Sound of One Thread Popping

Along with the dentist's drill, the crack of lightning, and the words "I think we should talk," the sound of One Thread Popping stands firm in Anxiety's Hall of Noises Fame. This sound is no respecter of seasons or sex; it simply and indiscriminately sounds its snap and calls up a sturdy quorum of insecurities. One races to the mirror to check all angles, then begins to spew out resolutions and recriminations. The scale is resurrected, understudies like Butter Buds and Sweet 'n Low begin substituting for the stars, and the closet is suddenly filled with interesting shoes. Sitting becomes an agony—one must remember to pull the sweater over the bulge—and stooping is definitely out! No longer comfortable in any of your clothes, you prepare a uniform, a single ensemble to act as a baffle between you and the rest of humanity, and begin to worry excessively. You acquire peculiar mannerisms and behavioral styles—become a little shifty-eyed in public, laugh too hard at fat jokes, grow a beard, overspend at the Clinique counter, and get undressed in the dark. You decide it's time to move your body around, tone it up and trim it down, but you certainly can't be seen in this shape, so you decide to put it off. The word "exercise" begins to chafe and nettle—it seems to jump out of every magazine and mouth —and you find that you have no safe place to land but under the quilt and the covers, where you hope to dream it away.

When morning comes, and it does, you may decide to feed the

Flaw, which is now begging for "bad" food—a bagel or a Brown 'n Serve sausage—or, you may, like Joyce Nester, decide to brave the bullies at the Exercise Class.

SITUATION #1
The Exercise Class

Having heard more than one thread pop when she pulled on the wool pants, and having decided she certainly could not start jogging until she lost fifteen pounds, Joyce cleverly disguised her voice and called a local health club. She avoided those that advertised on TV—too many perfect human specimens with which to contend, all trim, toned, and tan, lolling about in Jacuzzis, waiting to scoff at excess poundage. The club she picked assured her that the personnel were all nonthreatening, that six classes were scheduled per day, that the clientele were all women, and, yes, of course, many of their members were "out of shape and over thirty."

She selected the 4:00 class (to "beat the rush at 5:00") and now, wearing her black leotard and tights, circa '64, peeks into the exercise room searching out one woman fatter than herself. The room is filled with Twigs. Some are wearing leg warmers, knitted affairs which augment the size of the thigh. A few Leaves are sporting colorful sashes looped around their stems, while others are attired in wild berry tank tops, tucked into Lilliputian running shorts. To her far right, a dazzling length of Seaweed is doing a backbend; to her right, a Sprout in a lemon leotard is doing the splits. There is not a stomach in sight: there is only waistline *slack*.

A Branch approaches, asks if she's registered and would she like to *weigh in.* "Sure!" she answers in an unnatural voice tinged with wild aggression, and while following her over to the *scale,* Joyce becomes inordinately involved with the texture of the mock grass carpet and longs for high heels. "Let's see," murmurs the Branch, "you're just at one . . . forty . . . nine. We'll put that on your personal chart and each time you come in you

can compare that with . . ." Lost in a maze of pulpy associations, Joyce does not hear the remainder of the spiel . . .

A Stalk smartly saunters by, casting no shadow. Joyce thinks
she hears a snicker, but knows for sure she saw the flicker of a
raised eyebrow. "Would you be interested in a massage?" the
Stalk inquires pleasantly. "There's an available opening right
now." "Ah . . . well, no, not today . . . I just want to take the
class, you know . . . *work out,*" Joyce replies, hoping to pass
herself off as a New Woman, perhaps a Jane Fonda who interestingly, and quite by accident, happened to swallow a lamp.
"Okay . . ." says the Stalk, her eyes lingering a bit too long on
Joyce's upper arms, "you may want one later . . . if so, just let
me know."

Inching over to the exercise area, Joyce positions herself in the
back of the room, a little to the left, where she can watch herself
in the mirror, yet remain invisible to the Vine who seems to be
in charge, and who is now counting heads—ten Ferns and one
Bush. They all appear to know one another, an observation
geared to make Joyce feel odd, peculiar, and big. Two of the
Ferns are wearing ankle weights and, while discussing the
merits of five-pound versus ten-, raise and lower their slender
limbs, grazing their cheekbones with their calves in the process!

Not knowing what to do with her face, Joyce now pretends to
a gymnastic knowledge and begins to vigorously exercise her
wrists. However, after ten turns to the right and the left, she
perceives that one cannot continue this practice indefinitely.
Bending over at the waist, she attempts to touch her toes, a
move she instantly regrets, when she finds herself awkwardly
stuck very near to the current hem length.

A newly arrived Perennial takes a position next to hers and
Joyce eyes her enviously. "You're in such terrific shape . . . you
must come here regularly," she asserts boldly, longing for a
friend to validate her life. The Perennial surveys Joyce from
nose to knees. "Nope," she says, "first time in six months," and
with that utterance, bends at the waist, sandwiching her head
between her ankles, which she agilely grasps with her hands.

Joyce stares at this acrobatic feat with awe and horror. It becomes quite clear that this woman is without inner thighs! Her

own bulges, lumps, and fat pads suddenly assume elephantine proportions. Gaping moronically in the mirror at her debauched self-neglect, she is simultaneously stricken with the perception that she is taking up too much space and is overwhelmed with the need to apologize.

The sound of disco music infiltrates the Garden and the Head Vine snaps her fingers, cuing the Plant Life into line. The Ferns leap into the rhythms with strength and gusto, bending, stretching, jumping, twisting, all in perfect synch. Joyce, too, throws herself into the driving beat and valiantly attempts to become as one with this amazing botanical chorus, but, Jesus! she doesn't know what they're doing! *No one told me about steps! No one mentioned routines! Am I the only one who doesn't know?* While flailing about on her feet, she wildly searches along the walls for a cosmic twin, a Wallflower who may have crept in late whom she can look to for solace. Her arms and legs frantically scatter and blur in the air—she's confusing up from down, back from front, and the music is mercilessly ahead of her feet. As the Ferns bend to the right, she lunges left, and as their arms stretch heavenward, hers are down in hell, totally missing the essential bounces and beats. Her pulse and nerves are playing handball with her heart, she's begun to sweat prematurely, and her cheeks have turned a strange shade of puce. Vowing to keep up and keep on, she tries to observe the Vine Instructor, *plus* do the breathing, *and* follow the steps, but makes a gross miscalculation, smacks a young Bud right in the lips, and instantly wishes she'd worn a mask.

"ONE-TWO, ONE-TWO, TO THE LEFT, TO THE RIGHT, UP-DOWN, DOWN-UP, IN-AND-OUT-AND-OUT-AND-IN, two, three, four," commands the Head Vine. "AND NOW—LET'S DO THE *CRUNCH!*" Eleven women with beautiful backs fall to the floor and, defying all natural laws, balance their weight on their tennis-ball buttocks and move their legs "TO-THE-CHEST-AND-OUT, TO-THE-CHEST-AND-OUT," fifty times and more, with nary a whimper or bang. "PUSH-UP TIME!" screams the Vine, "KEEP THOSE BELLIES OFF THE FLOOR . . . LET'S GO: DOWN-AND-UP AND DOWN-AND-UP AND HOLD, two, three, four . . ."

If it hurts, it must be doing some good, thinks Joyce as she crumps on the floor. But, while burying her nose in the mock grass rug, she finds she has acquired a pathological desire for a club sandwich.

When the class ends, she hobbles head down to the locker room. Although she is sweaty, hot, disgusted, and dazed, she refuses to enter that sauna and, further, will take her shower at home! After this humiliation, she certainly doesn't want to be seen nude (and she's not sure how to obtain a towel).

While sitting on a bench, her breath heaving, her feelings bruised, Joyce sees a group of women—Firs, Oaks, a few Shrubs, and a handful of Bushes—rush in. Busily undressing, donning leotards and tights, they laugh about "cellulites and lumps" and groan convivially over sore muscles and aching backs. A large woman with hips unexpectedly approaches Joyce. "You look like you've had some workout," she says, arranging her breasts inside a blue leotard. "Yes . . ." Joyce answers piteously. "Well," she says, now knotting her hair on top of her head with a barrette, "I admire your guts—that advanced class for dancers is a real killer."

On her way to the exit, Joyce stops for a moment to look in on the five o'clock class just commencing.

"Ladies," she clearly hears the Head Vine state, "no overtaxing of muscles—especially you first-timers. And if you don't understand an exercise, give me a signal and I'll explain it. We don't want anyone to walk away from here feeling bad."

While the summer months in the sun or the splitting of a crucial seam may prod many fearful people into anxiety-laden predicaments—situations they wouldn't have imagined they were capable of entering—a broken relationship is the right prescription for others. After the initial pain of rejection and/or separation has diminished, there does come a time when your pep talks to yourself pay off. In a sudden burst of enthusiasm and hope, you decide to make a New Life with a New Body and leave the Flaw sputtering by itself in the distant past.

SITUATIONAL ANXIETY

SITUATION #2
At the Health Club

The divorce and the flu were the motivational nudges Ron
needed. In the wake of both, he observed himself in the mirror:
a roll of fat threatened to obscure his belt; subtle chins had
crept under his pectorals; thin, sloping shoulders, an office pallor
. . . no! This was not the reflection of a worthy adversary! He
remembers college: then he was a man in "fighting shape," fleet
of foot and quick of limb, able to leap tall coeds and coaches—a
man in absolute control of his physique. Something happened.
He now vows to catapult himself out of the mass of moping iso-
lates into the membership of—the Body Elite. "Float like a butterfly, sting like a bee," he muses to himself as he packs his gear.
"Pow-pow." Two jabs and a lateral shuffle to the left send him
off to the Gym.

The sexy brunette receptionist reminds him of facility loca-
tions—*will there be more like her down at the pool?* He edges
toward the locker room pinching more than an inch on his middle, envisioning the disappearance of all this superfluous flesh
by the time he's ready to swim. A Mountain, dangling a diaper-
sized athletic supporter on his wrist, opens the locker next to his.
Ron stares, then blanches: . . . *couldn't bat a ball across a living room,* he smugly muses, grabbing for his sweat pants to conceal his Fruit-of-the-Looms. A nude piece of sculpted Lava
walks in and joins a naked Doric Column. "Whaddaya say?" he
hears the Lava growl. The Column massages a granite leg and
rumbles something barely audible which seems to be, ". . .
thought I'd come in and jiggle the old fat today." *Jig-gle-the-old-
fat,* Ron mocks silently, his face fixed in crazed smirk, *what
jerks!* Pulling his sweat shirt over his pants, he catches a peripheral view of this duo, quickly ascertains that all men were not
created equal, and slinks out of the room.

On an island in the center of the workout room, glistening-
bodied Olympians in bulging red and blue bikinis are preening
and waging savage war with Universal equipment. Ron lingers

around the edge, pulls at his cheeks, and pretends to assess the
merits of a squat bench. Raw Power is flexing his triceps, and
Brute Force is belching the iron he pumped and swallowed for a
midday snack. Muscular Density, a short chap with sharply
defined tendons and connective tissue, grunts, then releases a
massive barbell and glares at Ron. Panicked, Ron makes a circu-
lar "okay" sign with his thumb and forefinger, then awkwardly
backs off, fondling the tube of a hip flexor and kicking the leg of
a bench press on his way. "What a creep," he whispers to himself with a sudden wave of superiority . . . *probably makes an X
for a signature.*"

Ron moves onto the oval track, stepping out in a slow,
confident stride. Five or six others are running the course, and in
front of him a shapely blonde with hair swinging like a metronome above her turquoise sweat suit captures his attention.
Strengthened by the notion that his quadriceps have gained
definition, that his deltoids are padded with rock, and that he
may have found a date for dinner, he holds a steady pace
behind her. A lean, ascetic Centaur flies by, filling him with a
sudden and unreasoning hatred! Ron picks up speed and sprints
past the blonde, closing ranks with the galloping enemy, but the
burst is short-lived. His heartbeat has achieved alarming momentum, he's panting for oxygen, and he's stricken with the
desire to nap. The blonde has now passed him, along with an elderly couple in matching sweat suits. *F_____ pedestrians!*
he thinks, observing their effortless strides. Heaving and puffing,
he slows down and prays his pulse rate will go unnoticed. The
Racehorse overtakes him again, this time grazing Ron's arm. Ron
heroically resists the impulse to smash him in his otherworldly
eyes and blast him out of his arrogant endorphin high. However,
unwilling to take the chance of looking foolish, he jogs off the
track and conceals his painful gasps for air in a series of mascu-
line hamstring stretches. "'Way to go . . . !" someone yells out
from somewhere in that room, and Ron fires a deadly glare at
the gaunt runner who, he's convinced, sounded that jeer.

"What narcissism!" he says out loud on his way back to the
locker. After removing his sweat suit and securing a towel firmly
around his waist, he slips on his Zorries. "Pure crap!" he murmurs at the door to the sauna and, having convinced himself

that his own inner life is far more profound and rewarding, enters the hot room—and freezes!

The platforms are crowded with naked men, elbows pressed on knees, squeegeeing sweat off brows and chests. *Where the hell am I supposed to look!* The only vacant seat is on the third tier. Cautiously avoiding skin contact, Ron climbs through a sea of black and tan, acutely conscious of his own blinding whiteness. At the second tier, he rattles off a garbled "Excuse me," and loses his footing as well as his towel very near to the nostrils of a bronzed Gladiator, who shoots him a look of suspicion and contempt. "Sorry, man," he mumbles, clearing his throat, then scrambles up to the vacant seat, inadvertently grazing someone else's firm forearm with the soft slope of his own. To his left, in front, two Titans are discussing the Super Bowl, a subject on which he is infinitely knowledgeable, and as he tries to think of a penetrating comment with which to prove his worth and earn his tenure at the National Conference, a voice from his right murmurs, "pretty hot, huh . . . ?" and Ron perceives he's being "approached." *Can I take this guy in a fight?* he instantly thinks, then, steeling his jaw, he turns and finds himself eye to eye with True Grit. "Good for sustained endurance," Ron responds, adding a manly chuckle, then punches his own palm. Having no idea why he said that, he faces front and is immediately beset with a heavy bout of paranoia. Trapped and overwhelmed with the desire to urinate, he silently counts a full 300 seconds, then, in a cleverly devised jailbreak, pushes off from the thighs, mumbles something meaningfully charged concerning the ethos of fitness, and escapes down the tiers.

In the hall he surreptitiously checks his torso and becomes violently enraged when he finds the roll is still there! Furious with himself and with *this stupid culture which encourages cheap, puerile substitutes for real strength of character,* he decides to try the steam room.

The air is filled with hazy fog, and within the clouds of steam he discerns strange figures and forms. Vaguely disoriented and ready to attack, he hangs back by the door, hugging both his towel and the tile walls. Tense, alert, and revved to defend against whatever may be lurking in the billowing white, he wipes the flow of liquid from off his chest and waits for "a pres-

ence" to bump him. Something skims his calf: he whirls around
and wallops the air, then instantly perceives he has confronted
his towel. "Heh, heh . . ." he snickers audibly, praying those
witnessing his feckless swat will judge him mercifully. Feeling
weak, fluish, hot, and drained of essential fluids, he finds the
edge of a bench and sits, forcing himself to begin another
300-second count. At 182 seconds, however, having failed to
prove to whoever may be watching that he's *a man who can
take it*, he sheepishly slips out the door and heads for the
showers.

While keeping a tired eye peeled for antagonists, Ron lathers
up and, though experiencing a creeping exhaustion, makes a display of loudly humming an old school fight song. Back at the
locker, while changing into his swim trunks, he sneezes and
closes his watering eyes. Unwilling to call it a day, he summons
up a hardy snort and heads for that facility known for its hard,
sinewy competitors and brazen nymphets—the Pool.

There are three people milling around the blue rectangle. Two
he recognizes as the matching sweat-suited couple from the
track; the other he perceives as an easily forgettable, flabby
stranger. Unaccountably disappointed, he relinquishes his "Most
Valuable Player" pose, relaxes his stomach, lets his shoulders
naturally sag, and jumps in.

"Nice dive!" says the fat, bland stranger as Ron emerges from
the deep end. Pulling his trunks out of his crotch, Ron offers him
a tough but modest smile. "You work out often?" the stranger
continues. Giving this question some thought, Ron swings his
wet hair back off his forehead and sucks in his gut. "Nah . . ."
he replies casually, "just stopped in today to jiggle the old fat,"
and, having said these words, reaches down to massage his granite leg.

SELF-PERCEPTION AND
SELF-CONCEPT

For those who suffer a poor self-image of the body, the anxieties
accompanying any physical displays of the body, as in the above
situations, are most distressing. Set adrift from identity anchors
such as clothes, important affiliations, or verbal excellence, you

and your leotard—or trunks—become a naked statement of your own self-perception. And that's the most significant aspect of the entire body-image problem: the *self-perception* that forms the self-concept.

Above and beyond those messages you received from school chums and dinner-table gossip years ago, how you were treated in your home as a child functions as a fairly accurate indicator of how you view yourself today as an adult. If a parent or other important persons from the past tended to be belittlers, fault-finders, or harsh critics, that experience could easily have been transformed into a sturdy perception about you as a person that you cannot shake. Expressed and unexpressed disapproval can be psychologically manipulated in a number of ways. In order to finesse the painful "felt" judgments, a translation process begins. That cloudy feeling of "wrongness" is filtered through a series of self-critical ruminations and then fixes on the most vulnerable of targets: that which is invisible to the eye—the intelligence—and that which is most visible—the body. When one feels an overall inadequacy about themselves, there is a strong tendency to localize that inadequacy and project it out onto the body. Your size, shape, facial features, hair, posture, voice, and sometimes even smell—everything about your physical person—become suspect and are pulled into a murky vat of bad feeling. That feeling balloons, metamorphoses into a perception about your entire being, and becomes firmly ensconced in the mind as your dubious identity.

The physically and/or emotionally reluctant parent has much to do with the external image you carry around of yourself today. If affection or caring was withheld from you as a youngster, you probably looked to your siblings to see how you were measuring up. If the son was the favored child in the family—given the clothes, generous allowances, the new bicycle, *and* the admiration—the daughter could have come to *think* of herself as unacceptable and, as a consequence, *see* herself as homely, plain, gawky, or fat. In order to compensate for those unlovable feelings, she might have promoted them further by becoming defiant and uncaring about her appearance, or, she might have made herself highly seductive, covering her "wrongness" under a disguise of flashy makeup and sexy clothes to prove *through others* that she was, in fact, "okay." Conversely, if the daughter was favored—made to feel attractive, cuddly, respected, *and* loved—the son might have come to see himself as unprized, unworthy, a flop, and counteracted that response by becoming sloppy, unkempt, and morose, or by camouflaging his "wrongness" with the uniform of the local street gang.

This proposition, of course, works with all combinations: the dynamics between sister and sister, brother and brother are just as competitive and act as precursors to the same anxieties—you weren't as pretty, thin, voluptuous, vivacious, or intelligent as your sister then, and you're not now. You weren't as handsome, muscular, athletic, popular, or adept as your brother, and nothing seems to have changed. Comparisons abound, and the formula, created years ago, is carried out into the adult world and clung to with remarkable tenacity: *If* you could become physically acceptable—pretty or handsome—*then* you would be loved, admired, famous, successful . . .

YOUR PERSONAL PHOTOGRAPHIC RETROSPECTIVE

Since this image problem is so firmly entrenched within your psyche, it might be time to stop and take a solid, objective *look at yourself* from an external perspective. This can easily be accomplished by collecting pictures of yourself—by creating your own personal photographic retrospective. If you can possibly obtain the old family albums or even assorted snapshots from the past—baby pictures, childhood snapshots, teenage and young adult photos—you can begin to launch a historical image expedition.

Take a look at the group shots. Notice the positioning of family members, where they tended to place themselves and next to whom. Look for the body posture and attitudes of parents, siblings, other relatives, and, of course, yourself. Is there evidence of physical affection? Is anyone touching, and is anyone touching you? Are there arms wrapped around shoulders, waists, or necks, and is that arm stiffly placed there for the benefit of the photographer, or is it draped with a genuine feeling of intimacy and warmth? Are the people smiling spontaneously, or are they wearing posed "say 'cheese'" expressions?

Where are you in these pictures? What is your attitude? Do you appear often as the serious, self-effacing member; as the family "clown," making faces and sticking your tongue out at the camera; or as someone who seems to gravitate toward one particular family member wearing an expression of hope?

Also look for shifts in your own expressions and body posture from picture to picture, year to year. Was there a point in time when you suddenly appeared quite different, when you put on weight, started wearing heavy cosmetics, took on a sad, pensive quality, or blossomed into a false smiler? And is there a gap in the sequence of photos? Was there a year when you totally disappeared from the pictures? Try to remember what was happening in those periods of time—what caused the shifts and the absence.

You might want to sit with these memories for a while, reflect on the emotions they summon up, and compare them to your present feelings. You weren't born negatively disposed toward your looks—something happened. Once you've gained an insight into the past, go over the photographs once more. This time, consciously switch your vision and look at yourself through the eyes of a loving parent or sympathetic friend. If that baby, child, or troubled teenager elicits compassion, try to remember that he or she still resides within you and needs to be treated with care and respect.

Consider this personal photographic retrospective as a consciousness-raising session or an enlightening technique. It could ultimately act to alter your conditioning and provide you with an important embryo for a changing self-perception.

However, the anxious are influenced by not only family dynamics, but also standards set by the region in which they live, the schools they attend, the neighborhood, specific block, climate, political movements, social class, and professional ambitions. Yet, although the character of a particular community of people may encourage a certain "look," the nation, via the media (and specifically magazines, movies, and television), sets a standard of beauty and desirability which promotes even more anxiety in those who accept that "look" as an entree into social Nirvana. Those who continually strive to achieve that "look" and that perfection find themselves in perpetual competition with celluloid ghosts—distant cultural figures whose lives bear no relation to the realities of one's own. The struggle then becomes a *substitute* for genuine experience and frequently is catapulted into an obsession. At this point, you become a worthy candidate for burn-out.

If you are continually pitting yourself against a Jaclyn Smith or Diana Ross, Robert Redford or O. J. Simpson, your anxieties concerning your own image undoubtedly ascend to stratospheric heights. People who only see the external beauty of another ultimately become jammed: their vision becomes limited, constricted, and compressed, and exists in a locket-sized frame. Your poor self-perception could easily be creating an unreal response to life and blinding you to those aspects of yourself which offer pleasure, comfort, and even joy. Celebrity figures usually achieve their status through diligent work on a specific area and concentration on a particular talent of their own. You might begin to focus on the areas in which you excel, be it mechanics, sports, business, creative expression, conversation, or humor . . . Start integrating those facets of your character into the total image of yourself. Once you've accepted your own abilities *and* potential, and have ceased rejecting who you are, your self-perception will begin to shift and assume a more positive direction.

"Different is nice, but it sure isn't pretty, pretty is what it's about./I never met anyone who was different, who couldn't figure that out," sings the young dancer in the song entitled "At the Ballet." That insightful lyric, written by Edward Kleban for the hit show *A Chorus Line*, captures the essence of the body and beauty image anxiety endemic to our culture. "Different" is an anathema to acceptability, and when one feels left out or rejected, there are always several features with which to substantiate the snub. Your behind is too big or too flat; your breasts are too small or too large; your nose is too sharp, too wide, and "tilts just a tad too much to the left"; your eyes are set too far apart, too close together, are small, hooded, not the right color; your lips are too thin, too thick, and the teeth are certainly not perfect—"maybe I'll have them capped, or bonded!" Then, there's "these damned stocky legs." If you do find something which you *like*, something in which you take pride, well, that's easily eclipsed by the overwhelming evidence of saddlebag thighs! which, of course, is the feature everyone is talking about!

You probably have a deep conviction about your looks that has become unshakable. Perhaps it's time to start building a trust factor into your character by asking someone whom you know and whom you feel genuinely cares about your welfare just how he or she views you. Query a sister, brother, close friend, neighbor, colleague, and be specific! Tell them you're tired of feeling unattractive, different, even "ugly." Ask for an honest assessment. Find out what this person sees as your strong points and then if, indeed, he or she views your own personal *bête noire* as offensive. Use the answers you receive as INFORMATION—not as criticism! You might discover that this person has secretly been put off by a slovenliness in your appearance, or by the dark, somber colors you habitually wear, or by the way you slump when you stand—something about which you have been totally unaware! Then, again, you might find that the feature you most fear and loathe has completely escaped his or her notice! In any event, you will have ventured out of your bell jar of complexes and gotten some honest feedback.

Much like Joyce Nester, the woman at the exercise class, a bad self-image leads to distorted vision. You become a pushover for approval or disapproval from the outside world, and a patsy for your own misguided self-perception. Consider this moment in the life of an anxious woman:

You've just had your hair cut and it turned out beautifully—it's exactly the way you fantasized last night when you were flipping through magazines for styles. You're wearing an outstanding new dress which hangs just right and complements your skin tones and shape. Your makeup turned out perfectly and the mirror reflects the super image of a woman you actually *like!* What's more, you even feel a little smug about the whole package.

Your husband, mate, best friend, neighbor, drops in, takes a look and says: "What did you do to your hair?" After a flash-frame of horror and homicide, you might snap back, "I washed it and it shrank!" Or you might begin to blush and stutter . . .

"My hair? You don't like it . . . three people told me how well it looked . . . see, it's perfect because it covers my ears which jut out, and it emphasizes my eyes, which are too small . . . and, well, it distracts attention from my hips, which we all know are too large . . . you don't like it . . . *Well, I like it*, and I'm the only one who counts!"

Of course, that's not true. *You* are the last one who counts here! Your self-confidence plummets, your judgment is called into question, your taste is rendered tacky, and you're hurled back into all of the hideous anxieties concerning your person that you always suspected were absolutely true. You may even change back into your old, known uniform, pull out the Crazy Curl to redo this mess on your head, and wear a scarf and sunglasses for the next two weeks.

Now, listen again. What the other person said was this: "What did you do to your hair?" No judgments, no criticism, no slur! But in your vast insecurity and rising anxiety, you interpreted that question as a scorching rebuke and found it necessary to beat this person to the awful punch by letting him or her know that you know that he or she knows that you have flaws, and that you didn't for a minute think you were getting away with them!

This miserable self-perception not only creates a litany of verbal defenses ready to be flung at anyone who vaguely threatens your moment of body or beauty glory, it also colors your encounters with complete strangers who may or may not be suffering from their own poor body image. At a business lunch, one woman finds that the woman across the table avoids looking at her face, and perceives that this second woman finds her too unattractive and unacceptable to confront directly. The first woman loses her power and her edge and flubs the account. In reality, the second woman may herself be terrifically self-conscious about her own looks, or be privately suffering from indigestion. A man in a department store is told by a lean and muscular salesman with an acorn in his belly, ". . . and I won't go to the beach until I get rid of this flab." The listener leaves with no purchase, and is sacked out for a week, during which time he blurs his mirror image to avoid looking at what he now sees as a

basketball being dribbled in his own midsection. A raised eyebrow, a curt glance, a tight smile from someone else, and the
"bad feeling" announces itself and takes command.

If you find you are continually disabled by what you construe
as society's snakebites of disapproval, you might try this technique. Find the one, two, or three features about yourself that
you openly (or secretly) like, and write them down in a notebook. Then think back to the compliments you have received
from friends, your mate, a stranger in the Ladies' Room at Saks,
the neighbor with the new car with whom you stopped to chat.
At some point, someone has told you about your lovely hair,
disarming smile, fine sense of color, unique sense of style, interesting collection of ties, or beautiful hands. Write down everything you can remember—as foolish as it sounds! and keep
the notebook in a private nook of your own. The next time
you're zapped by a case of "bad looks," bring out the list and refresh your memory. This method has been most successful with
any number of people who sink into despair when they feel the
"good looks" deck has been unfairly dealt.

However, if you're truly disgruntled by the way you look, why
not give the image a change? Get your hair restyled, shave off
the beard, change your lipstick and blusher, and buy a new
outfit—one that is completely out of character with your usual
style. If you always find yourself purchasing thigh-length wrap-
pers to hide the bulges, try on a few waist-length short jackets
(you might find yourself standing taller). If you've always worn
"earth" colors to play down your body, buy something colorful
(it could lift your depressed expression). If you've always
tended to be a conservative dresser, experience wearing something loose and free . . .

If you're really stuck and can't budge from your pattern, you
might inquire about a consultation. Many of the larger department stores now offer this service free. A "Shopper" will interview you, find out about your life-style, take your sizes, and set
about the task of coordinating a wardrobe. The consultations are
private and, if your schedule is very busy, they'll even shop for
you, gather a collection of clothing, and then arrange for an appointment where you can evaluate the selection.

When you get the goods back home, you may find that you're

actually scared and begin to regret your decision. Before you write the new clothes off as a total caprice, wear them around home for a while, then to a neighbor's house, the grocery store, the movies, and, finally, to work. It may take time to accustom yourself to the new look.

Ironically, the "wrongness" you feel about your body image often has a sense of "rightness" about it. Many times the feeling of inadequacy is so familiar that one does not know how to live without it. As was mentioned earlier, those who are overweight have a particularly rough time with image. Over the past few years, this problem, as it relates to women, has been given careful attention. Many women will lose considerable amounts of weight, then gain it back after very few months. While the stoutness was fraught with self-conscious anxieties, the new, slender shape sometimes promotes new anxieties, which, at the time, seem insurmountable.

Having dieted strenuously and shed a couple of dress sizes, a woman may now find herself with a new external image which thoroughly delights her. However, unconsciously, she may not have been ready to shed the *need* for those pounds. Her old proportions may have served as a coping mechanism—a tangible reason to remain in the shadows, even underground. She may now find that she felt more comfortable with the added weight: less threatening to others and therefore treated with less suspicion; less powerful to others and offered more honesty; less scary to herself, for now, with the new, lean look, she becomes a contender, a person to be reckoned with in personal and professional encounters—someone who is *open to retaliation*. More important, along with the pounds, she may have lost her excuses for remaining passive. No longer able to postpone life because of this "weight business," she may suddenly understand that she used the pounds and inches as a scapegoat, a weapon with which to avoid risking intimacy or challenge. Nonetheless, she feels off balance, out of her depth, bewildered by the new confrontations set before her, confused by the attentions of others: in short, out of context with herself.

Along with purchasing clothing in the old, larger sizes, she might unconsciously find herself susceptible to colds and flu bugs, and, in some cases, even sustain an injury—a sprained ankle, a wrenched back—maladies to keep her at home, safely tucked away from the anxieties of the new image and life. Ultimately, unable to reconcile the outer image with the inner needs, she may begin to slowly reaccumulate the pounds and grow back into her familiar body.

Both men and women who suffer from overweight often use their weight to avoid intimacy with prospective lovers. That aspect of life is perpetually postponed, put on hold or in cold storage until that magical moment when the pounds and inches disappear and the *real* you will emerge from this fleshy costume. It's much easier and safer, however, to fantasize than to confront the risks and dangers out there. A common statement from those who are overweight and alone goes like this, "I feel bad enough as it is; if I go out there and am turned down, I'll feel worse . . . I guess I'd rather not know . . . Maybe that's why I stay where I am." This is a particularly succinct and honest statement and illustrates how a poor self-image can be used as a shield against the everyday threats of rejection.

If you, as an overweight person, have perceived one area in which you back off and "play possum," there are probably many other areas in which this system has infiltrated. Try to ascertain which aspects of your life have been shunted aside, deferred until the miracle of slimness descends upon you unbidden. You might come to understand that you haven't worked for a promotion, that you don't solicit new friends, have become wedded to weekend television, don't voice opposition, express anger, or make yourself known in a number of crucial areas. Many people, right now, are fixed in an untenable marriage or relationship simply because of their weight. They are afraid to vent their feelings for fear of being left, and if that should occur, they'll be subject to a forever state of loneliness.

If you're truly serious about changing these self-abusive patterns, you might have to start taking some new anxiety-laden risks. Choose one area in your life which you find troubling—perhaps at work—and slowly begin to assert yourself and your opinions in business situations. It will be frightening at first, but only because you probably believe the other people are thinking: "Why should we take him or her seriously?" This is a distorted notion, one whose validity must be tested and disproved by you. Once you've ventured this far, you may discover that, in short order, you've become hard pressed to keep quiet or down.

You're probably also avoiding parties, dances, lectures—public places where you can be seen and *judged*. The next time you're invited out, go to the party and, once again, make yourself known! Two events may occur: You may find that you're beginning to like yourself just as you are and be stunned by the pleasures you've been denying yourself for so many months or years. Then again, you may find that suddenly you're quite ready to change your habits and begin a schedule of diet and exercise which could significantly alter your life.

By the way, if you are a large woman and often feel you're being regarded as a pariah by the world of fashion, you're not alone. A fashion conspiracy seems to exist wherein large women are treated as second-class citizens who are only allowed to purchase polyester pants suits and seersucker shifts. This not only is insulting to the intelligence, but also serves as a dangerous trigger for self-recriminations and nagging doubts about one's importance. Fortunately this problem is receiving some publicity and, hopefully, the public and designer consciousness will be changed. In the meantime, there are specialty shops and special departments in stores which now cater to sizes 16 and above. Do some investigation at your local department stores. If they don't carry larger sizes, make a fuss! Don't accept this as a "given"; ask to speak with the buyers and complain. When enough women combine and make their requests heard, the sizing of designer labels could alter and save many women not only from the shopping indignities thrust upon them, but also from igniting a host of bad feelings about their image.

Of course, the anxieties surrounding a poor body image are not the exclusive properties of the overweight. Many people, specifically men, counteract their feelings of body inferiority by behaving with grandiose superiority. Like Ron in the Health Club situation, a sneer of disdain covers a multitude of insecurities and functions as yet another coping mechanism. The anxiety these people feel rests on the perception that if they act otherwise, they will be "found out." Someone out there will get an inkling of the *truth*, and the truth will open its big, ugly mouth and broadcast that they are not as good-looking, well built, powerful, or unafraid as they would have you believe. Many men who suffer from feelings of body inadequacy will make great physical displays of courage and bravado to conceal a fluttering pulse. Refusing to admit to feelings of insecurity, they try to suppress their fears (which could range from heights to violence) and jump headlong into daredevil activities. Attempting to appear mellow in the face of danger, some will eagerly join expeditions to scale the Himalayas, while others will toy with the notion of "taking that guy in a fight." When you've never climbed a fence, and the thought of having your face hurt heaves you into panic, these counterphobic responses only perpetuate the fear, augment the poor self-image, and simultaneously act to scare the hell out of you!

It would be prudent here to start taking your feelings seriously and stop proving to yourself that you're someone else. You don't have to sky-dive, scale mountains, or challenge the white rapids anymore—that system for coping with doubt has become worn-out and obsolete. It might be wise to go back again and look at the old photographs. Is there someone in those family snapshots to whom you still feel compelled to prove your worth? Perhaps you'll come to understand that your father, brother, or another male figure who withheld approval and recognition in your crucial, formative years is still psychically cracking the whip. This insight should prove significant enough to begin observing how you behave in front of that secret audience you carry around. One way to ease the compulsion is to talk to yourself about the problem. Tell yourself the truth: "You don't have to put yourself in danger anymore. It's unnecessary." Hopefully, in time, you'll come to understand what it means to be a good parent to yourself.

While you're at it, you might check out how your secret fears are affecting the ways in which you judge others. When one feels oppressed and undermined, there is an unconscious tendency to ape the oppressor and become just as harsh and critical. If you're anything like Ron, you may look at others who reflect your own body problems as "easily forgettable, flabby strangers." In dismissing others on the basis of their external image, you're perpetuating your own worst fears. By taking on the mantle of those you deplore, those whose attitudes cue your anxiety, you unconsciously become one of the elitist crowd. Perhaps if you began to befriend those who reflect your real or imagined body flaws, you might become more honest, more accepting, and more generous with yourself.

Another interesting aspect of bad-body-image anxiety concerns the phenomenon of spacial dimensions and perception. Those who do not accept their bodies are without intimate knowledge of the body's capabilities and have little conception of the height, breadth, and depth of their reach. When the body is alien, these spacial perceptions become clogged. An inability to ascertain how far a raised arm extends, how high a foot should lift, or how much space exists between you and objects becomes manifest. As a consequence, the person is sometimes seen as clumsy—someone who stumbles into walls, bumps into furniture, or leans too far back in the chair at restaurants. These people never quite know how far is back, how close is front, or how near is the side. When reaching for a wine or water glass, it inevitably tips; when stepping over a telephone wire, they're prone to trip; and there's a bruise which intermittently shows up on the thigh from ramming it into the corner of the dining room table.

This ineptness is often linked to a physical unawareness and is closely related to the classical split between the body and the head. The body becomes the poor relation of the mind, a legacy that must be lugged around, dressed in uniforms, and treated with patronizing disdain. It follows, of course, that posture and carriage are neglected, and, many times, unless told, the person will have no idea that he or she is walking hunched over with their spines in an "S". Disconnected from "this thing below the neck," they may spend a great deal of time conpensating with the head, growing baroque facial adornments—moustaches, sideburns, and beards—or lingering around cosmetic counters where the "right" colors of lashes, lids, and lips become the prime focus for improvement. The body becomes recognizable only as an object on which to hang clothes, eliminate wastes, and to remind them of mortality. However, body avoidance has a cause, and if it's being rejected, subtly or blatantly, you may have to find new ways of accepting it back into the entire family.

If your inhibitions have conditioned you to walk with a slump and avoid eye contact by looking down, you may want to begin by changing this attitude. Perhaps what you view most of the time is the carpet or the sidewalk. If so, you're probably perceived by others as a person in a constant state of apology. Then again, you may be viewed as suspicious and shifty-eyed—character traits which cause people to take a wide berth around you, cuing even more self-consciousness. When you begin to look people in the eye, speaking or listening, you'll be perceived as more assertive and alert, and be responded to more emphatically and with genuine interest.

In order to change your posture, you may have to become sensitive to your body's messages—its aches and its pains. If you continually suffer from headaches, stiff necks, back pains (upper or lower), you might begin remedying these anguishing ailments by making some practical changes in your home. Look at the chairs and couches in your living room. Take special note of your favorite sitting place. Is that chair or divan a place where you spend hours slouching over, "relaxing" with a twisted spine? How about the mattress on which you spend approximately one third of your day? It might have run out of spunk some time ago and is now simply accepting your body's contours and offering no support. It could be time to buy a new bed, one that will help you to straighten out. Then there're your shoes. Three-inch heels may make you appear trimmer, sexier, and fashionable, but if they're a threat to your survival on the streets and in the office, try descending an inch. Women who change from high heels to flats several times a day are vulnerable to spine ailments, and therefore to a feeling of being ungrounded. Choose a heel size that is compatible with your life-style; you'll walk and stand with more authority and experience a better sense of control.

However, quite obviously, the best way to ultimately befriend your own body is by using it, which takes us back to our anxiety situations with Joyce and Ron.

The catch-22 in attending an exercise class when you're horribly self-conscious about the shape your body is in, rests on the fact that you really don't want to join a class until you do look better, and you won't look better until you attend. Therefore, you might as well make the trip as easy on yourself as possible. Do take a friend with you the first time out. In this way, you'll diminish the feeling of aloneness and oddness and provide yourself with someone to turn to when your anxieties spiral. That person could also prove most valuable in validating your perceptions about the procedure, as well as the level of the class. If Joyce had been with a friend, she might have trusted her instincts and accepted the fact that she was in above her head, competing with women who were, for sure, professional dancers.

If you haven't used your body in a while and you do sign up for a class, by all means speak to the instructor before it begins. Don't hide in the back row where you won't be noticed; introduce yourself to her and explain your particular problems—how long it's been since you've exercised, your need to go slowly, and your desire to have the routines explained more than once. Although most instructors will ask the students to push themselves that one step further, if you've been sitting behind a desk for seven years and your only exercise has been jumping into your car, taxis, or buses, you'll need to build up speed and stamina slowly. Don't be embarrassed to stop when you're overtired or hurting—the other women in the class have probably been at it much longer than you.

As for the Health Club, even if you do know the routines, if you've just gotten out of bed from the flu and haven't exercised for close to a year, you're not going to be ready to compete with Centaurs or Raw Power. If you're just too embarrassed to show yourself in a public place before you've become a "worthy adversary," you might first begin an exercise program in the privacy of your home. In this way you can build yourself up to what may be experienced later as your "physical debut" and enter the gym secure in your ability to present yourself as "a man who can take it." (Unfortunately, advertisements for health clubs and spas do not inspire confidence in those who nurture a poor self-image. The models seem to have been drafted from *Playboy* and Joe Weider's *Muscle and Fitness*. However, don't

be intimidated: real people with flaws like yours do make frequent appearances.)

Finally, for those who genuinely suffer from the situational
anxiety endemic to a poor body or beauty image, you might consider this question: If there were no mirrors in your home, how
would you ultimately perceive yourself?

TEN

Doctor, Dentist, and Shrink Anxiety

"Many illnesses are promoted from the third-rate to the first-rate by the anxious mind."
ERIC PARTRIDGE

WE ALL ARE CONSCIOUS OF GOOD HEALTH AND WE ALL WANT A clean bill attached to our records, but everyone's scared to go. Doctor appointments of any kind are universally accepted as occasions for hardy seizures of situational anxiety. The impending appointment is fraught with quintessential questions of mortality, abnormality, money, pain, and whether the Doctor will or will not take to you personally.

The ramifications of these visits are ominous and unpredictable. Many situationally anxious people find that their Symptom, previously noted as quiet, little, and benign, is now charged with eminent forebodings. They begin to flirt with the Inevitable, are humbled by the Unthinkable, and move to the rhythms of anxiety's swan song. Nothing is now what it originally seemed to be: the sniffles are a manifestation of fatal pleurisy; that sensitive incisor, a definite portent of jaw extraction; difficulty with authority figures, a sure sign of a terminal character disorder. The locus of existence now revolves around awareness of the Symptom, and the Symptom stands as a possible brush with death.

Anxiety, however, is a tricky magician. For some people, once the appointment has been made, the Symptom fades away. This miraculous event gives credence to the notion that the Symptom was psychosomatically induced, which gets them off the medical hook but encourages grave doubts pertaining to the soundness of the mind. While these people may initially welcome the disappearance of the Symptom, the memory of it lingers on and they soon find themselves seeking out signs of it, hoping, praying it will reappear.

There are still other anxious people who avoid making an appointment at all. Admitting to pain, hurt, or discomfort is not compatible with the plans for their lives. By maintaining a rigid attitude toward doctors, they can stave off a confrontation with what could be Final Knowledge and continue to hope that whatever may or may not be wrong (1) will simply get tired of waiting and slink away in the night, (2) prove to be the product of a temporary stressful event, or (3) will behave benignly until those researchers out there discover the ultimate cure.

In any case, whether you dramatize or deny the Symptom, if and when you do keep that appointment, certain truths will issue forth. Gourmandizing, smoking, drink or drug abuse, and all those secret promiscuities from your private underground life will be exposed, considered, explored, and perhaps taken from your playground. The Doctor, renowned as a healer of human ills, is metamorphosed into nothing less than the Grim Reaper of Authority—a specter of doom who stands ready to denounce your self-neglect, self-indulgence, and fun and, in the final analysis, just may inform you that your willy-nilly pizza days are numbered.

Compounding these anxieties is the vulnerable position in which you, the patient, are placed. A wide assortment of personal indignities are waiting in the examining room to attack and devour. On the M.D.'s table, private orifices are pryed open, felt, and viewed; on the Dentist's Barca-lounger, your mouth is objectified and stuffed with cold equipment; and in the Therapist's office, that wizard in the Eames chair plumbs the secret holes of your unconscious, trapping the hidden emotional sludge. It's difficult to maintain appearances when you're wearing a paper dress, it's impossible to speak intelligently with a saliva ejector hooked under your tongue, and it's hard to pass yourself off as a "normal" when Freud is staring into your soul, silently raking up your dark libidinal impulses.

Yet, while these indignities stoke anxiety's coals, another concern takes a giant step into your jittery awareness: *does the Doctor like you.* This is an issue of great complexity, for it means not only that your case be different from those run-of-the-mill common colds, cavities, or classical neuroses, but also that you make a lasting and favorable impression—perhaps even a conquest—through your carefully conceived case presentation. The benefits of this accomplishment have far-reaching implications. If you can indeed penetrate that aura of infallibility, you stand a good chance of (1) getting an emergency number for weekends and evenings, and (2) being remembered.

Although patient profiles vary, there are distinct differences between the kinds of situational anxiety you may experience on your visit to these three professional people: the Medical Doctor almost always provokes scary issues of life and death; the Dentist is associated with pain; and the Therapist summons up images of embarrassment and exposure. These three orientations are often confused by blanket issues of money and approval which slip in and out of each appointment. However, variables notwithstanding, these distinctions should provide insight into the discontent, ambivalence, and situational anxiety in the patient's mind.

SITUATION #1
The Doctor's Office—Checkup

Before Michael goes to the Doctor, although he consciously fears bankruptcy, waiting, and the rectal exam, he tells his wife this: ". . . just for the record, Jan, you know where the Will is, don't you? Second drawer of the white file, far wall in the office. Sam—the attorney's name is Sam . . ." However, when he arrives, the snazzy address, original art on the waiting room walls, and the reading material—*Forbes, Gentlemen's Quarterly,* and the *American Collector*—revive his surface concerns: they all point to a substantial nick in his wallet.

Right now, he's looking at that self-satisfied receptionist whose manner suggests three generations of Women Devoted to the

Fierce Protection of Doctors, *who knows about my hemorrhoids!* (She had a subtle smirk on her face when he checked in.) These other people in the waiting room aren't helping to ease his anxieties either: Junior League ladies, wealthy widows, and Type A corporates with rep ties and Bally wingtips, *who've never known a moment's pain and have the cartel on longevity* . . . Although Michael dressed carefully for this visit to avoid these feelings—wears his power suit and shoes for authority and a cotton Oxford shirt for authenticity—he nonetheless feels compelled to make a showy display of elitist exasperation, and at intervals emits a snort of upper-class annoyance.

Michael has witnessed the Doctor's chumminess with certain patients, people who obviously travel in the same social circle and call him by his first name, something Michael has never dared to do, *even though he calls me "Mike."* The receptionist, too, displays an intimacy with *those* patients: she is appropriately flirtatious and blushes when they call her "Lizzy." *Lizzy! . . . always been "Mrs. Lincoln" to me . . .*

The sound of chatter and muffled laughter emanating from the rooms beyond convince him that the Doctor is enjoying some light banter with a *healthy and important society patient, when it could all be over for me within weeks!* Michael mentally scrambles for a few amusing anecdotes of his own with which to compete, but can only remember an old Henny Youngman joke, the punch line of which completely eludes him. While Michael frantically wags his crossed leg, a tall distinguished gentleman, bearing a remarkable resemblance to William Buckley, emerges from the inner sanctum, followed some fifteen minutes later by a woman who's *a dead ringer for Dina Merrill!* Michael's stomach lurches and his face stiffens. Again he perceives just why he's so often given the old medical brushoff and begins to grind his teeth.

Simultaneously he is stricken by the thought that his *symptoms may not be all that significant*—perhaps he exaggerated their importance! But no, he's pretty certain he's on his way out. He did ask a woman in his office who knows everything medical. After all, *she's raised three children, knows all the diseases, symptoms, and cures . . . and (off the record), she said I was definitely suffering from a dangerous ulcer, maybe peptic, possi-*

bly even perforated, and occasionally FATAL, because "my sec-
ond cousin in Ohio is married to a man who had the exact same
thing and he was hospitalized, and then, well . . ." So, it's serious. However, it may not be noteworthy and, worse, Michael
fears that his symptoms may have disappeared! Horrified, he
secretly presses at his belly and is relieved to find he's still in
pain.

When he's finally ushered into the examining room, he's
handed a gown and paper slippers by a young, lively nurse. To
keep up appearances in his final hours, Michael subtly comes on
to her, but just as he's arranged his eyes to illuminate erotic
knowledge, she hands him a Dixie cup and says, "Don't give me
the first or last drops—just what's in the middle." These instructions are followed by a sly wink, which strips him of his sexual
prowess. He changes into his gown, prudently ties it in back,
and peers out the door into the hall. Finding it empty, he
shuffles down the corridor, acutely aware that his feet are
crackling. In the bathroom, both his apprehensions and his inability to urinate intensify. *I can't go. Nothing's coming. How*
long should I stay in here? I could lie and say I did, but forgot
the cup . . . But those concerns are short-lived. He runs the
water, looks to the ceiling, and Eureka! *What now? Do I bring*
this back to the room myself, or what? Is someone supposed to
meet me here? He certainly can't leave it on the sink—*it isn't la-*
beled! So he'll carry it back himself. Sneaking down the hall,
specimen in hand, he meets up with a gorgeous blond Valkyrie
wearing a fur cape and, in a trice, understands the impulse to
faint. Grinning sheepishly, Michael offers her an exaggerated
shrug of apology, watches her visibly recoil against the wall,
then scurries back to the safety of the room.

The instruments in the examining room tinker with his worst
fears: *things to poke, slice, insert, pierce . . .* Maybe he'll open
the drug cabinet and kill some time by reading the labels on the
sample pharmaceuticals, but no, someone could fling open the
door and misconstrue his intention . . . think he's *a closet addict*
or something. He decides to weigh himself instead, and just in
case he's being secretly observed through any two-way mirrors,
he steps on and off the scale whistling an upbeat version of a
Mahler theme.

Incarcerated in that room, folding and unfolding his arms, he paces and waits *for the Great Man to appear.* Preparing an angry diatribe which his symptoms *will more than justify,* he checks his watch for the forty-sixth time. "This is outrageous!" he says to the box of rubber gloves, and decides to dress, get the hell out of here, and find a real Doctor who respects the Hippocratic oath. "Okay, five more minutes," he says to the tongue depressors, "and that's it!"

The door flies open and the Doctor breezes in, his white coat and stethoscope flapping fore and aft. Michael receives a flash of a dazzling society smile, but before he can return it in kind, the Doctor has already looked away and, after checking the tab on the file, murmurs, "Well, how're you feeling, *Mike?*" Without waiting for the answer or the particulars of this visit, he launches an attack on Michael's body, knocking here, squeezing there, pressing, poking, and peering. Before Michael can utter, ". . . stomach pains, scared . . ." the Doctor has made an assumption and *thinks I'm here for my hemorrhoids!* "No, you see, I'm here because . . ." but his words are muffled by the instructions to "lean over," "relax," and "move back."

Michael cringes inwardly, *there must be a "right" way to do this* . . . and tenses up because he knows that the Doctor is judging his performance, pitting him against the pros. Uncertain as to whether he will or will not defecate and/or emit a foul noise which will bar him from medical offices on both coasts, Michael scrunches up his eyes. He tries his damndest to relax, to loosen up—*he's gonna hurt me! I know it . . . and he's gonna get impatient and annoyed and won't like me*—but the harder he tries the tighter he becomes, and he knows his shrinking extremities are proving conclusively that he is, indeed, a true provincial.

"Okay," says the Doctor, retreating. But now Michael's stuck with this mortifying business of getting back onto his feet. *What expression should I have on my face?* If he seems too blasé and unconcerned, the Doctor might think he's gay; if he seems too shaken, he'll be construed as odd, maybe even unstable; if he makes a joke, the Doctor could believe *I got off on it!* and suspect him of a kinky aberration—certainly not the kind of person to invite into his societal clique.

"So," Michael begins after adjusting his face, "I think I'm in trouble: I've got these pains here, and . . ." but a series of interruptions commence. Other patients in Examination Rooms A, C, and D are also waiting, and this assembly-line approach to medicine keeps the Doctor hopping away for "just a few minutes," which translates into a mean of fifteen. The telephone buzzes a few times, and he hears the Doctor prescribe, advise, and order, as well as chat with his wife, cousin, colleague, and son, which all suggests to Michael not only that his case is uncompelling, but also that he's been forgotten.

As the Doctor drops the receiver, Michael abruptly steals this opportunity to define his symptoms. The Doctor listens, *why did he raise his eyebrow?* and seems to absorb, *what does that nod mean?* then suddenly whisks out of the room, which Michael construes as either a sign of impending doom, or that the examination has been concluded. Not knowing exactly what he should do, he slowly dresses and worries over whether he should simply barge into the Doctor's private office, or linger around the hallway and hope someone will find him. It's quite obvious that *if I was part of the "inner cabal," I'd know what to do,* but he isn't, so he sort of hangs around the closed door feeling inept. Building up a sufficient rage and *ready to get some straight answers!,* he bursts inside. No one is there.

The Doctor flies into the office, blurs through the room, and sits behind his desk. Furious, Michael brushes lint off his power suit and again rattles off his symptoms, this time dropping words like "duodenal," "gastric," "esophageal," and "pyloric," *just to keep the rosters straight on who's who and what's what.* However, he hears himself back as confused and unschooled, and just as he finishes up, the Doctor, who has been doodling on a prescription pad, answers another call. "Sorry about these interruptions, Mike," the Doctor says, "we've had a number of *important emergencies* today." He then launches a familiar dissertation on the evils of "stress and tension," the need for "proper rest and diet," speeding up as he ticks off a follow-up lecture on "the high occurrence of gastritis among today's burned-out professionals who are competitive, chronically fatigued, heavy smokers, and drink excessively at business lunches." He assures Michael that this life-style has everything to do with not only his hemorrhoidal condition, but also his stomach pains, and the woman in his office? "Well, everyone likes to think they're a Doctor . . ." He prescribes a diet, which Michael does not hear, discusses the need for exercise, which Michael blocks out, and writes a prescription for a new medication, which Michael does not need.

"But I'm *sure* this is an ulcer!" Michael says, eyeing him with deep distrust. The Doctor rises from his seat, cuing the end of the interview. Michael stands, the Doctor shakes his hand and, before flying out the door, flashes another dazzling smile. "One more thing, Doctor . . ." Michael hollers, trying to hail the flapping white coat, *just one more question, damn it!* . . . but the Doctor has disappeared.

On his way past the receptionist's desk, he toys with the idea of asking her the cost of this visit, or maybe collecting insurance forms, but he nixes that impulse . . . *it's kind of pedestrian to bother her with something as mundane as Blue Cross.* When he returns to the office, *I'll have my secretary give her a call . . .*

Later, while trying to reconstruct just what was said in that office, Michael decides that, although this particular Doctor is noted for his gastrointestinal expertise, he still feels uneasy. He makes a note on his calendar to ask Joe and Charlie for the names of their men.

However, it's months later, and he hasn't done that yet. He doesn't know if there actually is a better man; he suspects his guy might just have been having an "off" day; and, although his stomach still hurts, he really doesn't know how to ask for his medical files without hurting the Doctor's feelings.

SITUATION #2
The Doctor's Office—the Gynecological Examination

She's been through Assertiveness Training, Executive Seminars (in three major cities), Self-Actualization, and a course in Tran-

scendental Meditation. Yet, when Jessie walks into a gynecologist's office, she turns to mush.

Unlike Michael, she has few compunctions about changing
doctors (*none of them makes me comfortable*) and within one
year has seen three. The first was Dr. Miller, an elderly gentleman, who was given to saying, "There, there . . ." The second
was a younger man who wore Gucci shoes and insisted on being
called "Jack"; and the third, a woman, Dr. Bridge, who had to
be no more than two years older than Jessie—perhaps much less.

In January, when the itch got bad, she broke out the underpants, the plain whites with no drooping elastics, performed all
the necessary feminine hygiene rituals, and went to her appointment with Dr. Miller. While filling out the Personal History
chart in the waiting room, she was attacked by nerves and forgot how to spell "diaphragm."

"Nice to see you, nice to see you," Dr. Miller said as he entered the Examination Room. Viewing him for the first time, she
perceived she was with the wrong man. (*I can't ask him to
check my diaphragm! He'll know I "do it." Oh, stop it! . . . he's
a DOCTOR, for God's sake! Yes, but he'll disapprove and lose
respect. Listen, you're a grown woman! So what, he's fairly conservative—I can tell by his glasses. Then just tell him about the
itch. What itch? It's not there now!*)

Her toes shook as she slid down the paper and secured her
feet in the cold stirrups, and she found it difficult to keep her
knees closed in that position. "Scoot down, scoot down," the
kindly Doctor said, "and relax . . . just going to look at your
'whatchamacallit' . . ." She looked to the ceiling and thought of
England, then at the nurse lurking in the corner, but her real
awareness was focused on the disembodied voice emanating
from an alien male hairline visually located between her sheeted
knees. The voice spoke of current happenings—the snow storm
in Detroit, his new grandson—non sequiturs culled from life and
geared to distract. "There, there . . ." he finally said, "your
'thingamajig' is just fine . . . fine. You can move back now."

During the breast exam, no one spoke. She shot a look at the
nurse to see if she was watching and then pretended it wasn't
happening; he seemed to be listening for lumps. "You don't feel

anything, do you?" she managed to squeak out. "Not a thing . . . you're just fine," he said, adding a reassuring wink. (*Was that meant as a slur?*)

She dressed and went into his office for some final words. "I think I need a new dia—" she began, then, observing the family photo on his desk, changed her mind and expressed some concern regarding her cramps. "Common problem, common . . ." he said, ". . . nothing to worry about. A couple of Tylenol will fix you right up . . . you're a healthy young woman."

As she left that office, she understood perfectly why she never mentioned the itch.

By May she needed a bottle brush, and got the name of a younger Doctor from her good friend Ruth. This time she purchased new print bikinis, bathed, shaved her legs and underarms, and douched excessively.

Sitting in his waiting room, filling out a Personal History chart, she completely forgot the date of her last period and found herself stealing an answer from the woman sitting next to her.

"Hello, Doctor," she said, this time using her Assertiveness Training, "I'm Jessie Frank."

The handsome Adonis grasped her hand firmly in both of his. "Hi, there . . . just forget the 'Doctor' stuff—call me 'Jack.' You're Jessie, right? So, Jessie, what's your problem?" Straining to remember why she was there, her face became mottled, and her eyes adhered to his shoes. "Well," he said, looking at her chart, "never mind, we'll just have a look-see."

(*What do I do now? If I'm too facile and adept, he'll think I'm an exhibitionist—a woman eager to fling herself at him. If I'm too tentative, he'll think I'm inhibited and I'll lose my edge. What do other women do? What the hell is acceptable and . . . right? Oh, get on with it! No, I can't. This is humiliating—I'm paying a stranger to stare at me!*)

Feeling much like a fugitive from rationality, while he chatted with her vagina about the new Cultural Center, his new Audi, and a "nifty new restaurant down the block," Jessie looked to the ceiling pretending she was really in Montego Bay and that she was definitely somebody else. Further, the exclusivity between

"Jack" and her nether zone stopped her from asking questions, or in any way "butting in."

"Well, looks good to me," he said, finally addressing *her*.

"Um . . . what about the itch, I mean, I think I've got a yeast infection, oh, not terribly troublesome, but, you know, from time to time it . . . itches."

"Infection? I didn't see any signs of— Did you *douche* before you left home?"

(*DOUCHE! That's too personal . . . God! he thinks I worry about odors, that I did this just for the appointment, that I'm not always so scrupulous, that I may be naturally . . . dirty. It's really none of his business!*) "Yes . . . I always do . . . every day of my life," she answered defensively. (*Why am I lying?*)

"There's your answer," he said, pointing a class ring at his own temple. "Can't see the infection if all signs of it are washed away!" and Jessie immediately felt disgraced for being clean. At that point, she decided not to mention the diaphragm business. (*What if I'm wider than other women?*)

In a gesture of alarming intimacy, he then gently removed the gown from her shoulders and began the breast exam. Suspecting him for a moment of legitimized fondling, she then began to worry over how flat her breasts looked lying down, but worse, the room was cold and she was tense. (*My nipples are contracting! He's sure to think I'm susceptible to being touched, not just by him, but by anyone!*) Then, of course, she was terribly concerned, even panicked, by the lumpiness she felt the past few months, and when he said, "You're fine," she didn't believe him.

"Didn't you feel those lumps?" she asked.

"Where?"

"Right there," she said, pointing to the general area.

"There's nothing there," he said, giving another press.

"Yes, I felt it."

"Feel again and show me exactly where."

"Well . . ." she said, mortified at feeling herself in front of him and asking him to feel her again so he'd feel what she felt.

"That's nothing—it's a thickness," he said, and she feigned a measure of relief. "Do you know how to give yourself a breast exam," he went on. "Do you want me to show you how?"

"NO!" she answered much too loudly. "*I know all about that!*"

Sitting in his office, her legs tidily crossed, she reported her experience with cramps. With his hands in front of him, thumbs forming a tent, he rattled off, "Percodan for pain, Monistat 7 for the infection . . . Need any tranqs? Just kidding." After he'd written out the prescriptions, he handed them to her. "Good to meet you," he said, and as she walked out the door she thought she heard him say, "Take it easy, babe, we'll see you in six months."

By September she'd had two cold-fear pregnancy scares and was determined to get a new diaphragm. This time, however, she'd see a woman doctor, someone to whom she could relate, and she obtained the name of Dr. Bridge from her neighbor Sue. She bought sensible underpants with a cotton crotch, and bathed only. Having eluded all memory lapses while filling out her chart, she casually flipped through an issue of *Country Living*.

However, after meeting Dr. Bridge in person, she began to feel uneasy. This was not the Dr. Bridge in her head, the older, mature woman with a graying chignon and wisdom to disperse, but a slim, young person with short brown curls, very much like her own. (*Is that a permanent?*) "Hello, Ms. Frank," she said. "I'm Dr. Bridge."

After arranging her body on the rack, Jessie realized she was just as anxious in front of this woman as she had been with the men, especially since she was a *contemporary!* (*This is a whole new ball game, kid . . . never exposed this part of your body to a woman. Should I be doing it differently? Stop it! She's got the same things you have! That's what I mean . . . she'll know. Know what?*)

Dr. Bridge didn't sheet her knees or give her time to drift off toward the ceiling. As she examined Jessie, she spoke: "You've got a little yeast infection here, must be uncomfortable . . . By the way, so you'll know what I'm doing, I'm taking a PAP smear now. Are you having pains during intercourse? How about menstrual cramps?"

(*INTERCOURSE! What did she see? Something's wrong . . . I knew it.*) "Why did you ask me that?"

"Oh, because you wrote on your chart that you have heavy periods."

"No . . . about the pain during . . ."

"No reason . . . I thought the—"

"No, you can be honest, what did you see?" said Jessie, cutting her off.

"Well, those yeast infections can be very unpleasant sexually . . ."

"And you didn't *see* anything different or odd, did you?"

"No, no."

(*Whew! If she asks in which positions, I'll deny ever taking a position. How do I know what she's thinking or whom she knows!*) "Yes, I have bad cramps, too."

"Okay . . . I'll give you something for that. So, now, how's your diaphragm?"

"How did you know I use that?"

"You wrote it on your chart!"

"Oh, right," Jessie said, then exhaled and closed her eyes. (*I'm going 'round the bend!*) Before she could relate the saga of her old diaphragm, rubber rings had materialized and she was being "sized."

"I think that one will do it," said Dr. Bridge, writing a number on Jessie's chart. "Okay, any trouble with your breasts?"

"That's it?" said Jessie, waiting to hear an incredulous gasp.

"That's it," she said, and proceeded with the next exam. "Do you know how to do this yourself?" the Doctor asked. (*Does she think I'm a total dunce? My God, we're the same age!*)

"No . . . ah, no."

"Okay, let me show you. Laying-down-use-the-flat-of-your-fingers-on-the-opposite-hand-moving-from-inner-to-outer-on-each-breast-covering-one-section-at-a-time-with-a-back-and-forth-motion-got-it? Now, let's see you do it."

(*Do it! What the hell did she say? Is it outer-to-inner, laying-down-with-a-forth-and-back-motion-sectionally? Just do it, Jessie, don't be an ass! But, she'll know I didn't get it! So ask her again.*) Gingerly touching herself, Jessie begins to press and move around the edges but is overwhelmed by the idea of being seen doing it wrong. (*Don't linger anywhere, or look as though*

you're enjoying yourself— you could run into her at a party . . .)
"Is that right?"

"Pretty much so, but you'll have to start getting used to how your breasts feel at different times of the month. So, try to examine yourself often."

Sitting in her office, Jessie stole a glance at the Doctor's calendar and happened to see two items: "Dinner, Fred: 8:30," and "Women's Medical Seminar: 6:00." This information startled her: Dr. Bridge was a regular person, just like . . . herself.

It's December, and Jessie needs new medication. She's thought of calling Dr. Bridge (*I really did like her!*), but feels uneasy, even anxious about making an appointment. In any event, there's no harm done and it's all okay, because yesterday, Marie, from her office, told her about a wonderful new Doctor, an older woman who has written two books and seems awfully wise— someone to whom she can really relate.

These two situations, of course, reflect only a smattering of the behavioral range of anxious patients. There are multitudes of patient styles and attitudes all reflecting a basic fear of the white coat, a symbol which tinkers with the mind and weights it with dread.

However, situational anxiety is not limited to placing high on the big Medical Hit List in the sky, it is also triggered by a sense of the vulnerable, of being exposed, and of being out of control. To avoid the horror of the unknown, many people feel compelled to act out certain dramas and regain what they experience as their flagging sovereignty. In the first situation, Michael wore his "power suit and shoes" as much to ensure against imminent death as to obtain his Doctor's approval. In the second, Jessie incorporated the premise that a moving target can't be hit and engaged in "Doctor-hopping."

These approaches to the medical appointment are ostensibly quite necessary, for as every anxiety-riddled patient will tell you, doctors are not keen on cowards and have no time to coddle minor eccentricities like panic and such. Further, sensitive patients are quick to perceive certain known and little-known particulars about M.D.'s which make appointments hazardous to their mental health—specifically, their self-esteem. After querying a handful of anxious patients about their Doctor grievances, this compendium of complaints was formed:

"They're so damned busy—I always feel I'm taking up too much time."

"He's a fine humanitarian, but I wish he'd remember my name."

"I feel kind of insignificant—they're so preoccupied with Larger Issues."

"I think they're all trained to speak 'in tongues,' swiftly and incomprehensibly . . ."

"Mine seems to assume that I, too, graduated from the College of Surgeons, and I just sit there silently, pretending to understand."

"Doctors! Masters of solemnity and the art of the understatement."

"How come they limit my questions to three and their answers to two?"

"Anyone can interrupt them—except me!"

"They're above discussions of fees."

"When in doubt, they seem to prescribe a salt-free diet."

THE MYTH OF THE SCARY DOCTOR

Most people are aware that *how* the Doctor relates to the patient is sometimes more effective in diminishing anxiety than *what* the medical procedure entails. However, doctors are not always the Marcus Welbys in the mind, and even if they were, when anxiety takes hold, many people are hard pressed to see them as anything but frightening figures.

Although those grievances may have a ring of truth, the pervading myth of the Doctor as a tyrannical authority who exists in a rarefied strata ready to pronounce judgments is closer to the heart of the anxiety issue. As a patient who does want some control over the medical appointment and the important dialogue, you may have to think about whom you unconsciously expect to meet when you arrive at that office. Is it a father who yelled for no reason? A mother who demeaned you by checking your neck for dirt? The uncle who ignored you and made you feel stupid? Or is it a combination of people who, years ago, stopped you from talking—or thinking?

The Doctor is the perfect grist for the emotional mill which grinds out old distressing experiences, and he or she can easily be transformed into a specter from the past who was disapproving. The unspoken contracts you made with those historical figures are carried into the office and are unconsciously renewed with the new authority. As a consequence, asking for aid, counsel, or advice triggers a sense of helplessness, even shame. You may begin to feel insignificant, small, or "in the way," and presumptuous if and when you interrupt, ask for clarification, or express your concerns.

However, while many doctors do indeed evoke unpleasant reminiscences, there are others who become victims of the patient's distorted vision and fall into anxiety's time warp. Dr. Smith, the one who saw you through your appendectomy and was so kind to your child when she broke her arm, may unjustly have assumed the mantle of *all* medical miscreants and need to be reinstated as trustworthy. The Doctor who is truly formidable may have to be approached assertively and made aware, by you, of your requirements. If that seems virtually impossible, you may have to try another Doctor. In any event, before you go to your next appointment, you might try to objectively work at disengaging this individual from the ghost voices of authority in your head and approach him or her from a fresh, unfettered perspective.

EXPECTING THE "WORST"

There's nothing like a sudden physical discomfort to remind one that life is not infinite and that time rushes on. Norman Cousins captured the essence of this issue when he very succinctly wrote: "Most men think they are immortal—until they get a cold, when they think they are going to die within the hour." Anxiety often nudges those intimations of mortality and, when it does, the overstressed mind can become very creative.

There are four common scenarios which anxious patients sometimes find themselves acting out:

1. *Off-the-Record Patient:* To avoid hearing the rude shock of his incipient demise, information the Doctor is certain to mention during the examination, this patient has already called his brother-in-law, so he'll *know* what's really wrong. The brother-in-law says, "Listen, I don't know and don't want to get into this," but the patient is insistent. "Look," he pleads, "I know it doesn't count, but off the record, just tell me what you think . . . you studied anatomy in college, didn't you? Just off the top of your head . . . what do you think? Can't a nose bleed be fatal?"

2. *Doom-and-Gloom Patient:* After a coughing spell, this patient *knows* he will hear the worst, begins to get his affairs in order, and prays he will gain some eternity points along the way. "Look," he says, "if it's anything serious, here's where the money is . . . No, there are two other banks you don't know about . . ." Later that night, in bed with the lights off, he adds, "Listen, I know I've been a little tough to live with, testy, irrational, but I want you to know . . . I've really loved you . . ."

3. *Aching-for-the-Truth Patient:* The patient here *knows* something terrible is being withheld and would rather have it "given to me straight." "You can be honest with me, Doctor . . . what's *really* wrong?" "Nothing, your test results are all negative . . . believe me . . ." "No, look, I saw you blink—you don't have to worry, I can take it."

4. *Prescription-Panicked Patient:* Although the Doctor told her she's in good health, she isn't sure. The pharmacist looks at the prescription and says, "Fifty milligrams . . . hmmm." Panicked, she blurts out, "What does that mean—is that good or bad?" "No, nothing," murmurs the pharmacist. "But you said, 'hmmm'!" "No, I just said, 'hmmm.'" "No, but the way you said, 'hmmm'—why did you say it that way?"

These four thumbnail profiles are illustrative of the ability to mentally leap from what is experienced as a minor cough to the expectation of a major coronary. Jumping from a discomfort to a disaster can have serious implications for anxious people: the panic can at times change the symptom formation and mask the underlying problem.

If you find that a muscle pain starts you flirting with the possibility of a dread disease, you're absolutely overlooking all of the intermediate contingencies and acting the role of masochistic provocateur. An irritation could mean you slept poorly or that you bumped into something—it doesn't necessarily mean internal bleeding.

Many people become their own worst alarmists by utilizing what is known as superstitious thinking. By jumping to the worst first, they feel they will protect themselves from the shock of hearing the bad news or from the illness itself. Often, however, when you have convinced yourself that you are, for sure, at death's door, the fear becomes louder than the Doctor's voice and you cannot hear what he or she is saying.

You might try to help yourself off the medical fast lane by thinking in gradations. If the first thought you have is that of disaster, catch yourself at that moment and back down. Start with something small—a vitamin deficiency, the flu, a case of neuralgia—possibilities which are not geared to panic-attack intensity. In the meantime, make an appointment and have the realities of your fears tested out.

BEFORE THE VISIT

There are many practical steps that can be taken to prepare yourself for an appointment and which can help to alleviate much of the anxiety.

If you're shopping for a Doctor, first decide if you would be more comfortable with a man or a woman. Next, since it's important to have a sense of trust in the Doctor whom you choose, ask friends, family, or colleagues about their doctors. Find out what qualities they find in this person that may be compatible with your particular needs. Call the Doctor's office: obtain information regarding fees, and ask for the names of hospitals to which he or she is connected. You can also check out the Doctor's credentials by contacting the local medical society, or by checking in *The Directory of Medical Specialists*.

Once you've selected a Doctor, call the office and find out what the procedure entails. If you're going for tests, ask the nurse what you should expect. For instance, if you're going for a glucose tolerance test, find out how long it takes, what you should and shouldn't eat the night before, how you'll be feeling afterward, and what, if any, discomforts you may incur. As an emotional shim, you might want to ask friends if they know of anyone who has had this specific test, and contact that person as well. Once you are told something about the specific procedure, you won't be as prone to exaggerate your fantasies.

In order to ensure you are supplying the Doctor with the information he or she will need to better diagnose your case, before you go, write down your family's medical history. If you don't trust the accuracy of your memory, contact a family member and reacquaint yourself with some basic medical facts. Did anyone in the family have diabetes? How about heart disease, liver or kidney dysfunctions? What were the causes of deaths? Since anxiety often prevents you from remembering important facts which could prove invaluable in assessing your situation, be sure to include your own medical history, as well as the medication you currently use, and the drugs your system cannot tolerate.

Dr. Patricia Conrad, a General and Surgical Gynecologist, and Infertility and Endocrinology specialist, who practices in New York City, tells us "there are three major concerns which frighten patients: the fear of cancer, the fear of chronic disease, and the fear that the symptom may be psychosomatic and therefore untreatable with a pill." Because these concerns are so terrifying, Dr. Conrad says, "patients sometimes forget to tell me why they're here, and will ramble extraneously and tangentially. Fear of the unknown blocks the patient's memory and we have to use the process of elimination to get to the cause of the visit." In order to help the Doctor, Dr. Conrad suggests that the patient, "make a list of all the symptoms the night before. If you find that your anxiety won't allow you to read it out loud, hand the list to the Doctor and let her read it." For the patient who 'blanks out,' like Jessie, this is a most important piece of advice. And, while you're listing your symptoms, be prepared to answer questions such as: Where does it hurt? When does it hurt? How

long has it been going on? Have you ever felt it before this? Is it
an ache or a pain, sharp or dull or a burning sensation, and,
when do you feel better?

Finally, if you are a person who truly "panics," you might ask
a friend to accompany you. Pick someone whom you trust, in
whom you can confide, and whom you feel confident cares about
you. Brief this individual on your fears, the possibility of "going
blank," and how he or she can help you through the appointment. If nothing else is required, you'll at least have support
walking in and walking out.

DURING THE VISIT

If you've decided to go it alone, you might try to tell the Doctor
and the nurses at the outset that "this whole business is very
alarming to me." In this way, they'll be alerted to your anxious
state and perhaps be able to assuage some of those fears by
explaining the procedures as they're happening. Many patients
become so frightened that they cover their nervousness by mem-
orizing *Grey's Anatomy, PDR, Symptoms: The Complete Home
Medical Encyclopedia,* plus the latest issue of *Modern Medicine,*
and present themselves as competing authorities. Others feel
they can only "get through" this mess by entertaining the staff,
and the day before, they work up a number of jokes, some
snappy patter, and two amusing anecdotes. While these methods
may work to hide the fact that you feel unhinged, they work
against hearing and/or assimilating important information.
Therefore, try to avoid becoming an unforgettable personality in
this office, and take notes instead. If you feel foolish dragging
out the pad and pen, inform the Doctor that you do "tend to forget" what's been said and need to record it. However, if you become rattled while writing, you might say that you'd like to call
back later to verify the discussion, and that you may have a husband, wife, or friend call back for you. At that point, find out at
what time the Doctor is available to speak on the phone.

If you do decide to take a friend, ask if this person can accompany you into the examination room. Most doctors are quite
willing to allow this procedure. Then again, you may want your
friend to assist only at the end consultation. This person can

then act as your "mouthpiece," and ask all the questions you've completely blocked out, as well as describe certain symptoms you've forgotten, and take notes for you.

For those people who are embarrassed by exposing the body to the Doctor, you may have to try something a little different. It's very difficult to rise above body-consciousness and the anxieties which are triggered by being "touched." This is especially common with rectal, vaginal, and breast examinations—body parts which have become sexualized. For these exams, it might be prudent to use a little "detachment." During those uncomfortable moments, mentally take a short walk away from your body and try to objectify the procedure. In this way, you will no longer be discussing *your* breast—large, small, or erotic—you and the doctor will be involved with "a breast," a part of the anatomy which must be felt for lumps or thicknesses, and which needs care and attention. This also applies to the internal exam, prostate exam, and all other areas of the body which cue embarrassed responses. In this particular instance, subjectivity can work against you, especially if you cannot separate your inhibitions from your important medical needs.

By the way, the mystery of the disappearing symptom—that bizarre occurrence mentioned earlier—could easily be within your own experience. If you've had a burning sensation in your belly and complained about it on the phone, you may find you feel quite foolish when asked to point it out—it just doesn't hurt right now! This is a manifestation of denial which your anxiety has created, and most doctors are well acquainted with this contingency. Simply describe the pain as you have been experiencing it, and try to understand that, unconsciously, you may not enjoy admitting to being in need.

AFTER THE VISIT

If you are thoroughly dissatisfied with the experience in that office, feel that you did not receive the appropriate responses but could not confront that person, you may have to fire your Doctor and hire a new one. However, many people, like Michael, feel a sense of loyalty to the old Doctor and can't bring themselves to change. If this is your situation, you might think of the first M.D. as a trial run. The next Doctor you select could be viewed as a "second opinion" person, which should make the switch much easier for you. Firing doctors, or any professional for that matter, is difficult, but it can be expedited painlessly by phoning the office and requesting that your file be sent to Dr. _____ for a second opinion.

(By the way, if you find that you've been leaping from Doctor to Doctor for several years, you may have to assess that pattern of behavior and find out what's behind the inability to safely land.)

Finally, after the visit, you may want to immerse yourself in something enjoyable! Plan a lunch or dinner date, a game of tennis, or a good movie as a reward for having once again survived the Doctor ordeal.

However, don't be too complacent. When you go to your mailbox, you could find your anxieties once again flinging you about the house. What about the Dentist! and his yearly reminder, which has just dropped from your trembling fingers to the floor?

SITUATION #3
The Dental Appointment

IN THE WAITING ROOM

Muzak, that false anesthesia, will act as the first of many numbing experiences. It will take effect the moment you walk into the room. As you identify "The Very Thought of You" (as rendered by the One Hundred and One Strings), you will be checking out the decor. Slowly, you will become aware that the painting on the north wall is obviously PLAQUE passing as a landscape; the line drawing in front of you, an ABCESS cleverly disguised as a bowl of fruit; and that rather odd abstract event, a collage of found objects—BRIDGEWORK and TEMPORARY CROWNS interwoven with a cat's cradle of FLOSS.

It will be too quiet here. There will be an overtone of unreality, a quiet denial of the real, macabre practices gleefully performed in the ROOMS BEYOND. Flipping through a *National Geographic,* you will listen for untoward sounds, perhaps a groan. But wait! Don't feel disappointed . . . in a moment you will hear exactly what you've been expecting—the sound of the HIGH SPEED DRILL. "I knew it," you will say to yourself, then clear your throat and wipe the corners of your mouth.

THE DENTAL HYGIENIST

Her eyes will glitter. You will wish you hadn't eaten sausage for breakfast. She will first stalk your mouth with a SHARP INSTRUMENT, get a deadly fix on your central incisors, then hand you a cup of red solution and command you to SWISH. A mirror will appear and cruelly reflect the fallen ways of your teeth. In a trice, you will understand that you are the Dental Heretic and that she is the Inquisitor, ferreting out sins against PREVENTIVE HOME CARE.

"Do you see *that?*" she will demand, pointing an accusing finger at the ugly evidence of your oral baseness. You will squirm and wince and be seized by hygienic guilt. "That is PLAQUE, and you've got severe BUILDUP." She will give you ample time to consider this indictment before ordering you to RINSE, and then begin the SCALING process. You will clutch the arms of the CHAIR, scrunch your toes, and become cold and hot in the extremities. Your TONGUE will move to all the wrong places and you will seek out methods for redeeming yourself as wholesome. Laughter will emanate from another ROOM; you will attempt to hear what is being said to ascertain how normal mouths behave.

"DECAY!" she will announce, and even the mailman standing outside by the desk will turn to gawk at the offender. You will cower and avoid his eyes, steeling yourself for the X RAYS which are being prepared.

A LEAD APRON will press you in the chair and she will affix film in a METAL HOLDER WITH SHARP EDGES. You will whisper in an ingratiating tone: "I have a very low gag threshold . . ." Nonetheless, your gaping mouth will be filled with cold, harsh metal and your eyes will water. Before the awful heave in your belly takes hold, she will reappear—just in time to postpone a VILE INCIDENT.

As you rise from the chair, you will be stunned to find that she is a very attractive, vivacious young woman! You will understand that this segment of horror is concluded when she offers a radiant smile and says, "Hey, I really like your boots!"

THE DENTIST

He will be nine feet ten, and humming "The Very Thought of You." You will be two feet four—short of breath and courage. He will have conferred with the Hygienist and KNOW YOU GAGGED!

During the next forty-five minutes, the following items will transpire between you, the Dentist, and the Dental Assistant:

- You will observe the NEEDLE coming at you twice; both times you will bolt your eyes shut.
- "Are you numb yet?" will be asked three times; you will respond, "Not yet," six.
- You will sneak a look at his fingernails and nostrils.
- The Dental Assistant will give you seven sympathetic smiles— two will be construed as horrifying portents.
- You will ask the function of eight objects resting on the retractable table and remember none of them.
- The Dentist will say, "OPEN," throughout.
- Your early traumatic experience with a Dentist will be explained.
- He will say, "WIDER," eighteen times.
- You will spot a knob with the word GAS spelled in red—and shudder.
- He will relate two bad jokes and three fascinating stories.
- Excepting for a throaty sound approximating, "Aaah, haaa," you will be unable to respond.
- The Dental Assistant will smile knowingly eight times, three of which you will not observe.
- You will ask to RINSE nineteen times and be granted eleven.
- "LIVE NERVE" and the "DRILL" will haunt you for the duration.
- For twenty-two minutes, you will silently question his need for a FACE MASK.

- He will say, "This is one hell-of-a tight spot," four and one half times; the last attempt will be truncated by a breathy expletive.
- You will be convinced that your breath is "bad."
- "EXTRACTION" will loom as a persistent threat.
- You will ask him about his need for his FACE MASK.
- "ROOT CANAL" will be mentioned twice, unrelated to your case.
- They will discuss a tooth with a unique pattern of DECAY and you will understand the feeling of "dirty."
- You will explain an early traumatic experience with a Dentist.
- DRILL BITS will be changed.
- The term "ORAL SURGERY" will chill your blood twice.
- You will remove the hook from your mouth and/or adjust it too many times for an accurate count.
- You will beg off for "just a moment" continually.
- You will explain an early traumatic experience with a Dentist, and then, for no reason, giggle maniacally.
- On several occasions you will try to act like an adult.
- Before you are out of the chair, your hair will get caught in the plastic bib strings.
- The Dental Assistant will touch your shoulder, and you will make a note to send her something wonderful for Christmas.

Leaving the office, you will experience a certain light-headedness, a sense of control, of triumph. You may turn to a mirror to repair your makeup. If that is the case, you will be startled to see that you have applied a gash of Ultima Burnt Toffee from your lipline to your ear.

Returning to the Examination Room to say a last goodbye, you will be amazed to discover that the Dentist and you are exactly the same height.

Dentists are a most maligned lot. Like the old "in-law" jokes, there has never been a "good" Dentist joke, anecdote, story, or pun. Dentists make pain; dentists give pain; dentists never take pain away—dentists and pain are synonymous! No one ever goes gladly, willingly, or pleasantly; patients are hooked in via long canes; carried inside in nets; or thrown over someone's shoulders, kicking and screaming. From generation to generation, dentists are associated with fright, horror, and hurt. Even when the occasion is a routine examination, one is glad when it's over and, later, may even require a nap.

"Is he nice?" is the first question asked when shopping for a Dentist. "I mean, is he *gentle?* I had a terrible time with a Dentist when I was a kid and . . . does he use anesthesia . . . will he give me more Novocain if I ask?" This line of inquiry illustrates just how frightened people become when considering a visit. Even the words associated with the Dentist are scary. A common word like "chair" is charged with tension and suspense. It no longer means a seat with a back for one person, it means "trapped," as in "can't move" and "prisoner."

"How much does he charge for a filling?" is the second question asked, but usually only after the threat of oral torture has been diminished. Then expense becomes primary. There are no low-priced dentists, budget-conscious dentists, time-payment dentists. There are only dentists who see your mouth as, oh, about fifteen hundred.

Nonetheless, you *have to make an appointment.* You can't continue to smile or eat with that hole in your tooth and, frankly, it's beginning to ache. It's extremely sensitive to hot and cold, and your tongue is rubbed raw from toying with the edges. You'd make the call right now but your stomach is announcing the queasiness of a growing panic. Well, maybe you'll put it off for a week . . . no one will know.

Anxious patients are rarely keen on taking care of business and are known to employ delaying tactics, both obvious and subtle, to keep the Dentist at bay. There's a patient who always breezes in late armed with a colorful story to tell, and another who, although he's requested three blue appointment cards and called ahead to confirm the time, forgets to come at all. Some people make it into the chair, then flatten their chins against their chests and unclench their teeth just enough to slip in a dime. "Open, please," requests the Dentist. "Oh, sorry . . ." the patient responds, then throws his chin heavenward, and unclenches his teeth just enough to slip in a dime. Others might need to sit for ten minutes under gas before the Dentist can show his face in the room, and someone else, after four heavy doses of Novocain, might still refuse to admit that the gums have sufficiently numbed.

Stalling seems to be an integral part of the total dental ordeal, and those who utilize these ploys usually have some very specific notions about the man in white with the mirror in their mouths.

THE MYTH OF THE DREADED DENTIST

The idea of the Dentist as a monster man educated in the intricacies of agony is a legacy of conditioned thinking that has, for years, been an accepted notion in our culture. This circumstance is unfortunate for not only the dental establishment, but also the public. The jokes, bad stories, and slurs have created a climate of fear and misunderstanding which preserves the myth and perpetuates the panic. Interestingly, unlike doctors, dentists are not viewed as tyrannical authorities from the past who just might yell. They are seen as *pain-givers*. Reshaping this perception seems to be about as easy as sculpting a stone with water; however, there is one step you can take right now to help you shift the negative impact of the dental appointment.

It might be fruitful for you to reconsider your past experiences with dentists. Thinking back, how much of your present anxiety is based on undefiled facts, and how much is the product of absorbed myth? How much of the pain you presently anticipate takes its antecedents from conditioned thinking, and how much from reality? Further, how many times have you run to the Dentist in pain and left that office relieved and salved? By separating the myth from the genuine substance of your past experience, you may jolt yourself into a new and more positive awareness and begin to diminish one aspect of dental anxiety.

However, there are those people whose childhood memories are authentically harrowing, and the terror they experience when confronted with the "chair" is a more complex matter.

Dr. Alfred Carin, D.D.S., practicing in New York City, has had much experience with the very anxious patient, and puts the lie to the myth of the dreaded Dentist. "Many frightened people were terribly traumatized as youngsters," Dr. Carin tells us. "Their first Dentist was usually insensitive. While an accompanying family member perhaps held this child down in the chair, the Dentist came at him or her with scary instruments. Now, as adults, these people relive that fear each and every time they make an appointment." Dr. Carin believes that all patients, but specifically the terrified, should be treated with great sensitivity and concern. "If the patient is so frightened that I cannot look in his or her mouth, we may spend the first and second appointments just talking through the fear. During that time, I try to accustom them to the routine procedures, the equipment and instruments, and help them to desensitize the old trauma." Dr. Carin suggests that you, as an anxious patient, inform the Dentist of your fears, either when you call for the appointment, or as you enter the office.

Dental Assistant Ann Hodorowski offers another piece of sound advice: "If a patient is too upset to speak directly to the Dentist, he or she should try to communicate the problem to the Dental Assistant, who can then relay the information." Ms. Hodorowski believes that "once everyone is aware of the anxiety problem, the patient is better equipped to relax. However," she adds, "a gentle, reassuring touch on the patient's shoulder doesn't hurt, either."

Panicky patients would do well to follow this advice. Anxiety tends to thrive on secrecy and fizzle out when exposed. So, by all means, do communicate your specific fears to the Dentist. Ask him to explain exactly what he's going to do before he does it, and as he's doing it. Make certain he addresses himself to all your concerns. Try to call your own shots and take some control over the occasion.

By the way, when you phone for the first visit, and tell the office that you are one of those anxious patients, you can also request a ten- or fifteen-minute appointment. In this way, you'll have provided yourself with a time-circumscribed appointment and will be less prone to tormenting yourself with visions of an hour in the chair.

Dental Hygienist Linda Rosenblatt reports to us that "some people become so nervous just being in the chair, they ask for laughing gas for a cleaning." While this particular procedure is relatively painless, it nonetheless is connected to the larger dental picture and triggers its own brand of anxiety. "Many patients perceive my instructions on home care—proper brushing and flossing—as a personal attack on their total cleanliness. Others become horrified when, after rinsing with the red solution, plaque shows up on their teeth: they're convinced I won't approve of them! This," she adds, "is all part of the general nervousness they carry with them into the office." Since the Dental Hygienist is the first person a new patient usually sees, Ms. Rosenblatt suggests that the anxious patient begin by discussing their apprehensions with her. As with the Dentist, the procedures can be explained, questions answered, and the routines discussed as they're happening.

THE FEAR OF VERBAL BONDAGE

Although pain and/or physical discomfort play key roles in the dental ordeal, there's yet another aspect which ignites anxiety's short fuse here—the confiscation of the voice.

If you've always used words as a means of maintaining control, as a technique for reassuring yourself, or as a method for gaining needed recognition, and if you've always depended upon your verbal acrobatics to demonstrate your intelligence, what do you do when you're rendered mute? Once that saliva ejector is hooked in place, those defenses are gone! You can no longer vocally manipulate the event—debate, argue, amuse, or cajole. Your verbal weaponry, along with your coat, has been checked in the waiting room. You are now in dental captivity—trapped, and at the mercy of the jokes, laughter, singing, clucking, and snatches of conversation from those looming over you. Uneasy being seen as this mass of incisors and tongue, you may find yourself blinking out messages and rolling your eyes to prove you are, indeed, very much alive.

This is not a happy event for any real talkers, but for the verbally anxious the loss of control and its concomitant vulnerability can catapult even relatively calm people into a growing panic. In order to ward off that occurrence, it would be prudent, at the outset, to inform the Dentist that you will probably want to stop the treatment at varying intervals. Provide him with a prearranged signal. If and when you find your verbal apprehensions mounting, you can hold up a hand or one finger and, in this way, inform him that a brief intermission is needed. Once you've gained some trust and believe he'll be sympathetic, you may feel less anxious over the inability to speak.

By the way, if you happen to have a low gag threshold, you might also want to apprise the Dentist of this fact before the work begins. As you're taking your seat in the chair, draw up a verbal agreement with him, one that ensures you'll be given every consideration. If it's not intrusive on his work, when you feel the gag mechanism take hold, obtain his permission to remove the material from your mouth which is triggering the reflex. (Interestingly, some dentists have found that placing salt on the back of the tongue actually works to diminish the gag response. Ask your Dentist about it.)

SOME PRACTICAL GUIDELINES

Dr. Allan Carniello, D.D.S., also practicing in New York City, has suggested some sound guidelines for ensuring that you do receive the best possible dental care.

When picking a Dentist, he advises you to "seek a trusted and reliable referral source, a relative, friend, or known professional." Once you've selected a Dentist, "talk to as many of his patients as possible—pick their brains. Ask about the office: size, decor, personnel; then check out the routines and inquire about fees. Know what to expect on the first visit—and think positively —he's there to help you."

If you haven't expressed your particular anxieties on the phone prior to the visit, Dr. Carniello suggests that you be open and candid about your condition when you meet the Dentist. He further offers some valuable information concerning what you should expect from the Dentist you've selected. "He should go slowly and be as pleasant as possible—explain all of the procedures very clearly, and answer all questions willingly. Look for someone who is honest, understanding, sympathetic, and gentle, who demonstrates that he enjoys his work and is proud of it." As a final suggestion, Dr. Carniello adds, "Try to pick a Dentist who displays both confidence in his work and confidence in himself."

(While you're shopping for the right Dentist, you might want to inquire about hypnosis. There are dentists who are trained in this particular procedure and offer this technique as part of their service.)

However, if you find that your dental fears have now been quelled, but, for no apparent reason, you're still biting the inside of your cheek and grinding your teeth, you might want to consider professional aid of a different sort. Should you decide to take your anxieties to an Analyst, don't be too surprised when you discover that they have achieved mythical proportions and have run away with your mouth.

SITUATION #4
The Psychological Consultation

"Do you mind if I smoke? Yes? No? Oh, okay, just wanted to find out if smoke bothers you, you know, some people can't tolerate . . . Well, you've got a nice office here. What's that? Oh, sorry, I thought you said something . . .

"Guess you guys have a pretty tough time of it, sitting all day, listening to the crazies . . . (*Why did he flex his ankle?*) That's a good-looking chair; always wanted one myself. (*It's not only bigger than what I'm sitting on . . . it's higher.*) What brings me here. Oh. Well, I've been having some dental work done and, funny enough, my Dentist suggested I should come— (*Should I tell him any more?*) He thinks I'm very nervous . . . he's a good friend, you know. Says I grind my teeth, probably in my sleep, and the inside of my cheek is sore, maybe from chewing on it, and, yeah, I bite my nails . . . just around the cuticle, that's all. (*Don't say any more—he'll think he's got another crazy . . .*) I don't know if that's any reason to see a Shrink, but he said so, so I thought I'd take a crack at it.

"What do *I* think's behind it? Beats me . . . I can't help what

I do when I sleep! (*Why's he looking at my tie—the guy is sizing me up for fee! Maybe I came in dressed too expen-
sively . . .*) What do *you* think it's from? You're the doctor!

"Tense? I'm not tense. No, you're real easy to talk to. (*He
hasn't said a word!*) Oh, you mean in my *life* . . . No, my job's
going very well, I should be getting a promotion next month
(*you'd better play that one down a little*), although my boss did
leave the company and I haven't been able to meet with the big
guns upstairs . . . (*I'm not opening up that can of worms, oh,
no . . .*) Why? Do you think that's a problem? You don't know.

"Family life? There's nothing wrong with my parents, I had a
fairly normal upbringing, my first wife (*Christ! That's a dead
giveaway!*) even referred to it as 'storybook.' You know, I just
knew you'd bring them up. Why? Because you guys always
point the finger at parents and, well, I'm one . . . Oh, I've got
two . . . a boy and a girl, good kids. (*I can say that. I don't
have to be all bad.*)

"My wife, Beth? My present wife? We have the normal, run-
of-the-mill disagreements—money, in-laws . . . Sex? (*This guy
must be a Freudian—they always want to know all about that
stuff . . . well, I'm not going to tell him about the other women,
the fantasies, or the magazines . . . let him ask me!*) Sex is one
thing that's really good. The sex between us is good, good. Why
do you ask? Touching all bases, huh? Well, I'm pretty secure in
that area. Look, you're on the wrong track here . . . Yeah, she
knows I made this appointment. Yes, she thought I should go.
Say, you know, I heard through the grapevine that your brother-
in-law is a divorce attorney. You're not trying to drum up business, are you? Just kidding! Just kidding. (*He's got one lousy
sense of humor . . .*)

"I suppose you've got a lot of people coming in here who just
break down right in front of you—I see that Kleenex box by the
couch. Do you, ah, have your patients lie down and tell you
their dreams? My sister, Charlene, is involved in that . . . four
times a week, 'on the couch.' My father didn't think too much of
that. (*Ought-oh . . . that's a heavy number, back off—*) Oh, he
was a terrific guy, but I think it's okay, my sister really makes
the money, she can support her Shrink . . . (*Oh, Jesus, he's
going to think that was a hostile comment . . . probably hurt his*

feelings.) Look, I didn't mean anything personal about that; what I meant was that she spends a lot of time in that office, but that doesn't bother me . . . I think I'm really your kind of guy, and whatever you think I need, goes! (*How come he doesn't take notes? How can he remember what I'm telling him?*) Say, is it always so dark in here?

"You know, this isn't so bad. (*Is he going to mention that couch?*) So, why don't you ask me something—I don't know what else you need. No, I don't feel jammed, I just don't know what you're looking for. Well, I've pretty much told you about myself already. But you look like you've got a pretty good sense of humor, so I'll tell you this: Do you know I was actually worried about what to wear *here?* Could you believe it? (*Why am I telling him this?*) Changed my shirt and tie three times this morning, then forgot my glasses and left my checkbook too.

"No, I'm not usually forgetful, except after a night of insomnia. (*Is that all right to say? Yeah, it's fairly normal . . .*) I get it once in a while (*where is this leading?*). I don't know, or, I should say, I can't remember what I think about. (*I wonder if he remembers what I just said about my checkbook . . . how can he remember everything?*) Say, do you remember what I just said about . . . (*I'd better not bring that up again.*) Ah, nothing. Forgot what I was going to say. (*Don't be an ass! Of course he remembers, he's a bright man—look at his office.*) Well, I've got a lousy memory, and I'm a salesman; have to read the names of my calls before I make them . . . (*How is this guy going to remember when I'm telling him about my mother, wife, sister, and kids. I'll help him along a little.*) Now, my wife, BETH, that's my wife—and CHARLENE, that's my sister . . . Just want to remind you so when I refer to them you'll know who I'm talking about.

"Oh, yes, I was telling you about insomnia. I guess I think a lot about heart attacks, sex, people I'm angry at . . . Who? Well, my mother for one, she's really been pissing me off lately—she's never liked my wives. BETH is my third wife . . . guess I have trouble picking women . . . but this one's an okay gal, married now about six months. Don't get me wrong, my mother's not completely off the wall . . . my wife BETH can be pretty demanding, and my second ex, JANE, well, she was always on my tail about one thing or another. (*I'm not lying down on that couch!*) She was the great guilt instiller . . . (*That pillow isn't there for nothing.*) If I forgot a birthday or anniversary . . . I mean, I'm not saying I didn't deserve a lot of that abuse, but . . . well, that's water under the bridge. (*I bet I still have ten minutes to go . . . but if I ask, he'll think I'm uptight.*)

"Yeah, I guess I'm angry at my second wife, too. How is my wife demanding? (*What's he getting at?*) You mean BETH? Oh, for a minute I thought you meant JANE, my second wife. (*Where are the clocks in this place? Can't look at my watch; he'll think I'm anxious, or tense. I'll just sit back here and relax . . . make believe I'm very comfortable; otherwise he may suggest that couch . . .*) Well, my wife's a complainer, and frankly I'm sick of being accused of being 'cut off.' I'm up to here with demands—my wives, my mother, my kids, my job, my sister, with that knowing smirk! I mean, you can tell I'm a real talker— I've been talking now for a good hour, right? A regular monologue. (*This guy doesn't care about time! Aren't these appointments fifty minutes?*)

"So, what do you think? Think you can help me? Think I really need a Shrink . . . I mean, 'Analyst' . . . sorry. I really don't mean to keep saying that. (*He probably thinks I'm pissed off.*) So, how long do you think it will take? You must have *some* idea. Well, I thought a couple of sessions, just to get a few things straightened out. I don't want to make a career out of this thing . . . Also, look, I know this is a sensitive issue, but how much do you . . . What I'm trying to say is, until I get my promotion I'm a little strapped, and I don't know when that's going to happen because I haven't been privy to the decision-making up there, and I know they're bringing in a new person, and I wasn't consulted . . . Jesus! You know, they really led me on, and I was convinced I was being groomed for management . . . and my goddamned wife keeps pushing me to get a straight answer . . . (*Aren't we at the end of this session? Does he tell me to stop, or do you just keep going?*)

"Look, if I do come to see you it can only be once a week, and I'm not sure I'll be able to keep every appointment. But, what do you think? Guess you can tell I won't be one of your more 'interesting' cases—I'm kind of a healthy neurotic who's just a little troubled . . . So, do you think by next month I'll have this sorted out? (*What does he mean, 'We'll see'?*)

"Okay. So, thanks a lot, Doctor. I'll see you next Tuesday, 5:30 sharp . . . unless, of course, something comes up and I have to cancel. It was a real pleasure meeting you. Say, hope you jog or play tennis, squash . . . Sitting in that chair all day can't be good for your health. Well, anyway, so long."

(*I'll be damned if I didn't feel better when I came in— thought he was supposed to make me feel good. If he's such a big-time Shrink, how come this waiting room looks so chintzy? And that woman over there, what is she, spaced out? That was one hard chair to sit in for over an hour . . . Wait a minute! It's only 6:20! Seems like it should be later . . . Well, there's one thing I can feel good about: I think I put him at ease.*)

The first psychological consultation can be a very threatening event, and tends to call up a plethora of defense mechanisms in the prospective patient or client. This situation can be very tricky: one seeks out the help of a professional because of a dissatisfaction or unresolved conflicts in life, then attempts to present him- or herself to the Analyst as a "picture of emotional health" who made the appointment because he or she is "just a little troubled," "someone else insisted I come," or "only in need of a piece of practical advice," which may be how to save a marriage, advance on the job, or become a better parent. Of course, there are endless variations on the presentation, but the image one creates often becomes more important than the feelings he or she suffers.

There are four main reasons for this surface concern, and each one is of major significance to the anxious patient:

1. The Analyst could think you are genuinely "crazy";
2. The Analyst might discover your case is so serious, you cannot be helped;
3. The Analyst has never handled anything as far out in his or her entire career; and/or,
4. The Analyst will be frightened of what's going on in your head, and back off.

In order to circumvent the possibility of any one of these concerns becoming a reality, you, as a prospective patient, will only tell him or her "a couple of things" about yourself—and only those that are "safe" and generally construed as "normal." You're certainly not going to admit to picking toenails, being sexually aroused by people in boots, the frequent desire to muffle your child's demands with a shopping bag, or twelve years of lying to the IRS, because, really, any of those topics could start the Analyst to thinking.

Then, there are all those meddlesome thoughts that continue to interfere with your presentation, such as why he or she isn't talking, sniffed when you mentioned sex, coughed as you brought up money, or cleared the throat at the very moment you said you were not a competitive person. These responses *could mean* that the Analyst is bored and is probably thinking about the interesting patient who just left, is sizing you up for fee, or has already passed judgment and found you unacceptable as a prospective patient.

Compounding these complexities, some intermediate anxieties emerge—issues of timing and measurement: How long should you talk about your ex-spouse—"Have I spent too much time on that? I don't want to come off as someone stuck in the past, but I don't want to seem too cavalier and untouched by it . . ." How much depth should you give to your relationship with your mother, and were you too intense when you mentioned your lovers? "Am I making myself look too good? Or should I throw in a little bad now, or vice versa?" What should be censored, what needs to be protected, how much should be told and at what point, how much is enough and not enough . . .

A subgroup of anxieties plague your thoughts. The Analyst isn't taking notes, and you don't know how he or she can remember what you've said, especially since you, yourself, can't remember and just might be talking gibberish! At that point, you may season your words with phrases like "Do you understand?" "You know?" or "Are you with me?" just to keep him or her on their toes and nudge them into consciousness. Now, convinced your case is uncompelling, you begin talking rapidly, leaping from safe spot to safe spot, trying to avoid your own suspicion that the Analyst can see through your clothes!

Of course, this leads to an attack of self-loathing which is then projected onto the Analyst, further convincing you that he or she does not like you. A new set of defenses now unravel, and you catch yourself uttering thinly veiled hostile remarks—comments you know the Analyst has caught, which are followed by off-the-cuff apologies geared to ensure you'll ultimately be seen as a fine human being.

Now this is something of which you cannot be certain, so you might let the Analyst know that you know that he or she knows that you may be "just a little nervous"—but certainly not tense! You're as normal as the next guy, including the persecutor in that chair, so you might begin to verify this fact by saying, "I guess everyone feels a little jumpy when they sit here . . . don't they?" If you receive no response, you may begin to seriously seek out the Analyst's flaws.

By the time you walk out of the office, you're already worrying about everything you did and didn't say, and may be stunned when you remember that you forgot to tell him or her why you were there.

Of all the situations you're likely to enter, the psychological consultation poses the most unique set of paradoxes. While it doesn't differ from other anxiety-laden situations wherein the desire to maintain appearances is foremost, the nature of this particular situation makes the exposure of your anxieties not only acceptable, but also desirable. What you present to the Therapist is taken as information that can be used to help you explore and ultimately diminish those anguishing feelings of self-doubt.

It would be to your advantage to understand that your confused feelings and run-on thoughts are neither unique nor crazy, and that they probably reflect the anxieties you experience in many areas of your life. Anxiety can be viewed as an inner cry for help, and if yours is suddenly giving a fierce yell, you're in the right place for support. However, unless you're quite accustomed to discussing your feelings with family or friends, this experience can be a little frightening. You may be at a loss to know what to talk about, and then again may totally blank out.

IMPORTANT SUGGESTIONS FOR
THE NEW PATIENT

If you've decided to seek professional help, it's important to see more than one Therapist: make appointments with at least two, three at the most. It would be helpful for your decision if one of the three is of the opposite sex. When you phone for the appointment, ask about the fee for this consultation—some therapists charge and some may not. If asked how you found this particular Therapist, you may want to tell him or her, "I heard you lecture," "read your book," "read an article in which you were quoted," "heard you on radio" or "saw you on television," "your word-of-mouth reputation," or "a friend recommended you."

It's most important to prepare for the consultation. Therefore, do make notes for yourself concerning your specific area of trouble. Try to focus in on the issues most significant to your life, which could range from relationship problems—fear of losing your wife, husband, or mate; an inability to make or sustain a loving relationship, to achieve intimacy; sexual problems—fear of becoming impotent, being penetrated, your pattern of flitting from one sexual encounter to the next; job problems—fear that your business will fail, that you're not fulfilling your potential, that you may be fired; to trouble sleeping at night, bouts of insomnia, nightmares, or fear of the dark. You may want to write down then talk about your fear of going out on the street, of driving a car, of shopping in department stores; that you're suffering from loneliness, isolation, an inability to make friends; or, something more amorphous—utter exhaustion, irritability, boredom, and the feeling of burning-out. Any one of these areas, as well as others, can be jotted down and used as a preliminary focus for your consultation. However, to avoid "forgetting" why you're there, do prepare yourself with notes.

It's essential that you refrain from alcohol or drugs prior to the appointment—both will dilute and confuse the issues. If you have a drinking or drug problem, don't take either at least for an hour before you arrive; otherwise you may be too dulled out to hear or remember what's being said. Do let the Therapist know if you are on medication of any kind—Valium, pain-killers, antidepressants, amphetamines for weight control, aspirin for an arthritic condition, birth-control pills, et cetera. You might also inform him or her of any physical condition which may concern you, including low blood sugar.

You might want to arrive at the office a little earlier than the appointed time to acclimate yourself. Since you'll probably be a little tense, try to avoid diving into a magazine or newspaper while you wait—reading material will divert your mind from what you want to say and you may find switching back to your problems a bit confusing. Also, if there are others in the waiting room, your anxiety may lead you to believe you've gotten the wrong time, even the wrong day! Those people might not be patients—they may be waiting for someone else. In any event, please do not feel compelled to engage whoever else may be sitting there in a chatty conversation; once again, it will work to dilute your own issues.

When you do meet the Therapist, if you need to smoke, by all means ask for permission to do so. The consultation is not an endurance contest. If you don't inquire, your tensions will increase, and the desire for a cigarette may take over your thoughts. Remember, you're not in that office to present a picture of sound emotional health—that's not why you made the call or rang the bell.

It's most important for you to remember that *you* are recruiting a Therapist for yourself. Do ask questions regarding his or her credentials: where he or she trained, how long they've been in practice, to which associations they are affiliated. Find out about fees, how many times a week you'll need to be seen, the method—sitting up or lying down, hypnosis, behavior modification . . . You might also want to find out if they've had experience with your particular problems—has he or she worked with many business people, artists, writers, students, performers, professionals, homosexuals, bisexuals, people of your race or religion, people with drug or alcohol problems. Try to get a sense of the Therapist: is this someone who inspires a sense of trust, someone who will be silently or verbally responsive to you?

Do inform the Therapist of your history with therapy. Tell him or her about other analysts with whom you may have been in treatment, and for how long. If this is your first visit with a

Therapist, and you're particularly anxious, by all means talk about what you're feeling.

You might want to bridge your awkwardness by simply stating: "I'm nervous about being here," "I didn't think I'd ever have to see a Therapist," or, "I feel crazy coming here, but I wouldn't have come unless I was desperate." "I feel like I'm coming apart, having a nervous breakdown," or even, "I've been thinking about suicide." Let the Therapist know at the outset exactly what it is that you're feeling. Don't try to camouflage yourself—he or she will not be able to divine or guess what's wrong; they don't have magical mind-reading powers.

Try to give the Therapist a sense of what you're about; present him or her with material about your feelings and your life. This is where your notes will come in handy. However, if you did not prepare for the consultation, you might get stuck and have difficulty defining or articulating the confusion. In that case, talk around it. Discuss a recent or recurring dream, a fantasy, an ambition, an anger at a specific person. If that's too difficult, you might describe to the Therapist a day in your life— one day—or what it feels like to get up in the morning, or how you feel on Sundays.

If you totally blank out, by all means use this as part of the information you present about yourself. If you've never been to an Analyst in your life, and the thought of it throws you into panic, *talk about it*. You may blank out in many areas—at sales meetings, with customers, clients, at the office, with your boss—and the symptom is now revealing itself in its full form. You may want to consider this a fortunate occurrence, for now it's out in the open and ready to be examined. By informing the Therapist of your authentic condition, he or she can help you to further articulate your discomfort.

Also, try to remember, you don't need to learn any kind of psychological jargon for the consultation. Many people immediately bone up on Freud, Jung, Adler, Horney, and Perls prior to the session, then spend much of the time dropping theories and interpretations so as to create the impression of psychological sophistication.

It is also recommended that you inform the Therapist of your plan to visit one or two other people. You won't hurt anyone's feelings; the Therapist will probably be very comfortable with your desire to shop around. If you do decide to return to this particular Therapist, he or she will appreciate your need to avoid hasty decisions. However, you may want to return to this particular Therapist for a second consultation; during the first session you may be very anxious and later be unable to reach a decision. By all means, make a second appointment—you are allowed one more visit before making your final selection.

Finally, it would be important to remember that there are no perfect patients. There are only fantasies and notions of how perfection manifests—and even they are imperfect. Whatever you do bring into that consultation, however you present yourself, and whatever you say will be useful. The defenses can be explored, your worst fears openly discussed, and your negative feelings considered without critical judgments. This is one of the rare circumstances in life where situational anxiety can ultimately prove to be a rich gift.

Epilogue

THE SITUATIONS PORTRAYED IN THIS BOOK WERE SELECTED AS A focus for investigation because of their high incidence of recurring anxiety among people of many different persuasions. However, they represent only a sampling of the occasions reported as triggers. There are many other life events, occurring daily, monthly, or yearly, which set off not only massive amounts of anxiety for the duration of the specific situation, but also unpleasant anticipatory responses. Therefore, don't be alarmed if your particular *bête noire* was not highlighted here for examination.

With an eye toward perceiving the similarity in substance and in feeling, however, you might want to look at a few other situations which habitually plague people in our society and perhaps identify a few more of your own.

Situations which concern money are constant anxiety-provokers—approaching the end-of-the-month bills, balancing the checkbook, budgeting, or having a credit card canceled. National holidays, specifically New Year's Eve, and family holidays are all situations loaded with stressful associations, as are long and short vacations. Many people are victims of out-and-out panic when put into a travel situation—flying, riding a train or a bus, entering a terminal and then a strange city. Change, too, is a charged event. Moving to a new city or into a new home can be both disorienting and distressing, as can the situation in which the loss of one's home is threatened. Shopping in large department stores, small boutiques, or even supermarkets are frequently mentioned as causing alarm, and, of course, social events, including weddings, funerals, reunions, and public speaking, stoke anxiety's coals. Additionally, any time an important relationship with a mate or a friend is put into jeopardy, situational anxiety can emerge in force.

It is sincerely hoped that through the situations cited in this book you will have gleaned an understanding sufficient to aid and perhaps guide you through the anxious events endemic to your own life. Many of the suggestions offered here can easily be transferred from one situation to another. For instance, the information provided in the Birthday Anxiety and the Private Aloneness Anxiety chapters pertaining to planning ahead for the future can be applied to situations concerning money, holidays, and vacations. Travel and shopping anxiety can be treated with many of the suggestions offered in Public Aloneness Anxiety, and when a life change becomes threatening, you might look to the aids listed in New Job Anxiety. Social events are not dissimilar to the problems that occur in Dinner Party and Social Anxiety, and the chapter on Sexual Anxiety, in addition to offering methods for breaking down barriers and achieving degrees of new intimacy with sexual partners, may be useful to remember whenever personal relationships of any kind become disharmonious.

It would be prudent to remember that situational anxiety, as opposed to the "free-floating" variety, only lasts as long as the situation itself is present. While it can manifest itself in thinking processes and judgment, intrude upon concentration, and cloud perceptions, it is temporary—it will pass. However, along with adapting some of the suggested modes for lessening its intensity, you might want to reflect upon how many situations cue the same responses and begin to put together a pattern of your own personal conflicts. By using your own instincts, insights, perceptions, and wild thoughts, you may glean a better understanding of how your conditioning, and therefore your thought patterns, perpetuate false interpretations of events. *The repetitiveness and intensity of situational anxiety can be diminished.* When you become sufficiently in charge of your own thoughts, actions, and plans, many of those disturbing external influences will lose their potency to alarm.

Do bear in mind, however, that while many situations promote unwanted feelings, anxiety itself is not a totally negative or destructive phenomenon. The positive aspects are important to your life—they provide you with essential alerts to danger, urge you on to a variety of creative and constructive pursuits, and help you to achieve maturity as well as wisdom. Every anxious situation you encounter can be viewed as an aid, if not a gift, toward enhancing personal growth. Joseph Wood Krutch put the issue in fine perspective when he told us, "Anxiety and distress interrupted occasionally by pleasure is the normal course of man's existence." Without anxiety, you would probably not be alive.

INDEX

318

INDEX

guilt feelings and, 152–54
the job and, 155–62
money and, 161
neighbors and, 154–55
panic and, 152–59
preparing for the unpredictable,
162
procrastination and, 160, 161
reading and, 157
self-neglect and, 161
self-worth and, 153
sleep and, 161–62
the telephone and, 161
ten impulses for, 159–61
waiting anxiety and, 161, 170,
171
Laughter, 8
body anxiety and, 243
dentist anxiety and, 289, 295
dinner party anxiety and, 174,
181, 188, 194
doctor anxiety and, 270
new job anxiety and, 217, 240
Logic, 10, 26–27
Loneliness/aloneness controversy,
89–90

Macho pose, the, 31, 41
Manners, dinner party anxiety and,
173, 196–97
Marijuana, 109–10, 190
Masochism, lateness anxiety and,
160
Masturbation
private aloneness anxiety and, 92,
96, 100
sexual anxiety and, 66
May, Rollo, 8
Meaning of Anxiety, The (May), 8
Medical societies, 284
Memories
birthday anxiety and, 198
insomnia and, 118, 119, 120
private aloneness anxiety and,
115, 118–20
sexual anxiety and, 27–28
Memory
doctor anxiety and, 268, 278, 285,
286
new job anxiety and, 219
shrink anxiety and, 299, 302–6
Miller, Llewellyn, 192

Monday, private aloneness anxiety
on, 126–29
Money, 308, 309
body anxiety and, 243
dentist anxiety and, 292
dinner party anxiety and, 176
doctor anxiety and, 267, 269, 274,
281, 284
insomnia and, 118, 120, 121
lateness anxiety and, 161
private aloneness anxiety and,
105, 112, 116, 118, 120,
121, 126
public aloneness anxiety and,
138, 144, 146
shrink anxiety and, 298, 300,
302–5
Mortality, doctor anxiety and,
267–71, 282–84
Motion pictures
private aloneness anxiety and,
109
public aloneness anxiety and,
132, 133, 144–51
selecting, 151
Mourning period, sexual anxiety
and, 52–54
Music
dentist anxiety and, 288, 295
dinner party anxiety and, 177
private aloneness anxiety and,
107, 111, 130
Myths
dental anxiety and, 291–95
sexual anxiety and, 19, 29,
39,–40

Neighbors
birthday anxiety and, 207
body anxiety and, 256, 258, 259
lateness anxiety and, 154–55
private aloneness anxiety and,
116, 130
New job anxiety, 3, 14, 217–40,
309
ambition and, 219–24, 231–32
anticipation and, 229, 231, 234,
235
apprehension and, 217,
235, 237, 239
authority and, 220–23, 231, 235
burn-out and, 233–35

319

INDEX

    63, 73–76
  as a false concept, 54
  shrink anxiety and, 307
Performance (sexual) rating, 73–75
Personal information, transmission
    of, 30–39
Pets, private aloneness anxiety and,
    116–17, 124
Planning
  dinner party anxiety and, 174–78,
    183–85
    making lists, 173–74
    menu selection, 173, 176,
    183–84
  private aloneness anxiety and,
    115–17, 124–26, 130
Posture, body anxiety and, 263, 264
Power
  of attraction, 20–21, 26–29, 44,
    55
  new job anxiety and, 222–23,
    235, 236
Pregnancy, sexual anxiety and,
    63–64
Prescriptions, doctor anxiety and,
    274, 278, 280, 283, 285
Presents, birthday anxiety and, 200,
    202–4, 208–12
Private aloneness anxiety, 11–12,
    88–131, 309
  the aloneness/loneliness
    controversy, 89–90
  ambition and, 116
  anger and, 106–10, 118–20,
    125, 126, 129
  apprehension and, 3, 99, 104–5,
    106
  authority and, 91, 95, 100, 128,
    129
  boredom and, 88, 90–91, 126
  cleaning and, 97, 98, 102, 113,
    125, 128
  clothing and, 91, 98, 101, 112,
    120, 126–29
  creativity and, 116, 121
  danger and, 104–5, 106
  definition of aloneness, 89
  dinner party anxiety and, 195–96
  doubts and, 99–100, 103, 106,
    126–27, 130
  dread and, 92, 112, 130

drinking and, 92, 94, 109, 112,
    114, 118, 123
drugs and, 98, 102
eating and, 92, 97, 98, 108,
    111, 114, 118, 123, 126,
    127, 130
exercise and, 123
fantasies and, 110, 120
fear and, 89, 99, 102
  of the dark, 104, 106–12
  at 4 A.M., 117–23
  at 4 P.M., 112–17
friends and, 91, 105, 110, 114,
    116, 125, 128, 130
the future and, 116, 117
guilt feelings and, 110, 118–20,
    126, 128, 131
insomnia and, 88, 117–23
isolation and, 89, 91, 95, 97,
    102, 116, 123
the job and, 108, 112–16, 120,
    121, 125–30
joy and, 110
keeping a written account of,
    110, 117, 121
masturbation and, 92, 96, 100
memories and, 115, 118–20
on Monday, 126–29
money and, 105, 112, 116,
    118, 120, 121, 126
motion pictures and, 109
music and, 107, 111, 130
neighbors and, 116, 130
at night, 88, 104–12, 117–23
  "out there" concept, 95, 96,
    102
panic and, 104–5, 108–9, 112
perception and, 113
perfection and, 99, 113
pets and, 116–17, 124
planning and, 115–17, 124–26,
    130
professional help for, 122
radios and, 107, 110, 111
reading and, 109, 114,
    118–19, 122, 124, 130
self-worth and, 103, 110
shopping and, 91, 112, 125
silence and, 104, 107–12
sleep and, 92, 95, 100, 105–8,
    111, 114